DATA-DRIVEN ORGANIZATION DESIGN

DATA-DRIVEN ORGANIZATION DESIGN

Sustaining the competitive edge
through organizational analytics

RUPERT MORRISON

KoganPage

Publisher's note

Every possible effort has been made to ensure that the information contained in this book is accurate at the time of going to press, and the publisher and author cannot accept responsibility for any errors or omissions, however caused. No responsibility for loss or damage occasioned to any person acting, or refraining from action, as a result of the material in this publication can be accepted by the editor, the publisher or the author.

First published in Great Britain and the United States in 2015 by Kogan Page Limited

Apart from any fair dealing for the purposes of research or private study, or criticism or review, as permitted under the Copyright, Designs and Patents Act 1988, this publication may only be reproduced, stored or transmitted, in any form or by any means, with the prior permission in writing of the publishers, or in the case of reprographic reproduction in accordance with the terms and licences issued by the CLA. Enquiries concerning reproduction outside these terms should be sent to the publishers at the undermentioned addresses:

2nd Floor, 45 Gee Street	1518 Walnut Street, Suite 1100	4737/23 Ansari Road
London EC1V 3RS	Philadelphia PA 19102	Daryaganj
United Kingdom	USA	New Delhi 110002
www.koganpage.com		India

Writing and editing contribution throughout: Will Sheldon
© Rupert Morrison, 2015

The right of Rupert Morrison to be identified as the author of this work has been asserted by him in accordance with the Copyright, Designs and Patents Act 1988.

ISBN   978 0 7494 7441 6
E-ISBN   978 0 7494 7442 3

British Library Cataloguing-in-Publication Data

A CIP record for this book is available from the British Library.

Library of Congress Cataloging-in-Publication Data

Morrison, Rupert, author.
  Data-driven organization design : sustaining the competitive edge through organizational analytics / Rupert Morrison.
    pages cm
    ISBN 978-0-7494-7441-6 (paperback) – ISBN 978-0-7494-7442-3 (ebk)   1. Organizational effectiveness.
2. Organizational change.   3. Performance.   4. Management–Statistical methods.   I. Title.
    HD58.9.M667 2015
    658.4'0301–dc23
                                                                                        2015031280

Typeset by Graphicraft Limited, Hong Kong
Print production managed by Jellyfish
Printed and bound in Great Britain by Ashford Colour Press Ltd, Gosport, Hampshire

CONTENTS

ABOUT THE AUTHOR

Rupert Morrison is the CEO of Concentra, one of the fastest-growing analytics firms in the UK and winner of the Technology Innovation Award 2011 in the *Sunday Times* Tech Track 100. He led the creation of its OrgVue product, an integrated software platform with solutions including: HR analytics, organization design, transition management and strategic workforce planning. It was selected as one of four Gartner Cool Vendors in human capital management from an international field. Created based on experiences helping clients with business transformation, it is revolutionizing the way people design, transform and operate their organizations to sustain competitive advantage.

Rupert's approach combines his experiences of running a fast-growth tech firm alongside a wealth of experience in business transformation, supply chain optimization, and organization design projects. Having studied economics at Erasmus University Rotterdam, he has spent 18 years in consulting, helping organizations around the world. While at Concentra, and before that with A T Kearney, Rupert has worked on projects in a broad range of industries including automotive, FMCG, mining, government agencies, pharmaceutical and private equity.

Rupert grew up on a sheep station in the Wairarapa in New Zealand. He lives in London with his wife and three sons. He has a passion for rugby, which he coaches, and for completing IronMan distance triathlons.

FOREWORD

The economic environment is changing more rapidly than ever before. The practice of organization design is therefore a complex one, often subject to intense time pressure, full of traps and false turns and carrying the risk of substantial inefficiency and loss. You can either encourage people to align behind your strategic vision and hope human flexibility makes things work – or you can get to grips with the complexity. To handle complexity, you need tools that allow you to intervene and to understand your people, activities and products. Organizations are generating data on these things more and more quickly; this data is the lifeblood of the organization. But the traditional tools for harnessing and presenting this data – Excel, PowerPoint – are no longer enough. The revolution in data visualization is continuous; with the way we consume, interact with and understand the data around us changing all the time, organizations have a real chance to do things better. The human eye and brain can cope with enormous amounts of data as long as it's presented well. You can only bring about effective change in your organization if you can really see what is going on in it. This is where the insights provided in this book are brilliant. Because the complex can be made simple if you visualize it in a sufficiently intuitive way, organizational design activities that were previously too difficult are now possible.

What's different about this book from other books on organization design is that it gives a structured approach, from the top level macro steps to the detailed micro steps, drawing on the author's experience of what it takes to 'make it real' when it comes to organizational change. The book documents an entire methodology, going further into the detail than other books. Some areas of the methodology presented will evolve over time as greater understanding of the problems and new possible solutions emerge. The value of the book is in setting the direction and providing the energy to start to define the problem space, and to give the best possible current answers. It sets a direction that others will follow.

In the chapters of this book are ideas that have gestated over Rupert Morrison's 18-year career, informed by work with over 100 clients, and born out of his obsession with data, visualization and mapping the true complexity of organizations. They are ideas that have been discussed and refined around the camp fire, in the pub, over countless hours in front of the white board and above all through application in practice. What is also in this book is a remarkably honest account of the pains of growing a successful and innovative analytics company – a backdrop which makes Rupert's book all the more powerful for the insights he shares. This book is one of the results of his dogged determination, emotion, energy and unreasonable commitment. Rupert combines deep insight into the future direction of industries with the sheer nerve to seek to shape the future. The tenacity of his vision will prove invaluable for organizations wanting to make real long-term progress.

Chris Barrett and Giles Slinger

ACKNOWLEDGEMENTS

I owe so much to so many.

To my many colleagues who have provided detailed comments, debates, ideas and encouragement. They have supported the refinement and implementation of much of the thinking, teaching me and detailing specific concepts and applying methods in practice. Andy Birtwistle, Ben Marshall, Chris Houghton, Darshan Baskaran, El No, James Don-Carolis, John Candeto, Katelyn Weber, Manish Chauhan, Mike Walker, Nikolay Vaklev, Patrick Gracey, Robert Campbell and Tom Simpkins all significantly contributed to this book.

To the Concentra and OrgVue senior team of Peter Lanch, Adrian Downing, Nick Finch, Weelin Lin, Rodin van der Hart, Jamie Pullar, and William Ingram for their support.

To Anna Triantafillou and Annie Cope for the graphic design. A key theme of the book is the power of visualization, and without their ability to turn my whiteboard and PowerPoint sketches into understandable images a core thrust of the book would have been lost.

To Katy Hamilton, Lucy Carter, Katleen Richardson and Stefan Leszczuk at Kogan Page for their expertise and editing advice and being so flexible in the publishing process.

To A T Kearney and my many mentors and colleagues there for being such a great firm and providing me with years of invaluable learning. Especially Earle Steinberg, Phil Dunne, Charles Davis, Anne Deering, Jonathan Anscombe, Yves Thill, Sean Ritchie, Antti Kautovaara, Judith Orzechowski, Jim Pearce, Matt James, Par Astrom, Steve Whitehead, Steve Fowles, Paul Collins, Chirag Shah and Gautam Singh.

To those who have supported and made Concentra possible. In particular Ben Scott Knight, Richard Thompson and Angus Whiteley for going on the journey, investing and believing. Also to Tom Brown, Goetz Boue and Paul Graville for founding the original software development firm and helping to form Concentra 2.0.

To all my clients who I am unable to mention by name. Thank you for placing your faith in me and for your continued trust and support.

To Chris Barrett for his technical and data vision, ability to transform an idea into reality and his detailed comments and advice. Giles Slinger for his tireless work, edits on every chapter and helping to take the thinking to the next level. Julian Holmes for his detailed comments and in particular expertise on workforce planning and implementation.

Without Will Sheldon I would never have been able to finish this book. Thank you for your editing, rewriting and ensuring every argument, detail and base was covered every time.

To my family: my father who passed 25 years ago and my mother. To Henk and Alexandra, my four brothers and dear sister, my special Uncle Erik, Aunt Marg and dear Gran. To my three gorgeous boys, Hugh, Alec and Peter, who give me a reason to keep going every day.

To my dear wife Vanessa. Everyone who knows me well knows that none of this would have been possible without you. To you, Vanessa, the biggest thanks of all.

PART ONE
Introduction

Data-driven organization design

War is ninety percent information.

NAPOLEON BONAPARTE

Too many leaders treat organization design as an exercise in moving boxes around PowerPoint slides. Too many analysts spend their time in unwieldy Excel contraptions that fail to give an understanding of organizational reality. Too many employees are unclear about what their role in their organization really is. Too much siloed thinking occurs because it is impossible to pull all the elements of the organization together. Too much time is wasted designing and changing organizations, with limited value. I believe the current methods of organization design are falling behind the needs of the modern-day organization. Organizations are struggling to understand where they are, let alone realize their plans and aspirations for the future. I wrote this book because I believe there has to be a better way.

Organizations must adapt to survive. They are a constantly evolving system made up of objectives, processes designed to meet those objectives, people with skills and behaviours to do the work required, and all of this organized in a governance structure. That governance structure goes far beyond the reporting lines of an org chart. It is how people work together and agree on what needs to happen, from day-to-day to year-on-year. It is dynamic, constantly moving over time. The structure must be fluid but you have to maintain an understanding of it. To be understandable you have to make it visual, because if you can't see it then how can you understand it? The organization must create an environment for people to perform, for only when everyone performs to their potential do you have a hope of getting and then sustaining your competitive edge.

Even without the complexities of being part of an organization, people struggle to perform and meet even their most basic objectives. Every year on 1 January millions of people resolve to lose weight and try to get fit. We all know it's not rocket science: eat a balanced diet and exercise regularly. And yet 92 per cent of people who make these resolutions will fail to achieve their goals, with over 50 per cent giving them up after just six months.[1] If we struggle as individuals how can we expect to fare when implementing change in organizations where we can be dealing with hundreds to many thousands of people? It's like getting fit: the theory isn't complicated, but putting it into practice is extremely difficult.

I believe that those responsible for ensuring their organizations remain competitive must stop relying on old-fashioned office tools and isolated org charts when defining how they need to organize themselves to meet their strategic ambitions. Not only are the techniques used to create and deliver organization designs outdated, they don't go nearly deep enough for what businesses require. They are superficial and not geared towards execution. How many organization designs are effectively just redrawn org charts? My observation, based on looking at hundreds of designs and organizations, is the vast majority.

The history of change has always been driven by innovation and technology, an idea encapsulated in the term 'creative destruction' coined by Joseph Schumpeter, an Austrian-American economist, in *Capitalism, Socialism and Democracy*.[2] He argued that the constant evolution of industries revolutionizes the very economic structure they are part of, continually destroying it and creating a new one. The advent of the information age we live in today represents this process in high definition. The rise of information technology has a huge impact on industries, bringing with it greater opportunities and greater risks. Reflect on the downfall of big names such as Kodak, Blockbuster or Borders and the rise of Apple, Amazon, Google and Facebook. Those organizations finding new ways of creating and leveraging information are ruling our time. Those that can't adapt suffer a Darwinian extinction. At the heart of this story is the emergence of data and analytics as the means to drive business.

Organizations are lagging behind when it comes to applying these principles and methods of market success to their people. Organization design and workforce analytics represent a new and exciting area of innovation, and it is my hope that this book will disrupt how organization design is currently thought about and practised. The book will provide a toolkit to successfully design, change and manage organizations. An ambitious subject for one book to cover, but this is a book for ambitious people – for real-life practitioners seeking to challenge and improve organizations whether through large-scale transformations or gradual change. Most importantly, this book addresses how to make required organizational change real by using a data-driven approach; not just implementing change, but tackling the everyday problems we face as practitioners, which halt us from sustaining and achieving results and goals in the long term. This book is about getting things done and creating an organization that has the competitive edge.

Effective organization design and management

Organizations are by their nature extremely difficult to design and manage as they are affected by internal and external forces. They are constantly in flux; growing and shrinking, changing focus and direction, and developing both intentionally and unintentionally. The rise of technology, globalization and the knowledge economy means organizations are having to become increasingly complex in order to deal with new business demands. As Jay Galbraith has said,[3] organizations that used to be relatively simple and stable in terms of their structure are having to become increasingly adaptable and multifaceted to survive in today's complex world. Organizations have been evolving over time to deal with changes in markets, geography and technology, and with the information age upon us it is more important than ever for companies to be in control of, and effectively design and manage, their organizations. The consequence of the increasing rate of evolution is that organization design is moving away from being a one-off intervention to an ongoing, continuous project that can never be 'finished'.

It is no surprise that organizations are struggling to cope with this pace of change. In my personal experience of working on numerous design projects and research across a range of organizations, few if any felt they have been on top of their organization design. Over and above this, organizations are struggling to understand themselves in a data-driven way:

- 90 per cent of companies have chronic problems with their data, eg missing, outdated or inaccurate (as reported by Experian in their White Paper, 'The state of data quality' in 2013).

- Very few companies are successfully implementing HR analytics and in two-thirds of organizations, the majority of time is wasted on consolidating, repairing and manipulating data instead of analysing it.[4]

- 50 per cent of organizations are unable to track and monitor business performance as they would like.[5]

- Only 30 per cent of the 37 companies surveyed by the Corporate Research Forum in 2015 said it was 'true' or 'mainly true' that their workforce strategy/plan has adequate breadth and depth to provide the necessary workforce information for making good decisions.[6]

It is because of coming across these struggles time and time again that I have wanted to set out an approach that addresses these issues and helps tackle them. To do this we first need to understand why people are struggling.

Why people are struggling with organization design

While most companies recognize the need to develop ways of designing and managing their organizations, the processes by which they are doing so are flawed. The methods traditionally offered and followed are insufficient, with most people struggling to make headway. I believe there are five main reasons for this.

1 Organization design theory is incomplete

While there has been a proliferation of literature on organization design over the last decade or so, the focus has been on top-level processes such as strategy, organizational structure and company culture. By nature, theory is often quite high level, but when it comes to organizations the key is not just how to make plans, but how to implement them. How do you implement the detail? With no roadmap for the actual implementation of an organization design, it is not surprising practitioners struggle to put the board's grand plans in place.

2 Organization design is never fully implemented

The lack of literature is reflected in the actual practice of organizational design and management. The focus is on the big picture, not the detail of the execution. Seeing structural org charts as the end game rather than defining all the elements of the design is the root cause of much of this. Once management teams have defined the key areas of design or modes of management for the organization, their attention moves on to other things leaving those further down the organization confused as to what it means to them and how they fit into the plan. For example, individual objectives are not linked to high-level KPIs, and what competencies are needed for the organization to execute its strategy.

3 Organization design is seen as a one off intervention

After finishing many traditional consulting projects, I have always been left with the nagging question of what happened after I left a project. Support is often used in developing the summary design but the teams who do the design will typically move on prior to full implementation and without providing the tools to enable the ongoing need for refinement. As the world changes, so too should the evolution of the detailed design. But the capabilities to evolve the design are not created. This is endemic to the very nature and cost profile of consultants; they have to move on and never truly own the problem from start to finish. And neither does the client organization. It reflects a wider approach to organization design (OD) as a one-off intervention. Projects are solved and designs are put in place but there is no guarantee that the value from that project will last. Given the evolving nature of most organizations, OD must become a core competency.

4 Organization design does not harness the potential of human capital

Too many employees are unable to fulfil their potential owing to siloed functional, geographic, customer or product areas. They manage the indictors they are measured by regardless of whether that has a negative impact on the whole, often because they just don't know better. Accountabilities are unclear, so hours are wasted trying to work out how to get things done rather than just getting them done. Conflicts are not designed out, so they fester and grow. The right resources are not allocated in the right proportions to the priority areas because the priorities are not agreed nor the means for determining the 'right proportions' established. This is due to the fact the detailed holistic design is avoided because it is perceived as being too difficult and not sufficiently prioritized.

5 Organization design has not been data-driven

Given reason number four, this is potentially the most crucial point of all of these failings. In the organization design and management process the person who traditionally has been the most powerful in the boardroom is the Finance Director. It is the Finance Director who is usually the gatekeeper to decisions because it is he or she who is perceived to own the most valuable and relevant business data. The Finance Director has the ability to communicate that data in a meaningful way – everyone understands the concept of a bottom line. Organization design practitioners have been unable to gather meaningful people data and link people performance data to business performance data in a significant way. Decisions have, therefore, been made on financial numbers rather than people and process numbers. In many ways, redesigns and change and transformations have actually neglected the people at the heart of them and have failed to centre that change on maximizing people performance.

This book addresses all of these areas by bringing organization design and management practice up to date. It provides a flexible toolkit and road-map to address the everyday challenges thrown at us when designing an organization.

How this book will help you

This book is for practitioners and as such it deals with the detail: how to see processes through from the beginning to end from high-level thinking right down to the day-to-day questions such as:

- How do I ensure the optimal design for my organization so that it meets a clear business strategy?
- How do I decide between ranges of contradictory macro options?
- What is the best way to collect and sort data on my employees? And how do I make it practical and relevant to the organization?
- How do I align everyone so they are pulling in the same direction?
- What is the best way to rightsize the organization?
- How do I carry out an impact assessment?
- How do I manage change when implementing a redesign?
- Who is the best suited for a new position we created?

- How do I plan the workforce on an ongoing and long-term basis?
- How do I monitor progress?

In answering these questions this book has some simple philosophies:

1 Organizations are systems. Just like the human body, each part of the organization is connected, and changes in one part of the system can have unintended and unforeseen consequences in another.

2 An organization's people are its greatest asset, and the right people are a rare currency. Anyone who works with people data, whether in HR, strategy, OD, or as a consultant, is in one of the best positions to give insight into organization design and organizational management. The goal is to ensure the organization has the right people in the right places doing the right things; to align the organization from top to bottom in order to achieve the best possible results.

3 Organizations need to harness data and technology. The HR department in particular needs to become more data-driven. It needs to ask the right questions; collect the right data; present that data in a visual way; use the right tools for different functions; and gain maximum impact from that data it owns.

This book takes lessons from a broad spectrum of functions such as HR, finance and marketing, disciplines such as economics, psychology, sport, technology, and my experience in management consultancy and running a company.

When it comes to organization design you have to *make it real*. This book is about how to get things done, how to take plans from a whiteboard and put them into practice. Part of this journey is about getting things wrong. Things will always go wrong. It is how you deal with the unexpected challenges thrown up in achieving your goals and objectives that is the real yardstick of success.

This book is not a panacea. There are some things that can never be certain when it comes to organizations. Nor will this book change the fact that organization design is hard work. However, it will ensure the hard work is worthwhile and give you tools and processes to help you find your right path and get to the end of that path. It is not expected that practitioners will read this book cover to cover from beginning to end, but it has been written so each element of the book can be picked up for each challenge faced, piece of inspiration needed, or question needing to be answered.

Structure of the book

This book outlines the frameworks, methods and tools for OD and ongoing organizational management. In Part One I lay out both the philosophical and the practical foundations. Part Two will explore the big picture introducing the concept of macro design and outlining the process of creating a clear organization design through three steps: defining strategy; iterating the design; and creating a business case. This sets up Part Three in which I focus on micro design, arguing that this is the real key to an OD. Starting with the barriers to micro design I then go through a step-by-step process addressing how to build a baseline, set objectives, map fixed-value chain processes as well as dynamic changing ones, map competencies, and right-size your organization. Building on these methods, in Part Four I address how you turn theory into reality. I go through the challenges of moving something from paper into reality and address how in practice this is done by looking at impact analysis, selection processes, implementation and transition, workforce planning, communications, succession planning and talent management. I conclude with a note on sustaining the organization and the necessity of celebrating success.

The result is a step-by-step guide to making change in your organization successful and long lasting. This is not an easy journey and it isn't one you have to attempt in one go. It helps to break the journey into separate isolated chunks. Reflecting this, each chapter has been written to be useful in its own right. As long as you have read the Chapter 1.3 Foundations and core concepts, you should be able to pick up any of the chapters and get value.

Wherever there are challenges, there are opportunities. For practitioners working in organizational changes and transformation there is a real chance to take charge of the data and analytics now available within companies, and use them to impact business outcomes. Whether you are looking at implementing long-term change and a large redesign, or a one-off small-scale project, I hope this book helps inspire you to make the most of your organizational data and analytics to drive effectiveness and efficiencies in your business.

Final thoughts

Nothing of real value can be done quickly and without significant effort. It has taken me a good five years to write this book. The concepts and principles within it have been tested and refined through reading the great work of others, attending dozens if not hundreds of seminars, surveying experts, refining the tools through to actually using them, debating the approaches, constant reflection, and learning from my mistakes. I have been blessed with the support of many remarkable people. To master the concepts within this book, therefore, will take effort and commitment. It is dense with content and aims to provide a holistic approach to give you the knowledge and tools to sustain the competitive edge through organizational analytics. The many illustrations are in full colour to make it easier to comprehend and to make the concepts more concrete. I use real-life examples and expose some of my failings. I can only hope you get as much value from reading it and applying the thinking as I have gained from actually writing it.

Remember this

1 Organizations are difficult to design and manage as they are affected by internal and external forces and are therefore in a constant state of flux.

2 Current organization design theory is incomplete. A holistic end-to-end approach is needed: from your organization's vision to tracking your actual results to defining the entire organizational system.

3 The organizations finding new ways of creating and leveraging information are ruling our time. Leveraging organizational data will help you win in your chosen space.

4 This book is written for ambitious people who are prepared to do the hard work required to achieve their edge.

Notes

1 Norcross, J, Mrykalo, M and Blagys, M (2002) Auld Lang Syne: Success predictors, change processes, and self-reported outcomes of New Year's resolvers and nonresolvers, *Journal of Clinical Psychology*, 58 (4), pp 397–405

2 Schumpeter, J (2008) *Capitalism, Socialism, and Democracy*, third edition, Harper Perennial Modern Classics

3 Galbraith, J (2001) *Designing Organizations: An executive guide to strategy, structure and process revised*, Pfeiffer

4 Bassi, L, Carpenter, R and McMurrer, D (2012) HR Analytics Handbook, McBassi & Company, New York

5 Eddy, N [Accessed 28 March 2015], Eweek [Online] http://www.eweek.com/small-business/business-intelligence-analytics-top-areas-of-investment-in-2014-gartner

6 Colin Beames, Workforce Strategy Audit Survey Report, Corporate Research Forum, March 2015. Question 11 of survey finding. https://www.kpmg.com/UK/en/IssuesAndInsights/ArticlesPublications/Documents/PDF/topics/workforce-strategy-audit-survey-report.pdf

Challenges

Accept the challenges so that you can feel the exhilaration of victory. **GEORGE S PATTON**

Introduction

Redesigning an organization can often feel like preparing for battle. It takes courage, and the knowledge that along the way there are going to be casualties and a few scars to take away at the end of it. The first question you have to ask before any organization redesign is: 'Is the potential upside of the redesign worth the cost and risk of doing so?' And when I say cost and risk I don't just mean for the organization, but its people. Redesigns can have personal implications across all levels of an organization. So, is your problem really an organizational structure problem?

I have seen too many executives embark on a reorganization believing it will be an all-embracing cure for their problems. If you have systematic issues in your organizational performance or behaviour, merely shifting responsibilities and role titles may not be the solution you are seeking. Often senior managers face an immediate need to reduce costs, integrate an acquisition or provide a platform for growth, and it is concluded that the current organizational structure is not fit for purpose. The experience of heads of department going on 'magic weekends' and coming in on a Monday morning having dreamt up a new organizational structure on paper is a common one when speaking to executives. However, this can be an entirely pointless exercise. Redesigns do not, or rather should not, start with the aesthetics of an organization. You have to fully understand the root causes of problems and performance. Only then will you find a solution. I would argue recognizing the problems is 50 per cent of the solution. Let's go back to the original question: 'Is the potential upside of the redesign worth the cost and risk of doing so?' What this is getting at is, do you really need a major organizational shift in direction (as described in Part Two of this book) or can you focus on the detail, making tweaks and readjustments to particular aspects of the organization (as outlined in Part Three)? As I emphasize in Chapter 2.2, if you are going to implement an organization redesign you need an overwhelming case for change. Otherwise it just isn't worth it.

Knowing when to carry out a large-scale intervention as opposed to simply tweaking the detail is the reason taking a data-driven approach is so valuable. Organizational analytics help to uncover root causes, illuminate the scale of problems and, through scenario modelling and testing, give some understanding as to the potential impacts and benefits of change. This is one of the reasons I place so much emphasis on building a baseline of data in Chapter 3.2. Having a data-driven approach creates a virtuous circle in which the better your data, the better you understand problems, and the more focused and appropriate your response can be. However, sometimes there is no choice but to embrace wholesale change. And even when everyone is trying their best to follow the right processes for the right reasons, this change represents a huge challenge.

In this chapter I outline the challenges in the actual process of doing an organization design. Although they are related, these are not the specific challenges of implementation (something I address in Chapter 4.2) but the challenges of the design phase as covered in the macro and micro sections of the book. These are challenges I have lived through and come up against time and time again with clients and through personal experience. I have discussed them endlessly and read as much as I can on the topic. But nothing can prepare you for actually experiencing them. Therefore, I begin this chapter with my own first-hand experience of doing an unsuccessful redesign to highlight many of the traps and issues that are seemingly obvious but easy to fall into. I then explicitly draw out five types of challenges in doing organization design: the complexity of organizations, people and politics, data and analytics, personal limits and design processes.

These challenges represent both *hard-edged data-driven issues* and the *soft people politics and change* sides. They are intrinsically linked and both are fraught with traps, in particular the soft side. However, if knowing the root causes of a problem is 50 per cent of finding the solution, then addressing and thinking through the challenges of a redesign up front will at least give you a head start.

The reality of the challenge

In early 2008 a group of management consultants and I took on a London technology firm. We wanted to merge the business knowledge and method-driven approaches you learn in MBAs and consulting firms with the engineering skills of hard-core software development. With these joint capabilities, we saw an opportunity in the market: to create solutions and products for business operations problems that were common, difficult to solve and high-impact. I became the CEO of this new company.

At the start, like many small, high-growth companies we had an extremely fluid and informal organizational structure. Between the members of the senior management team we covered sales, delivery, finance and a couple of the business lines. Everyone did a bit of everything. We maintained and aligned the direction of the business primarily through our close relationships. However, after two years of strong growth, we needed to rethink our strategy if we wanted to continue expanding. To invest in the business we decided to raise venture capital funding. This required a rethinking of our ways of working as the old ways did not meet the more formal structures demanded by venture capital firms, nor was it sustainable. We needed to redesign the organization.

Hubristic management consultant that I was, I thought that my years of experience consulting and doing organization designs around the world meant I knew all I needed to about the transition that was to come. I was wrong. And I fell into two of the most basic of traps when redesigning the organization.

I designed around the people, not the needs of the business

There is a big difference between doing organization design as a consultant and doing organization design for a company you part own, know and love. For a start, you have long-term social relationships with those you have worked with for years, and any design that affects them is going to affect those relationships. The trouble started through the process of creating a business case in the pursuit of venture capital. Creating a business case and professionalizing the business meant clarifying every part of the business; formalizing the budget, setting out accountabilities, confirming roles and direct reports. In this instance, the result was a scenario in which each stakeholder wanted to assert his or her ownership over the management of the company more strongly. Everyone wanted a large, meaningful role with power that reflected his or her shareholding and status as a director.

I compromised long-term goals for short-lived peace

As a consequence of the first trap, I began to move things away from the best design that would deliver the long-term goals of the business. New senior hires were brought into the business to professionalize many of the core functions and help drive the top line. As I brought in the talent to support the plan my number of direct reports grew. The need of many of the senior players to have strong roles resulted in a series of profit & loss accounts (P&Ls) being generated. The idea was that if everyone managed their P&L, then together we would meet our targets. But this wasn't an org structure that was designed; it was one arrived at through negotiation and compromise. I knew it wasn't right, but didn't feel strong enough to stop it. Unfortunately, the business performance significantly declined due to lack of alignment, an internal rather than external focus and us simply not all pulling in the same direction.

How the reorganization affected the whole

- Trust was eroded between everyone in the company because everyone was treading on each other's toes and putting him or herself first. There was a huge amount of duplication of documents and decision-making.

- It was impossible to achieve the marketing objectives. For instance, the new marketing director was overloaded with different messages and points of view from everyone who effectively felt they had a veto on every decision.

- Finance was submerged by a deluge of work that stemmed from the P&L structure. Revenue recognition became the largest bone of contention. This was paper money that had no impact on either clients or our bottom line.

What this looked like in practice

We had lost our competitive edge. Symptoms of the organization included:

- There were a huge number of meetings because there were so many people who felt they had a veto. So if you wanted to get something agreed, you had to lobby hard. I am a great believer in everyone having their say, but too many voices and vetoes just lead to nothing getting done.

- External contractors were brought in to do training in areas that, if the business was running smoothly, would not have been needed, such as executive management and team building – a direct result of having a lack of alignment behind a collective vision (an area I come back to later in the chapter).

- As Managing Director I spent all my time looking internally rather than externally. Instead of chasing up prospects I was struggling just to keep the company running.

- Growth stopped and we fell well behind budget.

- Staff attrition increased. It was no longer a fun place to work – something we had previously taken great pride in.

- Things got so bad we had to implement a redundancy programme, resulting in the cutting of the whole marketing team together with various other roles.

In short, the business had begun to fail. Thankfully, we managed to address the problems in time. We changed the design, sorted many of the structural issues and got rid of those P&L structures. The toll, on an individual and organizational level, however, was massive. I think it is extremely common for highly successful firms to dance with near fatal situations as they grow. Ben Horowitz does a brilliant job of describing the pain and mistakes in building a business in his book *The Hard Thing About Hard Things*.[1] Our particular story is being replicated thousands of times around the world every year. The key is to identify the challenges at the outset, and deal with the conflicts head on.

Common challenges in organization design

When a business goes through significant change, the design is just the beginning. Organizations are complex and so are people. Bringing alignment through change as a whole and individually is a real challenge. The larger the organization and more embedded the status quo, the harder it is. People, as individuals, have their own personal goals, pride, weaknesses, prejudices and complexities. Bringing everyone onto the same journey creates natural tensions and represents an obvious communication problem. In this sense, the first two challenges in this chapter ('Complexity' and 'People and politics') represent *why* organization design is challenging, while the later three challenges ('Data and analytics', 'Personal limits' and 'Design processes') represent challenges in *how* to deliver the design.

Complexity

Getting and keeping the competitive edge come in part from understanding the impact a change in one part of the organization will have on another. No easy task. A good way to appreciate the complexity of this is to think of the human body. As David Epstein writes in *The Sports Gene*: 'The 23,000 genes in a human body make up a 23,000-page recipe book, which in theory provides direction for the creation of the body... but if one page is moved, altered or torn out, then some of the other 22,999 pages may suddenly contain new instructions.'[2]

If we think of an organizational system, change can have serious unpredictable consequences. It's not just about the people; it's their roles, objectives, processes, competencies and more. Change one tiny part of that system and that is going to have a knock-on effect on at least one, and probably more parts of that system. And that's just what you can quantify. What about the effect change will have on 'culture' or company values? As I found out, your design can have all sorts of unanticipated results.

There is a lot to think about. And although you can never prepare for everything, you can plan and think through as many scenarios as possible to ensure that you've covered and thought of as much as possible. If the unpredictable happens you just have to be flexible enough and quick enough to deal with it. This represents a real cognitive challenge – to have all the elements of the system clearly defined and in your head.

Solution: break down the organizational system

This is a challenge that I address throughout the book and explicitly in Chapter 1.3. I have tried to simplify it by breaking down the organization into what I perceive to be its core component parts: objectives, fixed-value chain processes, dynamic process (eg projects, risks) and competencies. Everyone will have his or her own way of thinking through the organizational system, but the most important thing is that you do think and are always thinking through it. Fortunately, technology is on our side. The historical tools of the organization design practitioner such as Excel, PowerPoint, Visio and org charting software are being overtaken by a new breed of technology that brings together data analysis, hierarchical modelling and reporting. This is making it easier to understand and appreciate the organizational system as well as to test hypotheses and organizational scenarios. The organizational system is no longer intangible, but something we can really get to grips with.

People and politics

The biggest mistake you can make is to redesign an organization around people rather than its intrinsic needs. This sounds obvious but when you are emotionally invested – compromised by the existing design – it is extremely easy to forget. It is easy to do anything for the sake of peace. You keep individuals happy in the short term but to the detriment of everyone in the long term. The people factor of any redesign will probably be your greatest and most constant battle. The first reason relationships within an organization are so tricky is that people see different things and interpret the world in different ways. Examples where people may not be aligned include:

- the organization's vision and mission;
- organizational goals;
- value propositions and articulations;
- interpretation of roles and job descriptions;
- attitudes towards ways of working, colleagues, clients or stakeholders;
- approaches towards reward, remuneration, peer recognition or career advancement.

This is just scraping the surface. It is made even more complex by the second issue: the natural tensions that occur within organizations. Targets may contradict each other. For example, some teams or individuals may be measured, rewarded and driven by sets of KPIs that may be in direct conflict with others elsewhere in the organization. For instance, goals about growing direct sales may contradict goals about profit margins or short-term quality. If I drop the price I may increase the sales but I will then reduce the percentage margin. Equally, in order to increase quality I may need to increase cost with a direct result on margin (assuming you can't charge more).

The third reason is motivation. Some people will act for the good of the whole while others are more concerned about their next promotion, or having the largest department. It is almost never the case that a manager will say 'My team is idle and I need to reduce its size.' Just as wages are sticky (ie they only go up), so is the demand for resource. This results in a constant pressure for more and more of the same. The number of staff evolves upwards and managers who shout the loudest get more (a subject I tackle explicitly in Chapter 3.7).

This is compounded by the evolving demand for skills. If you take the Schumpeterian view that macroeconomic change is driven by the combination of technical innovation with entrepreneurship, then you can see many industries struggling to adapt to requirements for totally new sets of capabilities. A good example is the need for retail firms to hire digital teams and become competitive in the e-commerce world or the need for automotive firms to hire software developers. (In Chapter 3.6 I explore how to quantify the sorts of skills required for an organization and how to manage the strategic gaps in those skills.)

Solution: ensure clarity

In order to minimize the risk of people seeing the world differently, have them see the same things. Have single versions of truth for all the key design elements. Tease out the variations in interpretation through structured discussion. The entire data-driven organization design process will do just this.

In terms of targets being misaligned, Chapter 3.3 deals with this point explicitly. It is inevitable that objectives will often be contradictory. The need is to expose those conflicts and ensure the reward mechanisms don't get in the way of doing what is right. Lastly, the third issue of motivation is harder to solve. This comes down to who is hired and retained. Do they sign up to the vision and values of the business or not? If not, tougher conversations need to take place. People who are ambitious and who want to be promoted should be welcomed, as long as they have the behaviours, competencies and performance to back up their ambition.

Data and analytics

The value that a data-driven approach can bring to organization design is undeniable, as I will demonstrate throughout this book. However, that doesn't mean it's easy in practice. The perception is that the main challenges with data and analytics are technical; for example: collecting, merging, storing, structuring, calculating, maintaining, visualising or cleaning. But in reality these are relatively simple to solve, and becoming far easier to solve in this age of rapid information innovation. Far more difficult to overcome are the social issues data brings. Data is emotive, and can be threatening. Sometimes this is unintentional, and other times data is used actively as another weapon in the war of office politics. After all, information is power. These social issues cause blockers, and overcoming them takes a lot of guile, focus and leadership. In my experience there are four types of blockers:

1 The manager or employee who is **apathetic**. They think it's not worth the effort to contribute their data or ensure it is correctly formatted.

2 The employee who is **fearful to provide data** because of how it may be interpreted, and the risk of being misrepresented. They fear those above them will judge too quickly, and make unjustified decisions without the 'whole truth'.

3 The manager or employee who uses data as a **passive-aggressive** weapon in the battle for office supremacy. They present charts and figures that implicate another department, or person, taking the scrutiny away from themselves.

4 The manager or employee who hides information from others because **information is power**. If they hold the information they can hold the power and use that power over other people. Often done by refusing to give data or by presenting complex charts and numbers to ensure no one quite knows what is going on.

One thing is clear: transparency is rarely universally desired. And, obviously, unfettered transparency isn't the goal here. The flow of information will always be managed, and often for very good reasons. However, my point is that even obtaining the basic information on your current organizational performance can be a real challenge.

Solution: be persistent

I believe if you want organizational transparency then you have to fight for it. The technical issues can be overcome. Whatever the reason, it is those secretive souls whom you need to take along the journey. First, it is not an overnight fix. It will take time and repeated effort. However, with each step it will become easier as data becomes a fundamental part of organization design and the execution of that design. Second, ensure that throughout the design process the value of the outputs significantly outweighs the cost of getting the inputs. People will embrace data if they get something from it and have ownership over it. Even playing back the insights will surprise many because they are so used to providing data into a black hole. Third, if they give data once and you will want them to do it regularly, find a way to automate the process as much as possible. No one likes reworking the same thing over and over again. Fourth, if it comes to it, you have to be tough. If the only way forwards is to enforce from above – and it is rare that such a heavy-handed approach is required – then sometimes you have to use authority to get things done. This book champions a data-driven approach. Although I have tried to structure every chapter in as informative and practical a way as possible, there will never be an out-of-the-box solution to implementing and creating a data-driven culture, especially if it is at odds with the organization's current way of doing things.

Personal limits

Work should be fun. Obviously it isn't all of the time, but then you have to be engaged and know that the good times come along with the bad. During the dark days described in the above case study, I put on 10 kilos and had a limited social life and reduced sleep. Night after night, week after week, I would wake at 3 am or 4 am with my mind racing. This was pervasive. Change is emotional and taxing. The main reason for such stress comes down to lack of alignment and trust. So try (using the methods outlined above in 'Solution: Ensure clarity' under 'People and politics') to limit the risk of this happening.

Solution: manage your resources

First, manage your time. A large-scale organization design is time consuming. This comes back to the first question we asked in the introduction: 'Is the potential upside of the redesign worth the cost and risk of doing so?' For example, can you do more by clarifying objectives or responsibilities rather than by changing organizational structures? I believe that controlled organization development is often preferable to large-scale redesigns. Most of what I describe in Part Three and Part Four can happen without large-scale macro redesign. However, if a major redesign is the only option then make sure you have the time and resources at your disposal. Creating a clear well-resourced plan is fully detailed in the project management section in Chapter 3.5. Given the complexity of the organizational system, each day of effort can feel like a drop in the ocean. Your mind can only deal with so much. So be fair to yourself: make sure the timelines and resource plans are realistic and make sure you have the proper support in place.

Design processes

Approaching an organization design with a comprehensive and consistent approach can be a challenge. You have to apply the same rigour across all areas of the design, and also bring everyone along the same journey. Organization design is more than just a structural issue. As I highlighted in the introduction, so often organization design is understood simply as org charts and who reports to whom. The org charts become the focus rather than what work actually needs to be done by each person. Linked to the issues of people and politics, people care much more about their position on the chart than anything else. There is a real challenge in communicating and getting adoption of design methods which go beyond a simple restructure and fundamentally address the way an organization functions.

Solution: connect the organizational system

In many ways this challenge encompasses all the challenges above and the reason for this book. The solution begins with bringing clarity to the bigger picture, the purpose of the redesign. Not having an agreed method to follow or process for getting from A to B will result in chaos or, at best, time lost as everyone tries to muddle through. Throughout the process you have to be rigorous about definitions and phrases. Throughout this book, clarity of terminology, processes and documentation are common themes. Break down the organizational system and ensure everyone is clear that the issues go deeper than an org chart, and that there will be no quick fix. Finally, take a data-driven approach so that everyone starts from the same points and begin to connect the impacts on the organization as a whole. This book clarifies a process that is both holistic and truly end to end, to help design the organization, implement that design and sustain the design over time.

Final thoughts

Any person or organization can lose their edge. In my own experience, despite having undertaken consulting OD projects a vast number of times, I have made the most basic of mistakes. Just knowing the theory doesn't mean you are always strong enough to practise it. These challenges hopefully throw sharp perspective on the journey to come. It may seem daunting, but as I stated, just identifying the challenges gets you halfway there. At times, it may appear to be so much that it just overwhelms. Don't let it. Enjoy the journey of addressing these common issues. Organizations are organic, constantly moving and seeking direction. There are never any perfect answers when it comes to the design. There are just a trade-offs to be made. In order to achieve your strategy, you need to have the right people, doing the right things, at the right time, with the right competencies, in the right numbers. They all need to be clear about their roles, how they fit into a broader context and are aligned. Or as close as is practical given the realities of changing business life.

> ## Remember this
>
> 1 Don't fall into the trap of thinking that a change at the macro level is necessarily the solution.
>
> 2 Designing to keep the political powerbrokers happy is likely to backfire and result in a high price being paid.
>
> 3 An organization is a system and small changes to that system can have unpredictable impacts.
>
> 4 You are going to need to 'fight for transparency'.
>
> 5 Manage your resources and be realistic about what can be achieved within a given time frame.

Notes

1 Horowitz, B (2014) *The Hard Thing About Hard Things: Building a business when there are no easy answers*, Harper Business

2 Epstein, D (2014) *The Sports Gene: Talent, Practice and the Truth About Success*, Yellow Jersey

Foundations and core concepts

There is magic in graphs. The profile of a curve reveals in a flash a whole situation – the life history of an epidemic, a panic, or an era of prosperity. HENRY D HUBBARD 1939

Introduction

Organizations are complex, constantly moving and can often seem unpredictable. Dealing with uncertainty is hard but it is a constant in business. The challenge is to get into the best position possible to make consistently good decisions in an ambiguous world. The only way to do this is to arm yourself with the right tools, both on a conceptual and a technological level. A great example of how to do this comes from the world of economics.

In 1959 natural gas was discovered in the Netherlands. Intuition would say that gas means money, better business and more jobs. Good for everyone, right? Unfortunately not. After finding the gas, there were job losses and increased unemployment. On the face of it, a completely illogical and incomprehensible result. So what was really going on? The discovery of gas led to the appreciation of the Dutch currency, which in turn meant that the price of exports increased. Businesses lost trade as markets were unable to afford the increases in price and the knock-on effect meant cuts and job losses across organizations.

This example is a fantastic demonstration of systems thinking, a situation in which one part of a system (in this case the economic system – the oil and gas industry) has a hidden connection with another part of the system (the manufacturing industry). The real question is, can seemingly unconnected relationships and unlikely scenarios such as the example above be predicted? It could, and in fact in economic circles these interactions are now modelled by economists, to run scenarios and predict the impact of the economic development of natural resources. The phenomenon even has its own name: Dutch Disease.

Why is this relevant to the organization? An organization has many similarities to an economy. For example, both have tangible and intangible drivers and both are extremely volatile. Both are extremely difficult to understand in full and to manage accordingly. Like an economy, the organization and organizational change can only be understood from a systems perspective.

In the same way in which economists model economies, can we begin modelling the organization in a way that connects the organizational system? Can we simplify the complexities of this system to understand it as a whole, see the 'unseen' connections and get a glimpse of seemingly unpredictable scenarios before they happen?

I believe we are part of an exciting time where the advances of technology are allowing us to gain a true competitive advantage by using data and analytics from across organizations to model and connect the organizational system. This type of insight doesn't happen overnight. It requires a long journey, from collecting and analysing the data, to understanding how it impacts the business and then implementing the changes needed for business improvement.

This chapter lays many of the foundational building blocks for this book: a mental model for organizational analytics and design. Starting from a theoretical approach to the organization, I set out three foundations:

- **Foundation 1**: The organization is a system
- **Foundation 2**: Organizational data is hierarchical
- **Foundation 3**: Organizational data is messy

The chapter then lays out a three-step approach to deal with each one of these:

- **Method 1**: Create hierarchical data structures
- **Method 2**: Connect the system
- **Method 3**: Visualize to analyse

This chapter challenges some assumptions in current design work, and throws out some of the tools that have traditionally been used. I hope it provides you with a fresh perspective, and a new way of seeing and understanding the organization.

Foundation 1: The organization is a system

Understanding the organization as a system is at the heart of this book's application of organization design. Organization design is not about who reports to whom; it is about what each role in the organization is required to do, what decisions need to be made, what activities need to be done, what competencies are required to do these things and which employees have the right set of competencies for each role. The connections are many and inter-linked. Treating the organization as a system is about seeing and closing the gap between these areas. Answering the sorts of questions like: What are the optimum number of full-time employees (FTEs) for my organization? How are my customers going to be served? What are the value chains needed to serve those customers? How much of my workforce should be in house versus contracting?

The idea of treating the organization as a system is not new, but the thinking is rarely applied in practice. Taking a couple of examples from existing literature, the organization as a system has been defined in the following terms:

> Designing organizations is the process of purposefully configuring the elements of an organization to effectively and efficiently achieve its strategy and deliver intended business, customer and employee outcomes.[1]

> Driving business strategy and operating context requires holistic thinking (systems, structures, people, performance measures, processes, culture, skills...); design for the future; not to be undertaken likely; a fundamental process and not a repair job.[2]

These descriptions are all very well, but what do they really mean? How pragmatically can we make sense of the idea of the organization as a system in a value-adding way rather than an academic concept?

Let's start at a high level. An organization has a vision, a reason for being. This is translated into goals, objectives and more broadly into a strategy in how to achieve these (see Chapter 2.2 for a detailed description of these terms). Objectives are then broken down and delivered by employees who fulfil roles within a reporting structure. Each role is associated with certain processes and competencies required to deliver the objectives and processes ascribed to that role. I could keep going round in circles, but the system can only start to be understood as a model. Figure 1.3.1 shows some of the elements of the organizational system and how they can start to be connected.

This model in Figure 1.3.1 falls short of covering all the aspects of the organization – models are never able to convey the whole truth. It only shows particular elements and connections of the organization, but it is a useful way to begin to understand the complexities of the system. At first glance it may feel complex and overwhelming. I recommend you take your time, step through it slowly and focus on each of the various connections separately. The questions highlight the sorts of thought processes you should go through. For instance, how do you translate the strategy to specific goals and objectives as will be outlined in Chapter 3.3? Once the objectives are clear, you then need to define who is responsible for each one. That is represented by the links between the list of 'Goals and Objectives' and 'Employees'. The datasets each have a wealth of information in them. For instance, the employee dataset will frequently have demographic, performance and reward data as outlined in Chapter 3.2. An example of a gap is the difference between required numbers of people and the actual supply of people (as explained in Chapter 4.5). There are feedback loops; for instance, I may have a target headcount in my desired org structures, but is that number right (as is explained in Chapter 3.7) and does the top-down financial implication of this headcount match my financial goals? The system starts at two ends: the strategy and what the system needs to deliver to the customer. The customer dataset is drawn at the top, to signify their primary importance, with the employees right in the middle as the connection point between all the elements. Not every connection or nuance from this figure will make sense at first glance. That is fine. After you read more and more of this book, each of the elements of the system will become understandable.

I will reference aspects of this model throughout the book, putting each part of the organizational system into the context of the interrelated whole. Part Two covers vision and strategy, high-level goals, structural options and summary processes, while Part Three details objectives, processes, non-process, competencies and rightsizing. Part Four focuses on executing the plans developed in the macro and micro stages.

Exploring the organizational system in more detail, a good way to think through all its connections in practical terms is to think about a job description as shown in Figure 1.3.2. A job description systematically captures all the major elements of the organizational system. You have the person, the role, the salary and whom he or she reports to. You have a description of the objectives the person is expected to fulfil, the overall responsibilities, what he or she is supposed to do, and a list of projects that person will be focusing on and the competencies (ie skills and behaviours) required.

On this level, the organizational system conceptually is not that hard to grasp. However, in practical terms the issue is scale. Having one job description is quite simple but what about when we look at 10,000 or even just

FIGURE 1.3.1   The organizational system

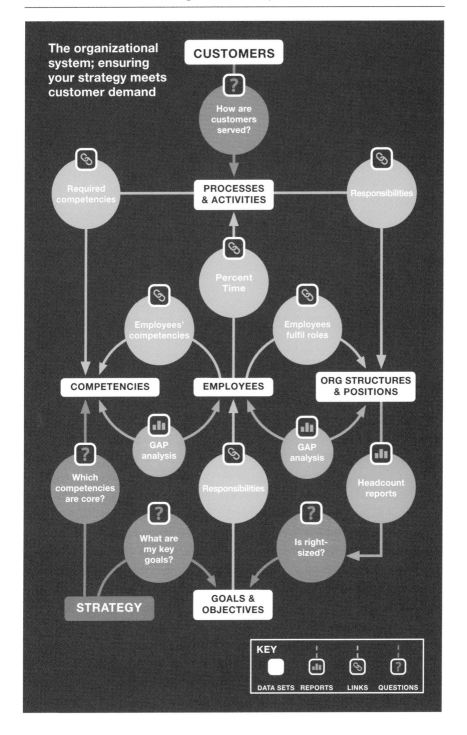

FIGURE 1.3.2   The organizational system as a job description

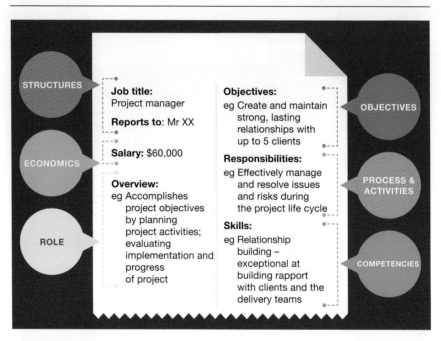

100? It is impossible to know how each person relates to every other person, especially across all functions – the brain can only process so much.

Unfortunately, it isn't always possible to keep organizations in small units. The complexity and size of organizations mean that often the basics are not understood, to the point where a large majority of firms I speak to don't know their headcount and certainly not their headcount over time, by function, location, grade and employment type (eg permanent versus contractor).

For example, I once worked with a fast-moving consumer goods (FMCG) firm who had roughly 20 manufacturing plants around Europe. They all produced the same products and by and large had the same processes. Within those processes quality control was crucial and strictly regulated. However, there was no consistency across the plants. The numbers of people working across quality control varied between two and eight. When we performed analysis we found that despite the difference in numbers, they were all covering the same amount of work. So, why the variation in number? At best they were just being inefficient and at worst creating a massive corporate risk.

This type of obscurity not only hinders business performance but also halts individual development and performance. If managers do not know what their reports should be doing, how can they give effective feedback? How well do you know they are doing in achieving their objectives? Are they on target or not? Do they have too much to do, resulting in performance suffering across the board?

To understand the interplay between all these moving parts we need to understand and break down the structural nature of the organization.

Foundation 2: Organizational data is hierarchical

The basis of my working definition of 'organizational data' in the context of organization design is data that has the person as the central unit of analysis. This is not the same as 'people data', which is a subset of organizational data and relates specifically to a person rather than their numerous connections and links across the organization. To put this in context, every part of the organizational system in Figure 1.3.1 can be understood as organizational data. Even if you approach a design from a specific process or competencies perspective, these areas of the organization always link back to a person. Understood in this way, organizational data has two far reaching consequences for the organization design methodology in this book: first, organizational data needs to be understood in the context of a hierarchy, and second, people data cannot be broken down into one unit of analysis.

The easiest way to understand the hierarchical nature of organizations is to begin from a simple people perspective. The natural structure of most organizations is one with a people hierarchy, built upon specific role levels and reporting lines connecting employees to specific managers. If we want to understand this simply, all we need to do is create a standard organization chart (Figure 1.3.3).

FIGURE 1.3.3   Organization chart coloured by department

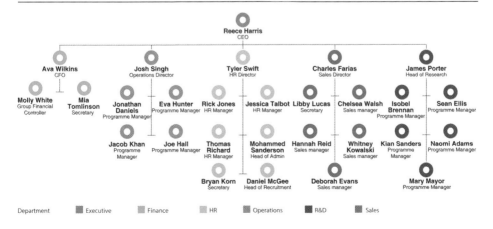

Unfortunately, far too many organization designs stop at this perspective. Design work is seen as a simple exercise of moving boxes around a PowerPoint slide. However, it is too simple to look at the design of an organization simply from a people- or even role-based view. This brings us back to my second statement, that organizational data cannot be broken down into one unit of analysis. What I mean by this is that within a person as a unit you have clusters of information linked to the person; for instance, a set of objectives, a certain amount of experience, competencies, strengths and so on. It is impossible to break a person down into one skill, or a particular set of skills. The result of this complication is that when understanding how the organizational system is connected you have to go much deeper than a simple reporting line. In reality, what you are dealing with is a complex interconnected, overlapping web of objectives, processes, competencies and so on. Because people do not change very fast, and are not infinitely divisible, when dealing with organization design you have to deal with ambiguity. Things never fit together perfectly.

This complexity doesn't mean we should give up, but that we need to understand how to break down the organizational system and see the connections. To do this we can apply the same hierarchical approach we took from a people perspective and apply it across the organizational system. In doing this, what you are actually doing is creating taxonomies for the various organization elements. Taxonomy is an area of science focused on classification or, put more simply, grouping things that are similar. It is a way of creating structures. A good example of taxonomy is the way Amazon organizes its products into different categories (eg books and audio versus sports and outdoors) and different subcategories (eg books, Kindle editions, children's books) and so on. Taxonomies are a great way of categorizing and subcategorizing data into logical chunks of information.

If you take the organization you already have taxonomies in the definition of the system: roles, objectives, processes, competencies and so on. Within each one of these there will be further subcategories. For example, if you go back to your org chart, it is likely that attached to the role titles are certain categories such as function, location, salary band, organizational grade. Or think of objectives. These start as overarching goals and cascade into more and more specific objectives and key performance indicators or KPIs (see Chapter 3.3). If you build out all these hierarchies you can then start to see how they relate to each other. Unfortunately, each area of the organizational system will not fit neatly on top of another. However, it gives you the building blocks for drawing the connections and links between them.

Foundation 3: Organizational data is messy

The organizational system is naturally complicated. However, one of the reasons so many struggle to understand the as-is of their organization, let alone implement an organization design, is a misdirected approach to data. In the previous section I highlighted one of the unique features of people data; that as a unit of analysis they cannot be broken down into a single unit. This has consequences for how you approach people data in order to make sense of them. This section looks at what data you are really dealing with when doing an organization design before highlighting the challenges that come with this organizational data.

Let's clarify immediately. Organizational data is not big data. At the time of writing this book there has been a huge buzz around big data and its potential business value. There is no doubt it is changing the way businesses are run. However, when it comes to people transformation and change, is big data really changing the way we design the organization?

There have been a lot of voices saying an emphatic Yes. For example, Jay Galbraith, building on his four structural principles separating an organization (business divisions, organizational functions, international units and customer segments), suggested that big data is a fifth structural principle when restructuring.[3] New functions will be the big data operations distinguishing themselves from the previous four structural principles that separated the organization.

I am not as convinced. Because of the hype there has been a lot of misuse of the term 'big data'. Big data is not the be-all and end-all, and thinking it is will mean you approach your organizational analytics and design in the wrong way. So what is the difference between organizational data and big data?

Big data

- **What does it look like?** Big data involves looking at upwards of tens if not thousands of millions of information points that are often extremely fast moving.

- **The challenge?** Their complexity, speed and volume. Big data can often be recorded in real time, involving millions of transactions over a short amount of time. For example, I once worked with a global FMCG firm that took out over $500 million of working capital across 180 markets through inventory optimization and better forecasting. This type of project represented a challenge in terms of the complexity of storing and analysing such large amounts of data in a useful and efficient way.

- **How to deal with big data.** Often when storing, processing and querying big data, and in the case of the FMCG firm, you would use a data warehouse (see Chapter 3.2 for a definition).

- **When do you use big data?** Examples include: marketing where big data allows more accurate customer segmentation through real-time analysis; in healthcare big data supports more targeted treatment for patients; in recruitment big data allows employers to screen potential candidates more accurately through CV and social media analysis; and in the supply chain business, big data helps reduce inventory wastage.

My view is that big data will affect how organizations do their business, but will not have a massive impact on the process of designing organizations. In reality, it is only for the very largest organizations and for very specific data, such as social media data on candidates or recruitment where dataset sizes are larger than a million data points.

Organizational data

- **What does it look like?** Organizational datasets are relatively small and contain the many-to-many* links of the organizational system.

- **The challenge?** The complex nature of organizational data means it is often incomplete and subject to (relatively) slow but constant change. For example, organizational roles can have numerous different titles making standard analysis near impossible. Traditionally, organizational data is held in numerous systems and documents including human resource information systems (HRIS), payroll systems and disparate Excel spreadsheets. The messy nature of organizational data is one of the things that make it so challenging, not its size. Most organizational data will contain millions of data points and connections at most. This pales in comparison to the volume and velocity you are dealing with in big data. It is the fact that the data is usually incomplete, constantly changing, hard to

---

*In a relational database, links (say, between cells or rows) can be **one-to-one** (eg: one person ↔ one National Insurance number), **one-to-many** (eg: one order ↔ several items) or **many-to-many** (eg: products anyone can buy ↔ customers who can buy any product).

maintain and linked in complex ways that makes the organizational data so hard to manage.[4]

- **How to deal with people data**. Traditionally, there has been a lack of technical tools to help understand the complexities of people data. I have horrible memories of working on designs late into the night to deliver a project, only to get told at the eleventh hour that a certain figure or graph was wrong. Cue frantic changes in Excel and PowerPoint to get everything ready for the final presentation.

Traditional relational databases (for a definition of a relational database see Chapter 3.2) such as Excel are great for many things, but they are just not set up for design work. Simple rows and columns do not allow you to truly understand the many-to-many links of the organization. For example, when doing process design, tables do not allow you to see how a process links to a role, what competencies are required for that role, and who is the actual person fulfilling that role currently, because they are bound by a one-to-one relationship. The only way forward is to stop thinking in tables and instead think in terms of graphs. Graphs have the ability to connect disparate aspects of the organization because they allow for the multiple connections contained in organizational data (for a more detailed description of a graph database see Chapter 3.2). The thinking behind this book and organizational visualizations used is underpinned by a graph-based approach to organizational data, to allow for the many-to-many links contained in organizational data.

Applying the foundations in practice

The way you see the world is the way you understand it. If you can't see something it makes it much harder to understand. In the context of organizational data and analytics, being unable to see the links and connections of the organizational system not only means it takes a lot longer to perform analysis, but also means a lot of detail is obscured and lost. What all organizations need is a new way to see themselves. They need the ability to look round the corners; provide context; connect the system – people, activities, processes, costs and so on.

In 2014, I worked with one of the world's largest fleet management companies who managed to do just that. Its business model is centred on optimizing the cost of serving customers while maintaining the highest standards of customer experience and satisfaction. However, the business had no way of knowing what happened to its money, from overheads to specific customer allocation. It wanted to be able to improve its understanding of its cost base, pricing and the services supplied to each customer. Where could it improve its processes? Where could it offer better prices? Which customer support activities added most value?

It all starts with the data, so the company held short interviews with 70 key people in the process and gathered together all existing operations data. After 10 weeks, it had a clear view of work volumes and their causes. The organization could see its total cost base from three different points of view – from the perspective of project, process or customer relations. This set of relationships is shown in Figure 1.3.4.

There were many surprising large variations in costs. For example, the organization expected its specialist Customer Queries team to take up 0.9 per cent of the cost-to-serve. But other teams from across the business were also responding to customer queries, which meant the actual costs were 3.2 per cent. This represented a huge opportunity to significantly increase sales. Using this information the strategy team could have practical conversations about how to re-engineer a more efficient cost-to-serve process: which activities it wanted to carry on, which activities it wanted to stop and whether any activities needed tweaking slightly.

FIGURE 1.3.4   Cost-to-serve model

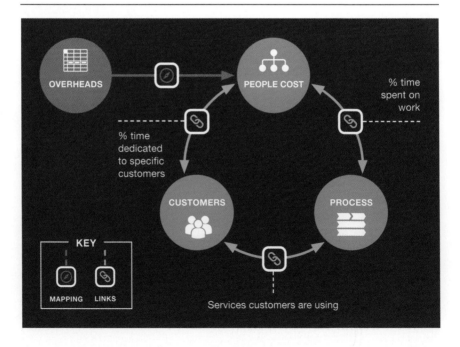

This is a great example of the value in mapping and analysing the many-to-many connections of the organizational system in practice. It is the only way to truly understand what is going on, what has happened in the past and, based on this, make the most informed decisions possible for the future. When faced with change, this model is what helps you decide which aspects of the organization you should keep and which you should leave behind.

So, how do you get past the numbers? How do you connect the system practically in a way that is manageable and understandable? How can you create an accurate design and consistently make good decisions? How do you get to the point where analysing past and present data happens automatically, and the focus is on predicting future trends, making proactive rather than reactive business decisions?

In the next section, I outline three methods that underpin my approach to data-driven organization design. These methods are not a linear process but a continuous and interlinked cycle of activities, which feed into each other to help understand and connect the organizational system.

Method 1: Create hierarchical data structures

As I outlined in Foundation 2, above, organizational data can be understood as a series of hierarchies. So, to understand and analyse the organization you need to build these hierarchies across the system. As is already probably apparent, hierarchical trees have quite specific terminology (see Figure 1.3.5 for an outline of key terms). In the context of taking a graph-based approach to understand the many-to-many connections of the organization, each position on any organizational hierarchical tree can be defined as a node. That is a connection point between multiple links. For example, a node in an org chart could represent a position that is linked to a person and a role, which are then in turn linked to numerous other data such as objectives and competencies. Equally, a node could represent an objective in an objectives tree or a process in a process tree. The node is purely an intersection point of information.

When doing organization design, like it or not, the trusty org chart is where most design starts. The org chart shows the layout of an organization in such a simple way and helps communicate the shape and structure of the reporting lines, as illustrated in Figure 1.3.3.

There is a common trap of reading too much into an org chart. It isn't where the box sits but what is in the box that counts. For example, when

FIGURE 1.3.5   Hierarchical tree terminology

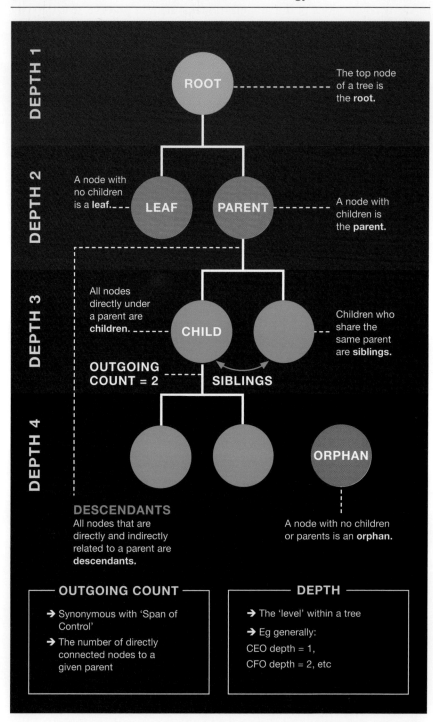

doing org design, people often obsess with where their box sits relative to the CEO. It is as if the distance from the CEO is the sole definition of power, grade, or potential salary. So does that mean those at the bottom of the org chart are by definition unimportant, regardless of anything else? Clearly not. I have seen org charts where someone's chauffeur is three from the top but where the lead technical director on a key future technological project is six away. There are times when the span of control or number of people below the position are assumed to be a proxy for importance instead. This type of thinking is flawed. Indeed, when I have experienced this first hand, one of the things that has always surprised me in allocating management was how we didn't want some of the most important positions to have a team to manage at all (ie no direct reports and a span of control of zero). The amazing thing – but it's logical in hindsight – is that (*a*) not everyone is good at managing, (*b*) many technical or sales roles suffer from the burden of management and (*c*) by not having a team, the influence of those individuals is not necessarily diminished in the slightest.

Doing org design is not about mapping and moving people and positions in org charts. You need to see beyond depth and layers, spans of control and size of control (the total number of positions below) and see what is in the box: the objectives; accountabilities; competencies; projects they are involved in; risk they manage; clients they serve. In other words, see the system. You need to understand the information flows and hierarchies across the organization to really understand how they fit together.

When building the hierarchies in practice across the organization, whether roles, objectives or processes and so on, a useful approach is the Mutually Exclusive and Collectively Exhaustible (MECE) methodology. This concept was developed by Barbara Minto while at McKinsey, a management consultancy firm, and is at the heart of her 'Pyramid Principle'.[5] The idea is that you take a high-level idea or action and break it down in a logical and structured way. Just as repeating points or missing out points in a presentation would have a negative impact on its overall message, not adhering to the MECE framework does likewise. The table in Figure 1.3.6 summarizes the two aspects of the MECE approach and how you achieve each one.

Using this approach is extremely useful when trying to break down work (processes), objectives, competencies, risk, projects and many more of the elements within the detailed design. Theoretically, if all organizational objectives are MECE then the organization is running at the best possible efficiency; there are no duplicated objectives and, when added up, all the objectives and subobjectives cover all the strategic aims (see more in

FIGURE 1.3.6   MECE methodology for building taxonomies

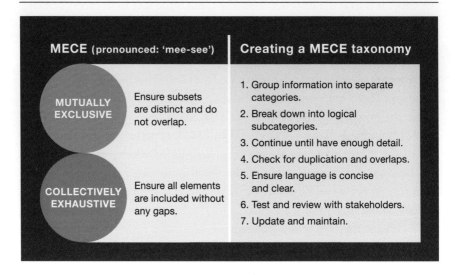

Chapter 3.3). In reality this is near impossible, but thinking it through in this way helps you avoid unnecessary blockers and inefficiencies.

The most important thing when building these taxonomies is to get the level of detail right. It is easy to define too much detail. For example, in the context of a work canteen there could be a process of 'Feed staff'. This can be broken down into five main areas: Manage the canteen; Buy the food, goods and services; Preparation; Service; Clean. From this, each element can be further analysed. For example, 'Prepare' could be broken into 'Meat', 'Vegetables' and 'Sauces'. These can be further broken down, and then again, and again, and again, as in Figure 1.3.7.

It is possible to break this down until you reach the point of absurdity. You could imagine that the process of 'Slice potatoes' could be further broken into sort potatoes; align them; cut them; and so on. Remember, though, all of these sets of information connect to one another so the more detail you create the more complexity you are going to have to manage. You have to balance detail against practicality.

Having created and visualized your taxonomies, the next step is to connect them to start defining them in the context of the organizational system.

Method 2: Connect the system

With your hierarchical information in place, the next step is to link these elements in what is a series of many-to-many relationships. At the end of the

FIGURE 1.3.7 Example process tree

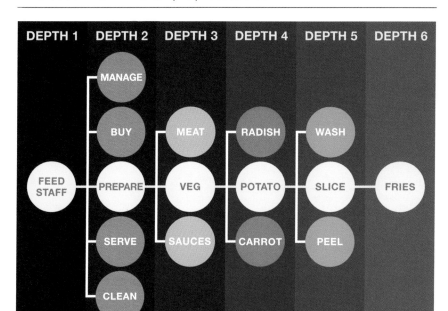

day, when doing an organization design you are looking at what and how much work needs to be done, and how to divide that work between your workforce. From the moment a founder brings on another person, an organization is born. From this point tasks are divided up: you do X and I'll do Y. As the volume of work, people and complexity increases, dividing the work and understanding who does what and for how long become harder and harder to manage. Taxonomies set the platform for bringing it all back together. For example, operations are split between functions and subfunctions. Work is broken down into a geographical context of what is done centrally or locally. Job grades are created so that the right level of task is done by the right level of seniority. Linking is how you can connect all these elements together.

Linking helps with a number of things:

- It gives clarity to who is required to do what and for how long.
- It helps ensure everything that needs to be done is covered.
- It avoids duplications of effort or things falling between the cracks.

Figure 1.3.8 shows, in the top two tables, differing ways of linking the organizational system through allocation of time and an accountability matrix,

FIGURE 1.3.8   Connecting the organizational system

Linking table by allocation of time

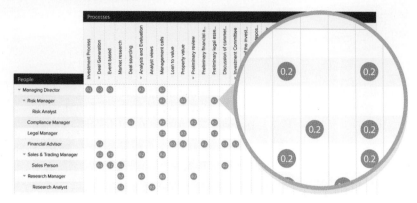

RAS matrix

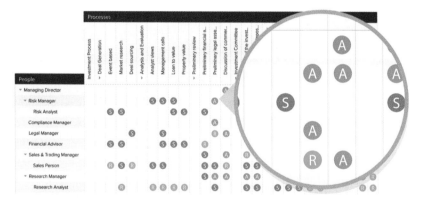

Org chart of RAS allocations

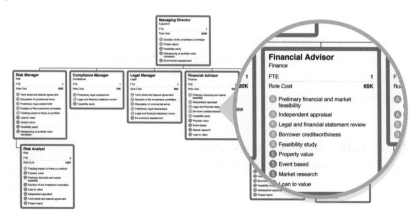

and then how those allocations can be seen within the context of the org chart. They both have positions as rows and, in this example, activities as columns. You can then fill in the gaps to mark which roles are connected to which activities and to see how this affects each person within the organizational hierarchy.

RACI, RASIC, RAPID – cut out the complexity

A tool often used for linking is the accountability matrix. I came across this method the first time I did an OD project for the sales and marketing function of an automotive company in South Africa in the 1990s. At 5.15 pm on a Friday in early summer, 15 minutes before I was due to join my colleagues for a well-earned beer, I got a call from the German office explaining they were urgently short of a consultant and off I went to the airport, files in hand and an angry girlfriend left behind for six weeks.

My experience of OD was limited, to say the least. I had just completed a restructuring of a UK automotive distributor, but it was obvious I was not the first choice. During the flight I had to prep for the 9 am kick-off meeting and, as part of that, for the first time I came across the RACI accountability framework. This framework helps determine who is Responsible (R), Accountable (A), Consulted (C) or Informed (I) for a set of fields such as objectives, risks, projects, processes, activities and so on.

A series of questions came to mind:

- What is the difference between being Accountable and Responsible?
- How important was it to really define who needed to be Consulted and Informed?
- What about other people who needed to be involved in actually doing the work?
- Making decisions is different from doing 'stuff' – what about all those who have a veto on a decision, or feel they do?
- The point of the A and R is that there should be only one person per role (ie single points of Accountability). But, what if there are two decision makers (ie two people have veto power)?

What I didn't think of until much later, but having done this numerous times since, is once this has been defined, how do you sustain it? How do you communicate it? How do you make it live? Too often we define things like a RACI as a one-off. People make a big fuss about whether they are *consulted* before a decision is made or *informed* after it is made. But this framework just creates an unnecessary amount of detail, and is completely unrealistic to maintain.

Whenever I did an org piece, whether using RACI, RASIC (the S stands for 'Support') or RAPID (a framework used by the consulting firm Bain with the specifications Recommend, Agree, Perform, Input and Decide), all those questions remained. In particular, I became tired of trying to explain the difference between R and A: 'The R needs to make sure it happens; the A gets shot if it doesn't and, yes, they are often the same person.' Equally, having debates about who exactly needs to be informed or consulted is fairly painful. If you debate that one for hours you really know you are going to struggle. Shouldn't the person responsible also be responsible for working that one out? Shouldn't we just say that the R and A are the same person? If it is a decision, should we need to know who needs to approve it (ie who has a veto)? From a workforce planning and resourcing perspective, isn't it important to know who needs to be involved? My conclusion was that you must be able to simplify the whole thing. In response to this I thought through an RAS method for the accountability matrix:

1 Combine R and A – just have R and define it as Responsible and Accountable.

2 Throw out I and C – leave it to the person Responsible to define who needs to be Informed and Consulted.

This just gives you the R – one letter for defining the one person who is responsible. Simple.

But equally there are scenarios where it is useful to:

1 define who needs to approve a decision to help clarify the governance;

2 think through who else needs to provide time to get the work or decision done.

This leads to a simple 'RAS' framework as shown in Figure 1.3.9. It is a simple way of making sure accountability settings for processes and activities are not held up by unnecessary conversations, meetings and complications.

Assigning accountabilities to each process and activity provides clarity to everyone, both the person responsible for any given activity and those around him or her. The example in Figure 1.3.8 has the Financial Adviser responsible for five activities and supporting a further four. Using this RAS framework you can allocate who is responsible for what and what is required from each role. It isn't easy to build an accountability matrix. It requires you not only to define the processes and activities, but also to think through the

FIGURE 1.3.9 RAS methodology

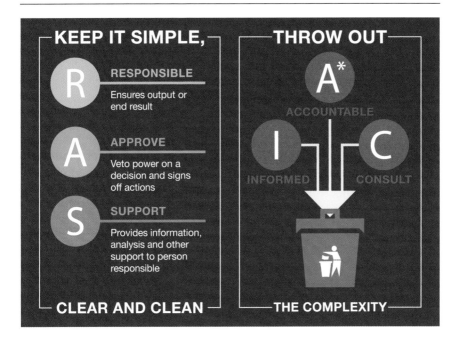

roles and define that link. It can be highly political and can often uncover cracks where either no one is currently responsible or multiple people are. So why bother? Why not just let people sort it out and get on with it?

First, it is true you can waste too much time on the detail. Referring back to the process of building your organizational hierarchies, this is why you need to make sure you don't overcomplicate things. If you have endless hierarchies and detail there is no point connecting everything in infinite detail. So, to make sure you don't go too far, start at the top. Connect the highest levels and then cascade down. Make a judgement call when you think you are going into too much detail and prescribing too much. After all, people can build the matrix out at a team level if they feel the need to formalize roles and focus. Part Three of this book defines in far more detail how best to do this and provides far more context-specific examples.

Second, putting a framework in place is useful, but it is not simply a box-ticking exercise. So to make it useful, make sure you think through the framework in practice and the amount of 'political noise' that will be generated by the numbers involved in the governance elements of the process design, such as the decision-making processes. This is expanded further in Chapter 3.3.

It is worth mentioning that I am not suggesting that the RAS method is the only way to build out these links. For example, instead of (or in addition to) the RAS matrix you could define the percentage of time that a person spends doing each activity, as with an Individual Activity Analysis (IAA – a method I outline in Chapter 3.4). Once this information is collected, you can define the cost of each activity and process that leads to a vast range of insights and improvement potentials.

The principle of creating an accountability matrix can be applied across all the areas of the organizational system. For example, you can link roles to process and objectives, process to competencies and, therefore, indirectly link roles and competencies together. Suddenly, the pieces of the jigsaw begin to fit together. You are starting to build out your graph. You can begin to analyse and get insight into which competencies are most in demand. If you then define which competencies each person has, then you know where the greatest gaps are and can prioritize your training and recruitment of specific skills. You can also begin scenario modelling. For example, what if you improved the efficiency of a given activity, then who would be impacted and what would the FTE reduction be? Part Three details how to do this and the ramifications of doing it in far more detail.

My final note on this section is that these connecting principles set the platform for high value-adding analysis by performing 'data mashing'. This is the process of bringing disparate sets of data together to look for and uncover new areas of insight. For example, combining your people data with sales data or network data to see where the hidden connections are. The possibilities are endless. However, the key is to get the basics in place so you can really start to explore how your people both impact and are impacted by areas across the whole.

To fully understand these links you need a way of presenting and interpreting that information. And here we come to the final and, in many ways, the most important method: visualize to analyse and understand.

Method 3: Visualize to analyse

The process of visualizing and analysing information is the foremost principle in understanding the many-to-many links and connections of the organizational system. It is the very essence of this book. Having looked at a range of definitions, I understand analytics as the revelation, understanding and communication of insights from data. In other words, analytics is more than just having and looking at data. Analytics if used in the right way helps to drive performance and better decision-making, uncover issues, solve them and see the results. As part of this analytical process, visualizing information can connect the seemingly unconnected, give deeper and better insights across the organization and improve the organization design process. For example:

- What sorts of recruitment channels provide the strongest performance with above-average loyalty? If you know that, you can concentrate the focus and recruit more high performers.

- Which managers have the most engaged, highest performing teams over a sustained period? If you know that, then getting to why this is the case is much easier.

- Which projects have inexperienced/low performing teams? Are they the most critical projects? Do you, therefore, know the balance of staff by experience, tenure and performance? This could mean the difference between the most critical projects failing or driving results beyond expectations.

- Which risks are being actively managed and, therefore, reducing the probability of them happening?

The list is almost endless.

One of the hardest parts of organization design is not actually working out where you are going but working out exactly where you are. You need to visualize data to analyse and understand the organizational system. Rows and tables of data tell you very little. Organizational data may not be big data, but that doesn't mean that it isn't still sizeable. Also, given you are bringing data from across the organizational system, no table is going to be able to show you the links which connect the system together.

The business case for visualizing information has been well made; using visuals over text can decrease learning time, improve understanding and increase the retention of information.[6,7,8] This is not only useful from the point of view of your own understanding of the organization, but how you report and communicate messages to others. It's about turning data into outcomes. Data tells a story, and you need to do that story justice. Know what messages you are trying to communicate and use your visualizations as illustrations. It's all about choosing the right chart for the right data and putting it in a logical order.

The simple point is that colourful, interactive images are a lot more exciting and satisfying than a row of Excel tables. Figure 1.3.10 puts this in sharp perspective.

FIGURE 1.3.10   Data table versus sunburst visualization coloured by engagement

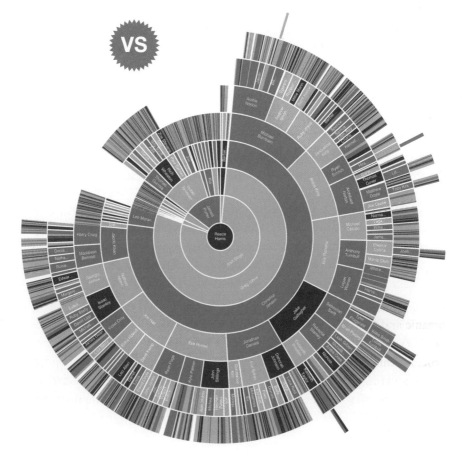

The table of data and the visualization in Figure 1.3.10 hold the same information. The Excel file simply lists the reporting lines, engagement index, the depth and spans of control. The first row is the CEO, and each row is another position. The visualization is called the sunburst (you can see this type of image on the cover of this book). The circle in the middle is the CEO. Each position that reports to the CEO is shown on the next layer. The colour is the engagement based on an RAG status: Red for poorly engaged; Amber for just below average engagement; and Green for engaged. The number of layers can be differentiated by the distance from the centre. Early patterns in engagement can be picked up. This visual doesn't convey all the relevant information but it is striking, easy to interpret and gives the person looking at it an immediate impression. By making your people data full of impact you will achieve more, and enjoy the process as you go.

There is a big debate in the world of data visualization. On one side is an emphasis on being scientific and precise, reducing subjective interpretation of the data. One of the leading voices from this school is Stephen Few, who in his fantastic book *Now You See It*[9] emphasizes minimizing the number of pixels in visualizations to ensure clarity. For example, using clean line charts, box plots or scatter plots over pie charts or infographics.

The other approach is to tell an emotive story: to not only convey information but also get a reaction from it. An example of this is the use of infographics to tell a story. This is an area explored by David McCandless in his book *Knowledge is Beautiful*,[10] where the emphasis is as much on the power of the visual as the information it represents.

There is quite a clash between these two schools. The purist versus the poet, if you like. One blogger with a marketing background positions the debate strongly: 'Do we seek to make art or is our primary goal to inform people about the state of the world around them?'[11] The challenge is that while infographics are more engaging they can give a misleading view of the world. I believe you can actually get the best from both worlds, especially in an organizational context. Often when representing organizational data you need to convey clarity and understanding while also engaging and creating an urge for action. I would tentatively put forward an emergent third school: data visualization focused more specifically on hierarchical, organic and framework-driven information. This type of information naturally fits closely with organizational data, and brings together the thought process behind representing frameworks, models and structures with added clarity and insight from high-impact and comprehensive data visualization. I would argue that a great deal of organizational analysis falls into this third

FIGURE 1.3.11   Stacked bar graph versus sunflower visualization: performance ranking versus tenure coloured by location

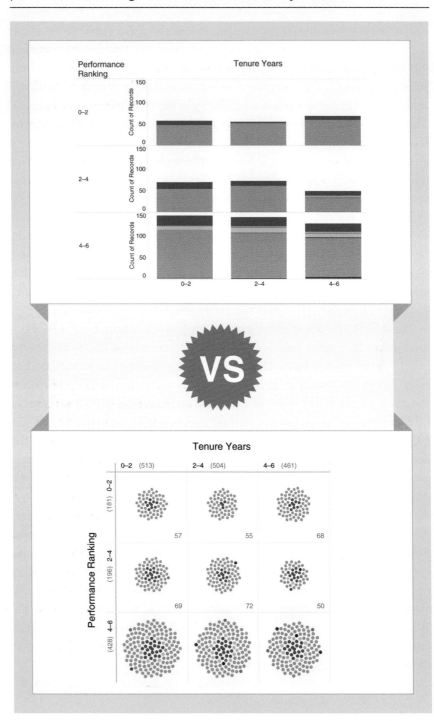

category. I leave it up to you to decide if this represents a new genre entirely or simply a practical application of data visualization taking the best fron the other two.

Figure 1.3.11 illustrates how the same data can be visualized in very different ways. The top figure shows a set of stacked bar graphs with the tenure ranges by performance scores. The sunflower figure below has the exact same information but shows each member of the various populations as a single coloured dot. I can see, for instance, that there are four people who have a tenure of 2–4 years with a 0–2 performance from the blue location. (The colour represents the locations of each employee.)

Hierarchical trees can be visualized in multiple ways and, in the context of organizational analytics and design work, they give the opportunity to see across the organization as a whole as you can visualize large amounts of information at once and present the organization for what it is: an organic, multifaceted system of people. Figure 1.3.12 shows several examples of hierarchical visualizations of organizational structures. Each one highlights a particular aspect of the organization. For example, Figure 1.3.12a allows you to see the organization as an organic whole. In contrast, the icicle chart (Figure 1.3.12c) helps to highlight the span of control and, when coloured by performance, whether there are any correlations between large spans of control and performance and any areas of the organization requiring particular focus.

If you are interested in reading more specifically on visualizing tree structures do read *The Book of Trees: Visualizing Branches of Knowledge* by Manuel Lima.[12]

I believe that data visualization and analytics are the key not just to understanding the organization, but having an impact, making things happen and driving change. It is a theme that runs throughout this book. The type of visual you should use depends on the questions. If you want to understand the layers and structural pyramid, then a box grid is an extremely effective way of understanding the 'shape' of an organization, as shown in Figure 1.3.13.

However, if you are also interested in the spans of control and the layers, Figure 1.3.14 brings that to life. The rows are the layers (the depth) and the columns are the spans of control (outgoing count). The numbers in each cell represent the number of employees with those spans for the given layer. This has been coloured according to a traditional blue-to-red heat map where blue is infrequent and red frequent.

FIGURE 1.3.12   Example organizational tree layouts

(a) Balloon tree layout

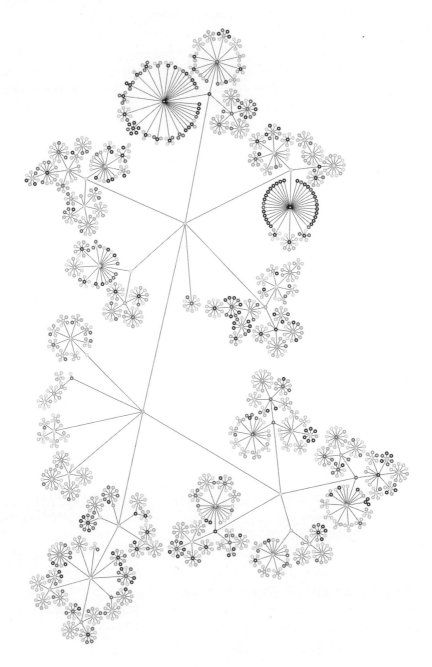

FIGURE 1.3.12 *Cont'd*

(b) Scaled balloon layout

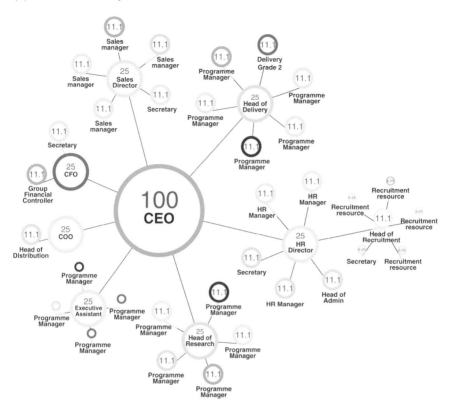

(c) Icicle layout

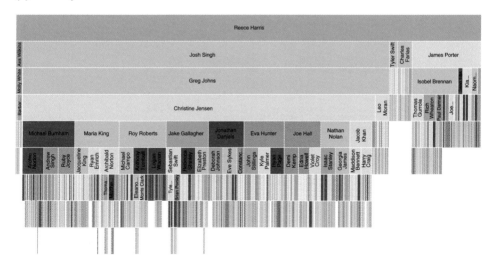

FIGURE 1.3.13   Box grid visualization of organizational depth (layers pyramid)

Count of Records by Records and Depth

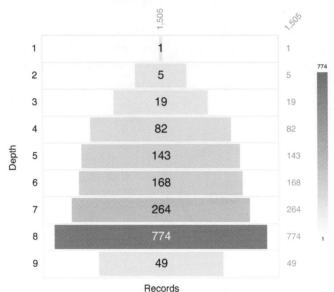

Records

FIGURE 1.3.14   Box grid visualization: heat map of depth versus span of control (outgoing count)

Count of Records by Outgoing Count and Depth

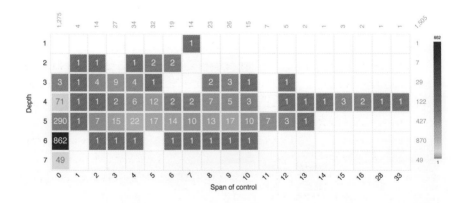

Span of control

A cornerstone of my belief in the power of data visualization and how it supports organization design is that visuals should be interactive, providing a seamless interaction with data from collection, through cleansing and analysis to manipulation and modelling. (The idea of cleansing data visually is one I explore in more detail in Chapter 3.2.) By playing with data visually you will make your life so much more enjoyable. The future is one where you can work with data visually, manipulating and changing visualizations that automatically alter data at source.[13] This is the Internet of Things applied to organization design and it is the logical next step from the touch-screen interactive technology we have come to expect in our everyday lives.

Model the to-be

There is so much value to be gained from visualizing and analysing the as-is of an organization. It is truly game changing to visualize and analyse future scenarios and decisions. This is the heart of good organization design, whether it is process design, objective setting, rightsizing or workforce planning.

However, at this point we are still in the world of moving boxes round a PowerPoint slide. We want to get to where, in the scenarios you plan, you can see all the elements of the organizational system shift with each change. Then you can see the gaps, the opportunities, the risks, and take action accordingly.

Tracking and sustaining performance

It is all very well getting the edge, but that in itself achieves little if you cannot sustain it. You have to find a way to track changes and performance over time. For example, take an objective. Can you set up a process so you can see the before and after effects of an organizational change?

Going through all these processes creates a virtuous circle. If you can see where you are you can plan for change; if you can plan for change you can make better decisions; if you track results you can maintain your understanding of the as-is and look for improvements – and so on.

With this in mind I see organization design as an ongoing process rather than one of intervention. Designs should be being tweaked, honed and improved all the time. It is only through data visualization and analytics that this can be made possible.

Final thoughts: see it as a journey

The concepts in this section and book are too penetrating to implement in one go as there is so much to define. In writing this book I have tried to break down each element of the system to make it easier to implement areas one at a time depending on your priorities.

By phasing the work, you should build institutional knowledge. The direction of analysis has to move from static snapshots to seeing change over time. Data is constantly changing and flow: both actuals and forecasts move. It is about seeing how these both change over time, their relationships with each other, what the gaps are, whether the gap is increasing or narrowing and whether you can find any causal relationships (for example, number of objectives owned by each person and the success rates of achieving the objectives) so that you can improve performance.

By creating, linking and visualizing your organizational hierarchies, the depth of analysis you can achieve is remarkable. For example, you can see the links between individual and objective performance, and then dive into whether an individual who is underperforming has missing competencies that are trainable, is overloaded with too many new objectives, or is working for a new manager who has historically had significantly higher than reasonable team attrition. Once the data is in place, you can really start to have fun and see the value flow.

Building an understanding of any framework takes time and I'm sure many of you will be thinking that this interconnected vision is a fantasyland, given that many organizations struggle to understand their headcount alone. But organization design is a journey and you can never do all the work or change everything in one go. I hope the methods and ideas in this book help to facilitate change at all stages of organization design, whether in answering the most basic questions or performing complex advanced analytics. The ideas in this chapter will help to navigate the remainder of this book.

1 See the organization as an interconnected system.

2 Build organizational data through taxonomies across each area of the system.

3 Organizational data is not big data, and contains many-to-many relationships.

4 Connect the organizational system through hierarchy building and by using links through percentage of time, competencies scores or acronyms like RAS in the accountability matrix.

5 Make it visual because the way you see the world defines how you understand it.

Notes

1 Mohrman, S (2007) *Organization Design for Growth: the Human Resource Contribution*, Centre for Effective Organizations, **07–10** (520), p 4

2 Stanford, N (2007) *Guide to Organization Design*, p 3, Profile Books Ltd, London

3 Galbraith, J (2012) The Evolution of Enterprise Organization Designs, *Journal of Organization Design*, **1** (2), pp 1–13

4 Slinger, G and Morrison, R (2014) Will Organization Design Be Affected By Big Data? *Journal of Organization Design*, **3** (3), pp 31–39

5 Minto, B (2008) *The Pyramid Principle: Logic in thinking and writing*, Prentice Hall

6 McDaniel, M and Einstein, G (1986) Bizarre imagery as an effective memory aid: The importance of distinctiveness, *Journal of Experimental Psychology: Learning, Memory, and Cognition*, **12** (1), pp 54–65

7 Patton, W (1991) Opening students' eyes: Visual learning theory in the Socratic classroom, *Law and Psychology Review*, **15**, pp 1–18

8 Verdi, M P *et al* (1997) Organized spatial displays and texts: Effects of presentation order and display type on learning outcomes, *Journal of Experimental Education*, **65**, pp 303–17

9 Few, S (2009) *Now You See It*, Analytics Press

10 McCandless, D (2014) *Knowledge is Beautiful*, William Collins

11 McDaniel, S [accessed 11 January 2015] Stephen Few versus David McCandless, Freakalytics [Online] https://www.freakalytics.com/blog/2011/07/08/stephen-few-vs-david-mccandless-my-thoughts/

12 Lima, M (2014) *The Book of Trees*, Princeton Architectural Press

13 Kristi, M (2014) Support the Data Enthusiast: Challenges for Next-Generation Data-Analysis Systems, Proceedings of the VLDB Endowment, 7 (6), pp 453–56

PART TWO
Macro design

Introduction

Industry executives and analysts often mistakenly talk about strategy as if it were some kind of chess match. But in chess, you have just two opponents, each with identical resources, and with luck playing a minimal role. The real world is much more like a poker game, with multiple players trying to make the best of whatever hand fortune has dealt them.

DAVID MOSCHELLA

When most people talk about organizational design they are referring to macro design. It is the sexy, fun part of design work. It's what the MBA schools focus on and it's all about the big picture. All too quickly, people think about the org chart and structure. People obsess about structure and jump in far too quickly. You have to step back and ask the really tough questions that are the fundamentals of the business. They include: Where do you want to go? Why do you want to get there? And, at a high level, how are you going to get there? The answers to these questions make up the backbone of your business, but they are often documented ineffectively and miscommunicated. They are also some of the hardest questions to answer.

The most important thing to remember, and yet the easiest thing to forget when it comes to the macro design, is that there is never a right or perfect answer; there is just a minimization of maximum regret. At the end of the day, who knows what you might have achieved if you had gone down a different road? But if you fail, you need to be able to look back and know that in the situation you made the right choice. Otherwise you are going to be giving yourself a lot of frustrated, sleepless nights thinking *What if...?* You cannot predict the future, and at some point you are going to have to take risks. To use the analogy of poker, this is when you put your chips on the table. It is when you make the decision to join the high-stakes game. However, the great thing about business is that while you inevitably have to take risks, it is you who decides what game you are going to play, who your competitors are and, to some extent, what rules you are going to follow.

At this stage of the design process you have to make trade-offs and only you (and your leadership team) can decide how to make those trade-offs. Once you have answered those where, why and how questions, you need to create a compelling case for change. There is no point trying to do something as invasive as change your organization unless there is an incredibly strong case for doing so. Once in place, you need to turn all of that into a distilled set of design criteria that can be used to support the decision-making process between the various options. As a recommendation on the path forwards emerges, so too does the need for a business case that will stand the test of time.

Macro design in practice

It is too easy to design the organization in a reactive and unstructured way. When I ran a workshop with a group of 12 senior HR leaders a few years ago on how they currently did OD, one of the participants talked about how two power brokers in her organization moved people around in a constant horse-trading battle. Several others nodded their heads and commented how they frequently witnessed similar behaviour. The risk organizations face is that by never taking a step back they lose sight of the whole and find themselves in a negative spiral.

Organizational redesigns are costly, time consuming and rarely much fun. Therefore, the case for change has to be overwhelming in order for it to be considered worthwhile. The macro design is something that should constantly be referenced, used and followed to direct your organization and the direction it is going in. This section, Part Two, sets out how to go about macro design from start to finish and assumes you are doing a wholesale change. However, many (if not most) redesigns don't focus on the entire organization but sub-elements of it. For example, redesigning the sales force, marketing or supply chain. The more frequent these mini redesigns, the greater the dynamic nature of the underlying drivers. For instance, as products and customers dynamically change, so too will the sales force, as explained in Chapter 3.5. The concepts still apply, but the level of granular thinking won't have to be as deep and frameworks such as multi-criteria decision analysis will rarely need to be used.

In many cases a redesign will not be necessary. The process of thinking about and answering fundamental questions about your organization helps set the path for the future, and it is always crucial that you should be clear about it. But macro change may not be necessary. Even if it isn't, the methods described in Part Three should still add significant value.

Structure and logic for Part Two

To start with you have to understand what you are talking about when defining macro design. Too often terms such as 'vision', 'strategy', 'goals' and 'objectives' get confused. Chapter 2.2 defines how each term relates to each other term when building an outline for your future organization. Having defined the journey, you need to translate this into a case for change. The case for change answers why you should do the redesign. How will this help deliver business success? And if you do need to change, how do you need to change? What are the design criteria that will act as a framework when creating your design? Chapter 2.2 is the reflective bit. It will make you stay up late into the night to work out exactly what you and the business want to achieve. But if done well, it is also one of the most fun things to do. There is nothing better than daydreaming into the future and thinking about what you and your organization can achieve in five, 10, 20 years' time.

Once you have the journey and the design criteria in place, Chapter 2.3 defines how to map the high-level value chain processes and then how to map the key accountabilities to the range of design options. The options are developed to best meet your design criteria. Who will be accountable at a summary level for what in your new organization? At this stage it is all about answering the high-level questions: the top two levels of the org chart and the summary 30–60 process elements. You are answering the 'what if' questions. You are making sure you don't suddenly wake up in a few months' time thinking: 'If only we'd thought about it that way!' This is partly about creating possible extreme options for the design so you can test boundaries. Being creative and running through all the options are absolute musts at this stage so that you can set up a review to determine which one is most suitable.

Finally, it's crunch time. You need to decide. Outlining the steps to a thorough options analysis, how do you choose the right design? What can we learn about effective decision-making with so many complex contractionary criteria? It isn't just about choosing the design, it is being able to communicate that design and persuade everyone to get behind it. Therefore, how do you create an effective business case that gives both a strong mandate and direction?

Macro design is about thinking. This thinking needs to be documented and communicated. In reality, the whole process is about answering a range of fundamental questions and documenting the answers to the questions. Those answers are actually your business case. The business case is nothing more than the documentation of those answers in a structured way. Don't wait until the end of your thinking to document your answers, but make the documentation a core part of the process. The macro design is going to be your compass over the whole of the detailed micro design and into *making it real*. It's what you should turn to in times of trouble to remind you why you are doing what you are doing. It's what you put in front of anyone who questions what you are doing so you can take them on the journey with you. The first step is working out what journey you want to go on.

Strategy articulation and design criteria

All men can see these tactics whereby I conquer, but what none can see is the strategy out of which victory is evolved.

SUN TZU

Introduction

To have a chance of implementing a successful organization design you have to know what you are trying to achieve from the design. Unfortunately, business language is full of jargon and words that are overused and misunderstood. Nowhere is that more true than with the term 'strategy'. It has come to mean so many things it almost means nothing. I frequently hear people refer to their strategy when what they are really doing is listing a set of goals. This isn't helped by the number of consultants who call themselves strategy consultants. What they are really trying to say is that they do important high-value work. Strategy is not the same as saying something is important. In the context of organization design, words matter. They set the tone and direction and they provide emphasis. It is crucial to be clear about what you mean by various business terms, and equally important to be extremely clear about what you mean when defining the key elements of your corporate and organizational plans.

This chapter gets back to the basics of strategic terminology and how to use specific terms in the context of defining your case for change and the type of organization you will need to execute your strategy, fulfil your vision and meet the ambitions of the organization. The chapter then investigates some constraints you may face before looking at how, based on your strategy and vision, you can set your design criteria.

Define where you are going and why

Before you even think about your organization design you need to start at the very beginning – ensure the vision, goals, strategy and mission are all crystal clear. These are the basis of everything the organization is and does. Many organizations think of themselves as being on a journey. If so, think of the tools you need to navigate that journey: a map and a compass. They tell you where you are going, the best route to get there, and that you are heading in the right direction. Your high-level organizational terms should perform the same roles as the map and compass.

In organizational terms, the vision sets the direction and goals – the *where* we want to get to; the strategy defines the plan and the *how* we should get there. We break the plan down into goals and objectives; into things that people need to do. The historian Alfred Chandler famously theorized that 'structure follows strategy'.[1] What happens if the strategy isn't clear? Simply, the design won't be clear and it will be impossible to implement. Equally, having a clear strategy can be one of the greatest enablers of successful organization design.

Of 34 organization design practitioners surveyed in collaboration with the University of Westminster in 2012–13, not one (0 per cent) said they were 'very successful' in their organization design.[2] This research included an in-depth survey that covered private, public and third sectors. Many other studies highlight that many change programmes fail, with Harvard Business School professor John Kotter famously claiming in 1996 that nearly 70 per cent of large-scale change programmes didn't meet their goals.[3] Significant progress has not been made and while there is clearly a large range of reasons, our research highlighted that not having a clear vision and/or strategy is one of the most significant.

The research we did found that 'people politics – protecting vested interest' was the number one barrier to success (a subject addressed in Chapter 1.2) and 'incomplete strategy' and 'lack of vision for the future organization' were the second and third barriers, as shown in Figure 2.2.1. Interestingly, having a weak case for change was not regarded as an issue, suggesting that there is typically a significant case for organizational change. In following up many of those surveyed, speaking to other OD practitioners and reading the literature on the subject, it is obvious that having clear answers to the 'strategic questions' is the single most important thing to get right. And you need to get it right from the beginning. It provides purpose for the new design and a way to make trade-offs about what you want from your design.

FIGURE 2.2.1   Top organization design barriers

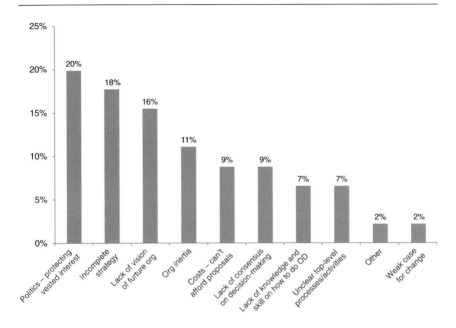

I am not a strategist nor have I done much real strategy consulting. I typically work on a broad range of operational and organizational improvement projects. However, given how important these terms are it is remarkable how many organizations I come across which seem to struggle with them. On the one hand, I find this pretty unacceptable given how fundamental it is. On the other hand, it is because it is fundamental that it is so hard. It is hard to define succinctly what we mean. We all know the adage 'I didn't have time to write a short letter, so I wrote a long one.' Distilling things to their essence takes time and clarity of thought. So perhaps we should always do more to challenge the assumption that the basics have already been well defined.

When training many teams, I find that part of the issue is that people don't fully understand what all the terminology means. So let's start there. Words and phrases used when defining high-level vision and strategy need to be thought about in terms of their purpose and audience. These statements are not just words on a page, but they are the inspiration for your employees and your customers. They should be the reason you get out of bed every day. They are the things that inspire you in your darkest moments and inspire those around you. You have to be utterly convinced by them.

Get your terminology right

To help address this I have created a slightly tongue-in-cheek diagram to show how all the terminology fits together (Figure 2.2.2). The image takes inspiration from SpaceX, an advanced rocket and spacecraft manufacturer with an ambition to colonize space.

Vision

A vision statement is a single sentence that explains clearly and specifically where you are trying to get to over the long term. In the context of Figure 2.2.2, this is to colonize parts of the universe. The vision statement defines the organization's purpose, but does so in terms of the organization's values rather than bottom-line measures (values are guiding beliefs about how things should be done). The vision statement communicates both the purpose and the values of the organization. For employees it gives direction about how they are expected to behave and inspires them to give their best. Shared with customers, it shapes customers' understanding of why they should work with the organization. This is potentially the hardest sentence to come up with because it has to be concise, useful, stand the test of time and speak to both employees and customers in an inspiring way.

Strategy

The strategy defines how you are going to achieve your vision. It sets out the direction and scope of the organization over the long term. It defines how you achieve your advantage for the organization by configuring resources in a challenging environment to meet the needs of markets and to fulfil stakeholder expectations. It is all about trade-offs. For example, in order to colonize space, the first step might be to develop rockets to get to Mars using liquid fuel technology. However, an alternative might be to develop nuclear fusion technology first and then move to get to Mars. These are the types of choices you need to make when setting your strategy.

Goals

Goals are the intended results you want your organization to achieve based on your vision and strategy. You could think of them as stepping stones. They are broad and do not need to be specific or measurable. This is what differentiates them from objectives. One of the SpaceX goals in relation to colonizing the universe relates to 'Structures Engineering' and a goal to 'have the most mass-efficient primary and secondary structures possible while exceeding all factors of safety'.[4] Once again, the key should be simplicity.

FIGURE 2.2.2 Reach for the stars – an example of strategic terms

STRATEGY
Build the space rocket technology and ecosystems
to get a human first to the moon, then Mars,
then to new solar systems. Use the technology
and resources in space to pay for investments in
engineering and the development of sustainable
resources that can be leveraged commercially.

→ How will we get there?
→ It's about trade-offs

VALUE
'Strive to improve.'
→ The Behaviour

GOAL
'Develop a sustainable
energy source.'
→ Desired results

OBJECTIVE
'Get a human on the moon
before the decade is out.'

→ SMART and aligned
to strategy

Your goals should communicate clearly the ambition for your organization, speaking naturally to particular parts of the business. Taking your vision statement, breaking it down into chunks which facilitate its fulfilment.

Objectives

Having created your goals, these naturally convert into defined objectives. Objectives should be SMART (Specific, Measurable, Achievable, Relevant and Time-bound) as described in Chapter 3.3. However, at this top level do not get bogged down in the detail. The objectives you set here should be high-level objectives that cascade down only to the top levels of the organization. The further detail of cascading objectives right down through the whole of your organization comes with micro design (Chapter 3.3). For example, an objective in the context of Figure 2.2.2 might be: 'By September 2009 became the first privately funded liquid-fuelled vehicle to put a satellite into Earth orbit.' Incidentally, this is something that SpaceX actually achieved.

Values and behaviours

Values and behaviours are what everyone needs in order to best ensure that the vision, goals and objectives are met. They form an important subset of the competencies described in Chapter 3.6. For example, a job advert on the SpaceX website stated: 'We seek future colleagues with a rare mix of drive, passion, scrappiness, intelligence, and curiosity to seek what's beyond the stars.' SpaceX was a lead news item in June 2015 when a launch malfunctioned. It's a feature of such ambitious projects that they will always encounter setbacks along the way. I hope SpaceX succeeds.

Mission

The mission statement is a summary, used for internal purposes (for example, 'To populate the universe to save humanity's existence for eternity by populating other planets in a financially self-sustaining and eventually highly profitable way'.). It pulls together key elements of your vision, goals and strategy. It is essentially a summary of your top-level direction setting with an inward communication focus. In one sentence it should communicate your organization's reason for being, and the end-to-end journey you are embarking on. It should be accessible so that new employees understand it, buy into it and come on the journey with you. It needs to talk about the high-level 'how' and not just the 'why'. In your mission statement, you mention what your organization currently does. Mission statements explain what the company is good at, who is the customer that they care about, and what the company does that might be really good compared with the competition.

However, it is not just about understanding the function of these terms and articulating their contents. You then have to communicate them effectively. Whether it's a video, presentation or booklet, make your story come alive and target that story to the intended audience. For example, implementations and transformations are increasingly using videos specifically targeted at employees to help communicate why a change was required, what is changing and what the benefits are. Whatever you do, be creative, inspiring and communicate the meaning behind the words.

At the end of this process you should have clear, succinct and engaging documentation of your vision, your goals and objectives, all summarized by your mission statement. I hope these definitions and the example help. I equally hope that when you do the design, you don't skip over this crucial part of the process. There is no doubt these elements are extremely tough to define – and they are the subjects of numerous other pieces of literature. What I want to get across, though, is the need to think, challenge and test before you do a design. Do not go into a design with the assumption everyone is clear on the direction of travel. And, if you bring up issues of clarity at the beginning, it is going to make the chances of success for your design so much higher.

This high-level overview is the reference point for every single decision you take and is the very heart of your organization. Only if you understand all these things can you move along the design process: creating a case for change, evaluating your design criteria, defining your processes, listing your structural options, creating an accountability matrix and creating your business case. Defining the case for change and setting your design criteria are the subjects of the second half of this chapter.

The case for change

The case for change is what should drive alignment across all stakeholders. It is crucial that all decision makers fully support each point with both their heads and hearts. This case is what you will use when communicating to all employees during the implementation phase, as described in Chapter 4.4.

Your top-level strategic definitions are reasonably static. Your organization is not. Whether you created them yesterday or two years ago, you have to work out where the organization sits in relation to achieving them. It is also worth stating that this is not a linear process. It is much easier to think of it that way, but all these elements are built simultaneously, are intrinsically linked and have consequences for each other. For example, goals should be built on current strengths, taking into account current challenges.

Your case for change should detail the key improvements that will take you from where you are today to where you need to get to. Start with what is good. What are the things you most want to keep? What are your strengths? The next stage is to detail the improvements. You can think of these in two broad categories: things that you are doing that you should stop or improve and things you aren't doing. A way to think of this is the analogy of moving house. Imagine you are moving: what do you want to take with you, leave behind or buy new? Undertaking this process is not simply about drawing up a list based on talking to senior-level individuals across the business. Equally, this represents the beginning of your communication process about the design. In Chapter 4.4, I devote many pages to the topic of communication. Recognize that going through the process of defining all the key points of change is the start of your change process: how you do it, whom you involve and what you say to set the scene not just for the answer but also for the buy-in and change programme. Take time to think about who needs to be involved at this very early stage.

In order to build the case for change, run an exercise that brings information from across the business. It should cut across functions, organizational levels and geographies. Don't just ask those at the top and don't simply list a set of challenges and improvements. For example:

- Define what is the impact of the challenges. What would be the result of fixing it?
- Clarify the scope of the challenges; for example, if the issue is 'a suboptimal innovation process' then what does that really mean? Is the scope of the issue:
  - all innovation processes across that value chain or specific elements?
  - all geographies and products or subgroups?
- Is the challenge a symptom or the root cause of an issue?
- Translate resolving the challenges, as far as possible, into numbers: numbers that are ideally broken into meaningful categories. For example:
  - top-line growth;
  - cost savings and efficiencies;
  - improved customer satisfaction;
  - great compliance and reduction in risk;
  - improvements in innovation;
  - improvements in talent and key competencies.

In going through this process, it is always worthwhile taking a look at your competitors and other benchmarks. What are your strengths relative to them, and their strengths relative do you? What inspiration and ideas can you take away? Equally, are there ways of working you want to avoid?

In getting and keeping the competitive edge, you need to know how you are going to win in your given market. A great way of thinking about this is to think of your nightmare competitor, even if such a competitor doesn't exist today. How would such a competitor beat you in the marketplace? What kind of things would the competitor do? Describe your competitor. Give your competitor a name and personality. Have one of the team role-play being the competitor and talk through how they could beat you.

The case for no change

I want to be clear from the start: unless the case for change is overwhelming, stop where you are in terms of a major organization transformation. Change is messy, hard and disruptive. You have to do it for the right reasons if you are going to make it worthwhile. You have to take the organization on the journey, so unless the change ticks all the right boxes, stop. That doesn't mean you can't drive significant improvements. Often, focusing on a particular area of the business will add significant value. Indeed, many of the methods and techniques described in Part Three and Part Four of this book can be undertaken in isolation and will deliver benefits, regardless of whether they are part of a wider programme or not.

From my experience, I think there are four broad change criteria that have to be met before you undertake major macro change:

1 It has to be financially sound. The change will result in you being much more successful and profitable from a financial perspective.

2 It has to be emotionally sound. Unless you are completely convinced in your heart that change is needed and is the right move, there is no point. Like the vision, the change has to be what gets you out of bed in the morning and what gives you strength to see the process through from end to end.

3 It has to be succinct. The case for change needs to be unambiguous and memorable. This is where communication starts. If you can inspire people and bring them along with you on the journey, the ability to go through the process of change is much more achievable.

4 It has to stand the test of time. Given the upheaval that comes
with change, it is only worthwhile if it is something that will last.
If you can look forward three, five, or even 10 to 20 years and see the
benefits change will bring then the effort in the short term becomes
worth it.

None of these is a strong enough reason on its own. They rely on each other.
For example, a change may be financially sound, but if people do not believe
in it and cannot understand the change, that change is never going to happen
or be a success.

Detailing the case for change

To develop an emphatic case for change it is useful to detail the challenges
to your organization currently against your high-level ambitions. One of the
ways of doing this is to take your goals and objectives, and translate them
into actions. Next, translate those actions into the negative and positive
impacts change will have on the organization. From this analysis you can
assess whether a big change is the best path forward or whether you can
make the desired improvements through small steps. Whatever you decide,
I cannot emphasize enough how useful and important this exercise is. If you
do it well just once, and really challenge yourself to think about all these
areas, it will be your go-to guide for years to come. It creates consistency in
the long term for your organization, whether you make a drastic change or
not. At the end of the day, whether you decide to proceed with major change
or not comes back to trade-offs. Only you and your leadership team can
make the decision of whether the medium-term disruption caused by a large
organizational change is more worthwhile than small tweaks to medium-
sized improvements in your organization. However, you cannot make this
decision until you have understood the constraints facing you and whether
your desired direction is feasible or not.

An example is one client company that was locally organized with strong
country business units. It took the company far too long (it should have
cut the time by half or one third) to bring new products to market. It was
not benefiting from scale, which resulted in too much stock and suboptimization of supply, and it was doing many of the basics things poorly because
it could not pull its key capabilities together, like engineering or procurement leverage.

Constraints and risks

We all live in a world of constraints and uncertainties. Organizational change is particularly risky with many constraints and hidden traps. Understanding and documenting them early on mean they can be best incorporated into the thinking. One example is thinking of constraints and risks to various design options. Examples of constraints include limited budget; strong personalities and egos; risk of too much disruption; lack of alignment; competitive reactions; risk of losing key talent; customer intimacy requirements. These types of constraint will come up again and again during the design, not simply at this stage.

The benefits of dealing with constraints and risks upfront are exemplified in software quality process. When a developer writing code finds a bug, if it is fixed immediately it can take minutes. But if the developer sees it as the job of the quality engineer to find bugs and ensure they are dealt with or if the developer simply misses a bug, then the quality engineer has to find the bug, verify it is a bug, record it in a system, potentially explain it to the developer; the developer has to go back to his code and understand the issue, and only then fix it. Then it all needs to be re-tested and often the project manager needs to ensure this has all happened. If the bug is not found and the customer finds it, then the amount of talking between various parties (verifying, testing, re-testing and planning) starts to spiral. It is similar with organizational design. Addressing a problem upfront is a tiny fraction of the cost of dealing with it later. The project impetus for speed can cause derailing down the line. One of the most important rules in negotiation is not to value time over the deal. Momentum, pace, cost control and hitting milestones are clearly important. But not if they drive issues which derail an entire organization.

Too often, constraints and risks are listed in Excel or PowerPoint in a fairly superficial way. They are not really dealt with, but the team members can say they are dealing with them because they have a list. When writing the constraints or risks down, ensure you have identified the root issues. This is half the battle in overcoming them. Like many things, you must provide structure to dealing with these issues. How severe are they, how controllable, when would they hit and what is the impact? If it happens, then what? What are the mitigating actions? A typical list that might be produced has the issue, a score on impact and on the owner. These sorts of list are a good place to start. But that is all they are, a starting point. Chapter 3.5 elaborates further on how to ensure the organization is geared towards managing risks effectively.

The next step is for those worthy of managerial effort to be given a little more attention. For example, on budget: this is all to do with the business case. What are the criteria? Is the cash physically available? Does the payback period and/or Return on Investment (ROI) meet your financial thresholds? In terms of impact: impact on what? Is the impact of going over budget a threat to the survival of the business or does it simply mean a reshuffle of budget priorities and allocation? Think through: if the risk or issue is not dealt with, then what? What would you have to do? What would the financial cost be of that? What are the mitigating actions? How are you going to track that they are done?

A commonly cited implicit constraint is the ego of some of the senior team members. It is probably worth thinking through what is behind the inflammatory word 'ego'. We can rephrase this to mean: What is it that really motivates the individual? Why has the individual made the sacrifices he or she has to reach the position he or she is in? How critical are team members to the ongoing success and loyalty of the team? Often, it is autonomy and control over one's destiny that is the driving force, not the size of empire. Making assumptions can be dangerous. Equally, expecting someone to tell us straight what his or her issue is can be equally fraught. People don't always reveal the truth, especially if they think they are talking to the enemy. Therefore, list the potential reasons for the issue, and find a way to get answers. It is worth investing the time upfront to get to the bottom of these sorts of issue.

The last thing to say on this: many of the issues and risks will be mitigated through the proper execution of the micro design. However, options analysis (the subject of Chapter 2.3) requires thinking about the possible constraints, as there is no point having the perfect organization design if it is impractical and unfeasible to put in place. The section on 'Risk management' in Chapter 3.5 provides more insight into managing these points.

Setting the design criteria

If you decide that doing a full organization redesign is the way forward then the first step is to set out your design criteria. The design criteria are your guiding principles for any decisions regarding how to change your organization. They are entirely dependent on your vision, goals, strategy and the case for change. They bring these all together to provide a framework and set of priorities for any design work. They are integral to ensuring you choose the right design for your organization – something I will come to in Chapter 2.3. With that in mind, to set the design criteria you need to have a firm grasp on where your organization is heading, what the challenges are, and what the ideal is, as set out earlier in this chapter. This is where many of the trade-offs are made, and you have to decide which criteria are the most important. You have to prioritize. These will be your reference points for any design.

Often, setting design criteria is regarded as an excuse to set down a long list of aspirations. But resist the temptation as it makes the exercise meaningless. The list needs to be short and you should really focus on what is important. The criteria you select are dependent on what you are trying to do. To get to this point, take your vision, goals, strategy and the case for change. Use them to define the priorities for your design. For example, if your goal are top-line growth through production innovation, but you are slow at new product introductions because the organization is geographically controlled (for example, manufacturing, engineering, and marketing execution are all local), then a sensible design criterion might be 'New product introduction efficiency'. Having set out all of your design criteria it is worth just cross referencing them at the end with all the major elements of your case for change, to ensure they all align and will prioritize the desired improvements in the right areas of the organization. Once you have done this, you will have created the framework for your design, and these criteria will be at the heart of every decision made and everything you do going forward in your design. An example of some common design criteria include:

- improve product innovation and time to market;
- improve customer relationships;
- improve functional excellence;
- support the acquisition agenda;
- increase supply responsiveness;
- minimize cost;
- reduce the number of management layers;
- optimize tax.

Final thoughts

A commonly used term to define how an organization will execute its strategy is the Target Operating Model (TOM). The TOM defines how all the elements of the organizational system work. Unfortunately, the definition that many give of the term varies. I regard it as the summary structural design together with the value chain required, detailed processes and competencies. In other words, it is synonymous with the macro and micro design.

This chapter has looked at the big picture. All the elements defined in this chapter are critical to the success of not just the organization design, but of the business as a whole. In reality, I have only scraped the surface of these areas, but there are many other books out there that investigate big picture setting in detail. That is not the focus of this book. What I want to emphasize is that you have to ask the questions to get the answers. Never assume people have these answers when doing an organization design, so ask the questions. If there is confusion about the high-level business priorities then clarify them now, as otherwise implementing a successful design will be near impossible.

In light of this, having set out the elements in this chapter, I suggest a meeting of all the key decision makers to review the fundamentals. Does everyone agree and is everyone extremely motivated to take on his or her part of the task to make the change happen? If not, stop with the major transformation and move straight to the elements within the micro design. I believe a great deal can be solved through micro changes and doing the business basics well. However, sometimes surgery is needed. If that is the case, you need to define and choose specific design options and detail the design. This is the subject of the next chapter.

Remember this

1 Ensure the vision, strategy, goals, objectives and mission are all defined and understood.

2 Set out the case for change and only move forward if the case is overwhelming.

3 Detail the constraints and risks and think through them so that options moving forward are feasible.

4 Set out clear and concise design criteria to provide a framework and a set of principles to follow throughout creating and implementing the organization design.

5 Make sure all key stakeholders are aligned behind the direction of travel and are invested in the change.

Notes

1 Chandler, A (1962) *Strategy and Structure: Chapters in the history of the American Industrial enterprise*, MIT Press, Cambridge MA

2 Research conducted by Concentra and the University of Westminster (2013)

3 John, K (1996) *Leading Change*, Harvard Business School Press

4 SpaceX website [accessed 23 February 2015] [Online] http://www.spacex.com/careers

Structural options and business case

> *Whenever you see a successful business, someone once made a courageous decision.* PETER DRUCKER

Introduction

The goal of organization design is to create an organization that is best placed and most likely to achieve the strategy developed in Chapter 2.2. In doing this, the first decision you have to make is what your high-level organization should look like. Once that decision is made, everything else follows. The crucial work here is in ensuring the option you choose gives you the best possible chance of fulfilling and delivering your design criteria. The rationale behind the decision will be documented in your business case, and is the logic that will drive the detailing when doing the micro design. It will also form most of the collateral for the communication that is required when implementing the design, covered in Part Four of this book.

The decision-making process throughout both the macro and micro phases of design is never simply about the structure of your organization. Hierarchical structures play a key part in the organization, ensuring accountabilities and responsibilities. However, you need to think about your decision in the context of the organization being a collection of people who have to get work done to deliver a particular strategy. One angle that is gaining increasing momentum is to view the organization as a network. Organizations are not simply units of command and control. They need to be enablers of efficient information flows. Peter Hinssen argues in his book *The Network Always Wins*[1] that networks are far better at facilitating the flow of information than traditional hierarchical structures: 'Networks naturally turn information from ponds into rivers. Today's organizations need these rivers of information to handle the speed needs of the network society.'[2]

This does not mean hierarchies and networks are mutually exclusive. There is a balance to be made between rigid hierarchical structures and allowing flex in the system to encourage networked ways of working. In many ways, mapping and connecting the organizational system are a way of understanding and dictating high-level aspects of formal organizational networks. The key is not to overprescribe the connections and stifle the informal networks and self-organizing nature of an organization. Much of this comes into your micro design, ensuring you are practical about setting out how people will work together and that you are not overly prescriptive. In deciding your options and high-level structural design, you are laying the platform to direct the micro design in a way that fulfils, as closely as possible, your design criteria.

There is no universal truth in macro design, just a range of trade-offs between a range of desirable but often mutually exclusive factors. A decision has to be made, and you need to reach a conclusion that you are confident, on balance, meets the largest number of your design criteria. A good rule of thumb to use in decision-making is to minimize your maximum regret. For each option, what would your maximum regret be and how do they compare? In deciding between your options it is easy to become deadlocked between different needs, that is your design criteria. Therefore, how do you know you are using those criteria in a meaningful way? And how can you make sure you are making a good decision? It is not easy. As Professor Paul Nutt famously concluded in his book *Why Decisions Fail*: decisions fail half the time.[3] This is due to three blunders that essentially come down to bad practice when making decisions, rushing into decisions and poor resource allocation. With organization design, I see decisions reflect these three blunders all the time. Senior managers are keen to get to the answer straight away. Outcomes are mapped on a napkin, with boxes of the desired to-be structure, before anything else. As already stated in Chapter 1.2, people love the org chart because it is so tangible. And all too often, once one view is written down a psychological commitment is made to that answer.

This chapter will help you to navigate the decision-making process to ensure you are able to choose the best design possible. I start by outlining how to define your organization's high-level value chains and processes, and how to structure them for different design options. Using the design criteria you created in Chapter 2.2, I then set out a data-driven approach to options analysis based on the science of multi-criteria decision-making (MCDM). Finally, having made your decision, you need to turn your attention to creating a compelling and clear business case. This is the focus for the last section of this chapter. It is this document that, if agreed upon, will steer the remaining months of design and implementation work, and years of business performance.

Develop options

There are three steps in developing your options: first to define the value chain and summary processes; second to set out the best possible options; and third to map your summary processes to each option so you can clarify what they really mean. In the second step of developing potential options, ensure you give yourself the best possible chance of finding the route that will best help deliver your strategy and support your design criteria.

Define the value chain and summary processes

Understanding the organization as a system is one of the core principles of this book as outlined in Chapter 1.3. This is the first time you start mapping and designing that system, mapping your high-level processes to the high-level to-be organizational structure. I explore more detailed process design in Chapters 3.4 and 3.5. At this stage you only need to define your summary value chain and high-level processes. Once these are defined you can see the consequences of each design option by linking your roles to your processes. This does not necessarily mean your organization chart will look that different for different options. You might end up with two identical organizational charts for two options but fundamentally different organizations depending on the responsibilities attached to each role. Remember, it's what's in the box that counts.

To begin with, simply list where each of the core processes sits. You can do this by taking the key 30–60 chunks of work that are required for your organization. Then build them in a simple taxonomy that is ideally two or three levels deep (no more). Figure 2.3.1 is a simplified example. These summary processes help to define the true scope of each of the structural options after you have defined where the responsibility for each of these processes resides using the 'RAS' linking method described in Chapter 1.3 (I return to this later in this chapter).

Develop options and dimensions of design

Putting your value chain and supporting processes to one side for the moment, the next step is to develop different design options. Developing

FIGURE 2.3.1   List of summary processes

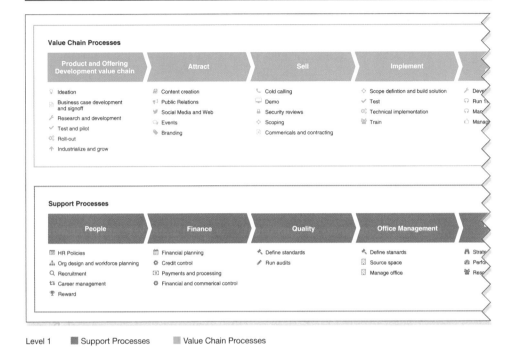

Level 1   ■ Support Processes   ■ Value Chain Processes

these options can be challenging, either because you have a blank piece of paper or, more likely, there will be a tendency to jump to the 'right' answer. I have often seen people come up with three obvious options and then stop without thinking through other possibilities. Or even worse, just going with the first option that is suggested. A helpful way to develop design options is to define some different possible dimensions of design. Here are some generic dimensions you might use:

- functions
  - eg HR, finance, procurement, supply, R&D, sales, marketing
- geographic
  - eg Organization for Economic Co-operation and Development countries (OECD); Brazil, Russia, India, China (BRIC); Sub-Saharan Africa
  - or even smaller categories, eg regional, country, state
- products and competencies
  - categories, brands and products
  - manufacturing centres

- market segments
  - customer segments, eg enterprise or SME
  - vertical industry, eg FMCG; government; life science; finance
  - channel, eg direct, value-added resellers, consulting firms
- process versus project based
  - Teams are bought together on a project-by-project basis. Each project may last several years.
- degree of centralization
  - Consider each element of the value chain and the degree to which it should be centralized between the centre, regions or local presence.

The best organization designs usually focus on a single primary dimension of design. So design options are typically formulated around a particular primary dimension with different secondary dimensions. For example, if you are considering options based upon products or geographies or functions, you might develop two product-based design options that treat the secondary dimensions of geographies and functions differently.

Not all the dimensions of an organization will be relevant to every organization and it is all right not to develop an option for every dimension. However, it may be helpful to develop some 'controversial' options that help test and enhance the final selected design and flesh out how secondary dimensions are incorporated. In any case, most organization design projects might consider three or four design options for evaluation. The ultimate design will often be a hybrid option of two or more of the design options.

For example, one of my colleagues was involved in the design of a UK central government department largely involved in designing and implementing policy. Traditionally, these departments are organized by policy area. However, an option was developed around the department becoming a projects- and programmes-based organization. Although this was not selected as the primary option, there was a helpful debate about how the department should be organized to deliver projects and programmes, and separate to the organization design, that led to a significant change in the way that major programmes were governed within the department in the final design.

Figure 2.3.2 gives some generic examples of design options set against a common set of design criteria and their respective advantages and disadvantages. There will never be a perfect option. For example, if customer responsiveness is crucial, then all things being equal you will want to have

FIGURE 2.3.2   Scoring of common structural dimensions against common design criteria

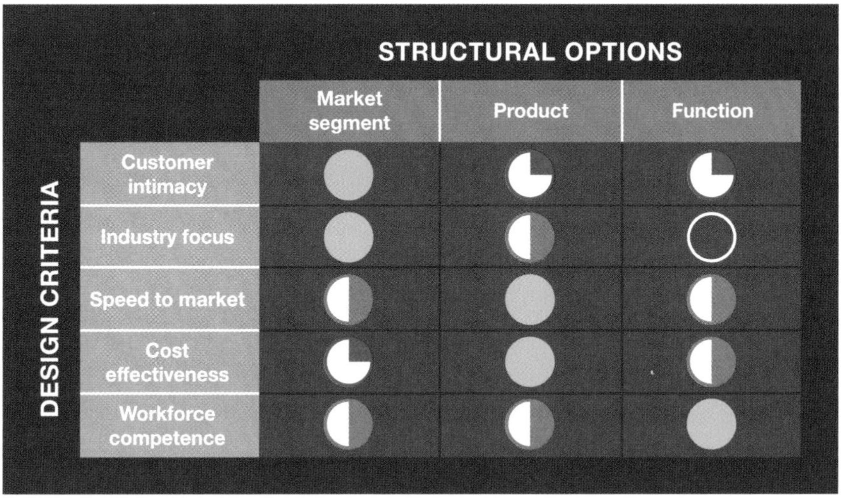

a more decentralized structure. However, if it is all about cost savings and efficiency then removing duplication and moving to a more centralized structure might be best.

In the example in Figure 2.3.2, the market segment approach is preferred if the design criteria for customer intimacy and industry focus were most important. This would be true in any service business where understanding the customer needs and being responsive are of paramount importance. The product dimension might be preferred if the keys to success are speed to market or cost effectiveness. This might be true where customer needs are generic but there are scale and efficiency in focusing on particular products or more likely product categories. This is often seen in consumer goods businesses. Finally, the functional view is preferred where the key to success is the different competencies required of the workforce. A functional option is often preferred for smaller businesses serving customers with similar needs across a narrow range of products.

In reality, it is rare that a selected model is based precisely on one dimension. It is often a hybrid depending on the function or value stream in question within a business. For instance, the sales function might be structured along geographic and product lines whereas HR might be based on function work streams; for example, a centre of excellence, shared service functions and geographical with local HR business partners (HRBPs). Because most organizations end up with a mix of structures, coming up with your options and understanding how a combination of structures might work in a matrix are the most important parts of the macro process. Examples of hybrid options include:

- front and back, eg technology firms
  - front-end functions such as sales and customer services are organized based on how the target market is structured into geographic units and/or industry verticals
  - back-office functions, those that are not client facing, are functionalized and centralized
- decider-provider, eg supply-driven organization like FMCG
  - all decisions are made centrally, such as what gets made and delivered, investments and which new products, while locally the manufacture and delivery are sorted
  - the execution of the decisions is done based on a geographic model.

When creating hybrid options it will be tempting to map a matrix structure. The idea behind a matrix structure is to try to get the best of different structural options by splitting reporting lines. For example, combining a geographic and function-orientated structure you might have a role reporting two ways, both to their function manager and geographic manager. The reporting lines will represent a different managerial relationship. For example, the function manager might have veto power on objectives and target setting, prioritization of work and performance evaluation. However, the geographic manager may control the day-to-day management, task allocation and support.

This type of matrix, although it looks good on paper, can often fall down in the long run. It can make reporting lines unclear and lead to miscommunication between employees and their respective managers. Just because an organizational structure looks like it should work does not mean it will in practice. Structure only goes so far in facilitating work, as I mentioned in the introduction. I think it is important to have clear reporting lines to ensure accountability, but have good process design to facilitate ways of working laterally (process design is discussed in Chapter 3.3). For example, in marketing functions you often have to work with people across the organization to create campaigns. However, as long as you know who is the approver for each piece of work it doesn't matter whom you report to in order to get things done. When building your options don't mistake reporting lines as a specified link dictating whom someone will work with. A matrix is often not the perfect solution, although it may look like it.

Avoid going with the obvious

A trick to avoid the trap of having limited options is, for every objective in your design criteria, to think through what would be the optimal solution for maximizing that single criterion, irrespective of all the others. So if you have seven criteria, then you might have a long list of at least seven options. From these, you could create alternative blends or scenarios. A generic framework I find particularly useful for ensuring you think through all the options is the 'Disney Method'. Created by Robert Dilts, it is a great way of getting the balance of creativity, problem solving and evaluation needed when coming up with design options. It can be used for workshops in teams, as well as a useful internal checklist to make sure you approach any type of decision-making in a robust manner. It sets out four thinking styles to take in turn when thinking through the issues: outsiders; dreamers; realizers; and critics.

- **Outsiders** – First, think from the perspective of an outsider.
  In many ways, play the role of the consultant. What are the objective challenges or opportunities facing the organization? The book *Designing Organizations* by Jay Galbraith is an excellent resource for reviewing a broad range of options in addition to the above examples.[4]

- **Dreamers** – As a dreamer, ask yourself: 'What do I really want my organization to achieve/look like in an ideal world?' Let your mind wander freely and come up with a visionary big picture with no boundaries, limitations or constraints. At this stage, don't let reality come into your thoughts. This is daydreaming and dream scenario time.

- **Realizers** – Having come up with all your options, ask: 'Can they really work?' This is about organizing ideas to put your plan into practice. How would each of those options work? What processes would map to what roles? What would need to happen to make it real? In part, this stage is simply about removing the options that are obviously impossible. This is the mode of thinking you should also be in when performing the options evaluation that I come to later in the chapter.

- **Critics** – The final viewpoint is that of the critic. The critic searches and uncovers the flaws. Test the plans, look for problems, difficulties and unintended consequences. Evaluate them. Ask yourself: 'What could go wrong?' Think of what is missing. In terms of the brainstorm, this viewpoint should come at the end. This is a particularly useful perspective to have when writing the business case (the last section in this chapter). It will help you think through the most important justifications and supporting points for your chosen option.

Map processes to options

Having listed your viable options, you need to define what each one means in an organizational context. Take the high-level value chain and processes you mapped out at the beginning of this chapter and allocate responsibilities to your top-level organizational structure. This helps to bring each option to life, helping you think through what your organization would look like for each option. It ensures you are clear about the differences between the options. It provides an understanding of where the work gets done, how decisions will be made and how each option will function.

For instance, within Figure 2.3.1, in the set of 'Support Processes', 'Office Management' has three sub-processes: 'Define standards', 'Source space' and 'Manage office'. In a functional organization structure with three local sales offices, the central HR function could be responsible for defining the standards for each office and sourcing the physical office space, including the contract management with the landlords. The local sales manager, for practical reasons, could be responsible for the day-to-day management of the office space. This is represented in Figure 2.3.2.

To finish defining each option continue mapping all your high-level processes to your high-level to-be org structure. As Figure 2.3.3 demonstrates, the same process can be mapped to more than one part of the to-be structure; in this case, the mapping of 'Manage office'. From a practical perspective, when building the options, try to keep the number of boxes per option to the bare minimum. For example, it would have sufficed to have only one box in the structure saying 'Local sales office' instead of listing each individual office. In this example I have shown only the responsibilities and this should suffice for most things. However, there are times when mapping out the core decisions and showing where each one needs to be approved will help demonstrate how the governance in each option will operate. The crucial point is to define how each option would work and to bring them to life. Having mapped them out, ask one person to represent each option and

FIGURE 2.3.3   Defining the responsibilities for
the 'Manage office' example

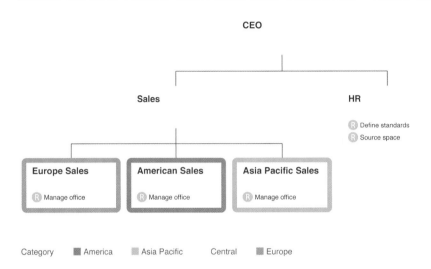

Category   ■ America   ▨ Asia Pacific   Central   ■ Europe

present it. Talk through examples using case studies, and discuss the differences and the strengths and weaknesses of each one.

In many cases it will be obvious which option is the best one. If that is the case, great! Move straight to developing and signing off the business case. Unfortunately, it isn't always obvious. There may be material differences of opinion with major trade-offs to be made because each option optimizes only a few of the design criteria. In this case, you need to make a difficult decision based on a set of, at face value, incomparable multiple criteria. In this situation, there are some useful data-driven methods to support the decision-making process.

Analysing and deciding your best option

Having developed your options you should have a good sense for the big idea behind each one: how they will work; an initial sense of which design criteria they most support; and where you have compromised the most. In making your decision, whatever you do, do what is right for you. Don't use an external benchmark as a default answer. I am not against using outside examples as inspiration for developing an options list, but when deciding what to do, you have to choose the option that is right for you, not for someone else. Equally, be careful about extrapolating a chosen option from one situation to another. For instance, the model that works brilliantly for a sales force in the United States may be a disaster in other smaller, less mature, more relationship- and family-driven economies such as in Southern Europe. The rest of this section is given to outlining methods to help you if you find yourself in a scenario where you have to make a complex decision between options. In making that decision, there are good and bad decision-making practices. I'll start with the bad.

Qualitative weightings

Carrying out options analysis and making decisions based on qualitative weightings are a common practice, though limited in its usefulness. The first step involves listing your options, giving each of your design criteria a weighting (giving each criterion a specific weight based on its importance in relation to the other criteria so that some criteria are taken into account more than others) and scoring the options against those criteria. This was the same approach used earlier in this chapter and can give a sense of which design dimensions are most viable. However, the approach is limited owing to its arbitrary nature and lack of differentiation between options. The limitations of this approach are illustrated in Figure 2.3.4, which shows each option ranked against design criteria by using a scoring method (1, 3, 6, 9) to create a larger range of weighted scores. Both examples have exactly the same scoring system but different weighting. In the top example the scores for Option 1 and Option 2 are very similar. Can you really decide to go with Option 1 just because it is 0.4 higher than Option 2? And yet, in the bottom example, just by using different weighting criteria the decision seems to suggest that Option 2 is the best option. Using this technique and the process of scoring and weighting can be very useful as it helps us to think through what's important. It also helps to highlight whether there is only one obviously viable option. But when there is no clear option, it does not really help to cut through the complexity.

Multi-criteria decision analysis

The challenge with the above type of options analysis is that you have to assess a large range of criteria against a range of options. It makes it difficult to really objectively quantify the viability of the options against each other at a holistic and granular level. It is well documented that people fail at making complicated decisions. Why? Simply, human beings have 'limited

FIGURE 2.3.4   Simple weighted average option appraisal examples

Rank	Criteria	Weighting	Option 1	Option 2	Option 3
1	Drive the innovation agenda/speed to market	89	9	9	3
2	Improve customer relationships	55	6	6	9
3	Improve functional excellence	34	9	3	1
4	Support acquisition agenda	21	6	6	3
5	Ease of implementation	13	1	6	9
6	Minimize cost	8	1	3	9
7	Improve communication and collaboration	5	3	3	3
8	Reduce functional or product silos	3	1	3	9
9	Support tax optimization	2	1	3	3
10	Minimize the number of managerial layers	1	1	3	9
	Total	231	6.9	6.5	4.8

Rank	Criteria	Weighting	Option 1	Option 2	Option 3
1	Drive the innovation agenda/speed to market	5	9	9	3
2	Improve customer relationships	5	6	6	9
3	Improve functional excellence	4	9	3	1
4	Support acquisition agenda	4	6	6	3
5	Ease of implementation	4	1	6	9
6	Minimize cost	3	1	3	9
7	Improve communication and collaboration	3	3	3	3
8	Reduce functional or product silos	3	1	3	9
9	Support tax optimization	1	1	3	3
10	Minimize the number of managerial layers	1	1	3	9
	Total	33	4.7	5.1	5.7

information-processing capacity'.[5] Although the example above seemed structured, it still involved the decision maker to simultaneously compare all the options at once and define scores directly as an arbitrary number. To help people make great decisions, we need a method that breaks down the problem into smaller, more manageable chunks so that our brain can process it and understand all the trade-offs between the options. Although there are many approaches, I suggest using Simple Multi-Attribute Rating Technique (SMART) as outlined by Paul Goodwin and George Wright in *Decision Analysis for Management Judgement*.[6] This technique is a great way of assessing options against one another in a situation where there is a lot of ambiguity. A simplification of their method is:

1 Create a value tree of the key attributes with weightings.

2 Define how each attribute will be measured through value curves and weightings.

3 Score each option and compare.

4 Run sensitivity analysis to see which scenarios would change your decision.

1 Create a value tree

In order to make the analysis a data-driven process we need to create a set of attributes in which the options can be assessed against a scale. This is not as simple as taking your design criteria and applying them, because the criteria can be very vague. For example, a key design criterion may be to create a structure that improves customer relationships. But how can you quantify this so that you can compare alternatives? Instead of quantifying a criterion it is easier to ask the question: 'How do we achieve this?' For example: How do we improve customer relationships? Asking this question helps direct more specific and measurable attributes such as 'average distance of staff from customers' and/or 'fewer managerial layers'. In coming up with these attributes you are actually creating a value tree as shown in Figure 2.3.5. The two main attributes you are assessing are cost versus benefit. You can then break these down into specific attributes to measure against. When creating your value tree, to ensure the attributes you measure against are as useful as possible, try to follow the principles of developing hierarchical trees discussed Chapter 1.3. The goal of this process is to learn about the values you are going to measure against in order to assess why one option may be better than another. If your tree is too large then any analysis would be too complex and would lose its benefit. The perfect value tree, like all trees, is more art than science and will require multiple iterations. It is worth saying that creating the tree is beneficial in itself as it clarifies which metrics are important to use and assess against throughout the whole design process.

2 Define how each attribute will be measured through value curves and weightings

Having set out your attributes, you can begin to assess how well each option performs against them. I am going to explain the technique with a simplified example. Imagine you only had three attributes to compare:

1 The first is how good each option will be at driving innovation. This is the key reason for the org change and is therefore given a weighting of 50 per cent.

2 The second is the restructuring cost. You give this a weighting of 25 per cent, but if the cost is above your limit, then regard it as unfeasible and automatically remove it from consideration as a viable option.

3 The third is the balance of customer-facing roles (local delivery, presales support) and central excellence (R&D, marketing). This is given a weighting of 25 per cent.

FIGURE 2.3.5   Multi-criteria decision tree example

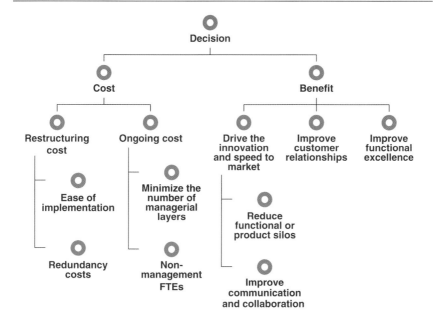

3 Score each option and compare

The first step is to draw value curves in order to compare each option against particular criteria as highlighted in Figure 2.3.6. A value curve gives a maximum score of 100 and a minimum of 0 against each attribute. The top-left value curve in Figure 2.3.6 demonstrates how you might analyse a value curve of cost. It shows that any option below a cost of $10 million will receive a score of 100. This is because anything lower than this cost will not have an impact on how the option is rated. So whether the cost was $8 million or $5 million, it would be rated exactly the same. It also shows that anything above $31 million simply isn't an option. It is beyond the budget so receives a zero, and that tells me the option is unfeasible and should be cut from the decision-making process.

Value curves can also reflect attributes that have an ideal in the middle. In the organizational context, this is often the case with ratios such as the size of one function to another or span of control. In Figure 2.3.6 the bottom-left value curve shows a simplified example of this. The ideal ratio between customer-facing functions and central R&D and marketing is 5 (for every customer-facing FTE there is one central FTE) and 5 is worth 100. The scores don't decrease too quickly if they are between 4 and 6, but anything below 3 or above 7 is given a 0.

FIGURE 2.3.6   Example value curves and sensitivity layers

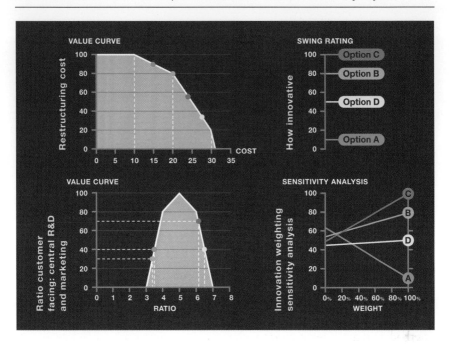

Of the three attributes, innovation, with a weighting of 50 per cent, is regarded as the most important. However, for this attribute there is no precise measure. The technique to use when there is no precise measure is a 'swing rating'. The technique requires you to rank each option against the best one. The best option is given 100 and every other option is rated from 0 to 100 relative to that best option. This is called the 'Swing Method'. Option C is rated the best, with Option A regarded to be only 10 per cent at good as Option C on this particular attribute. In terms of this innovation example, you could develop sub-attributes such as: speed to market; number of PhDs available; and cost. These can be combined with other swing ratings such as level of creativity or ability to pull knowledge.

Once I have all of these values, I combine them. So for Option A I get the following scores: Cost of 90 with 25% + Innovation of 10 with 50% + Ratio of 40 with 25% = 37.5. Option C gets the highest score (75) and, therefore, should be the option that is selected. But first, check you are truly happy with this selection and understand under what conditions you might change the recommendation.

4 Conduct sensitivity analysis

A final step is to perform sensitivity analysis. A lot of the values you have assigned to options against attributes are estimated. Sensitivity analysis gives you the opportunity to assess how the options would perform under different weightings to make the decision-making more robust. Given the weightings and scoring, as already stated, Option C wins with 75 points while Option B follows closely behind with 68. But what if people didn't agree with weightings? What if the importance of innovation was rated at far less than 50 per cent? At what point would Option C no longer be the best? The bottom-right graph in Figure 2.3.6 shows how the scores vary depending on the relative importance of the innovation weighting to cost and customer-facing ratio. For example, what would happen if innovation was only weighted at 20 per cent and the other two attributes weighted at 40 per cent? Then Option B would beat Option C, but only just. Looking across all the options on the graph it shows that in no scenario is Option D the preferred option. Equally, Option A becomes the best choice only when innovation is weighted at 12.5 per cent. Depending on the weighting it is essentially a choice between options B and C. What is so useful about this method is that it helps quantify how options perform, depending on the importance given to particular criteria. It helps people think through what are the basis and justification for making their decision.

Cost–benefit analysis

Another extremely useful analysis to compare options is to carry out cost–benefit analysis. However, giving a weighting to costs and benefits is tricky because they are so broad and cover such abstract elements of the design options. So to assess costs and benefits against each other, compare the options against them on a scatter plot. It is useful to plot out the options like this because it helps to stimulate trade-offs between costs versus benefits rather than trying to prioritize by weighting the number. To do this, aggregate the overall costs and benefits from your value trees for each option. An example of what a scored value tree might look like for one option is shown on the left in Figure 2.3.7. Taking these aggregate scores, plot them against each other for each option. The graph on the right in Figure 2.3.7 has the x-axis as the aggregate of cost scores while the y-axis is the aggregate of the benefits. I have illustrated this example with seven options. Once you have plotted the options, draw an imaginary line between each option, staying as close to the top-right-hand corner as possible (this is called

FIGURE 2.3.7 Aggregating and comparing each option

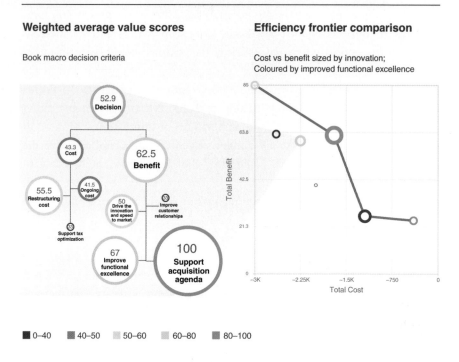

Weighted average value scores

Book macro decision criteria

Efficiency frontier comparison

Cost vs benefit sized by innovation;
Coloured by improved functional excellence

■ 0–40   ▨ 40–50   ▨ 50–60   ▨ 60–80   ■ 80–100

an efficiency frontier in economics). If an option is below the line, then it is always going to be inferior. Doing this highlights immediately which options are not worth considering as their benefits are not worth the cost or vice versa. In this case this accounts for options B and E. For the rest of the options (G, A, C, F, D) you can have an informed discussion between the cost–benefit trade-offs for each one. This technique is extremely useful in many contexts, not just organization design: for example, in making strategic supplier choices as part of a procurement process.

Further estimating benefits and costs

If you are looking for further differentiations between your options or you want to quantify the benefits or costs of a chosen option further to justify decision-making you can estimate benefits and costs in more detail. It is rare you will need to do this across all your options. If you do, to save time you could just quantify the key decision criteria drivers for all, rather than the detailed numbers.

In practice, the majority of the values will need to be calculated based on assumptions. For example, if you are further estimating benefits you are trying to demonstrate high-value benefits of a particular option based on firm numbers. With benefits there are tangible and intangible values. When it comes to those that are tangible, try to translate them into dollars. For instance, if you estimate a synergy of 20 per cent of teams X, then estimate the number of people in X together with their average cost. Don't just say the benefit is 20 per cent.

The intangibles will be harder to quantify and in many cases more significant. But again, try hard to translate these things into something you can quantify. For example, if the benefit is greater decision agility, then break down that into the value using the value tree. Greater decision agility might mean: getting to market faster; reduction in management burden; or an increase in staff engagement. So what? Taking an increase in staff engagement as an example, if there is currently a high staff turnover, then you can calculate the cost of staff turnover by breaking it down to: recruitment costs; upskilling costs; and lost sales for those in a sales role. Recruitment costs might be 15 per cent of the first year's salary, upskilling a further 20 per cent and lost sales 5 per cent of those in a sales position. From these sorts of assumptions, you can infer that a 30 per cent increase in engagement should result in attrition going from the current 20 per cent to between 12 per cent and 15 per cent. And, therefore, you can calculate an estimate for the actual benefit your option will provide. If the prize seems big, then spend more time on validating the assumptions and calculation logic. The more you can quantify the benefits case and tie it back to the design criteria, the stronger your case for change will be. The same approach is equally valid for quantifying the costs.

Develop and sign off the business case

Having developed your options and performed your analysis, you should be in a position to pick an option and write your business case. The business case should serve two purposes: first, to present to and receive buy-in from decision makers; and second, to act as a reference guide for the detailed design and implementation. It will be the backbone of your organization for the future. If you have been thorough in many of the processes described in Part Two, then the business case will write itself. Be clear about your recommended course of action, and using the work and analysis you have done already, make the 5–10 key points which support your decision. Whether the audience is composed of decision makers or those carrying out the implementation, you need to make sure it will resonate with those who engage with it throughout the design process. Think of it like a story, taking people along the journey of the decision-making process.

When you write the case think about what the key takeaways are, and make sure they are the points that come through. In writing this type of document a useful technique to think through is the Pyramid Principle (see page 39). For each section, start with the high-level points and break them down, documenting all the steps you have gone through in the macro design as you go. To help you think through how to write your business case, I have put together a simple generic structure and story as a 'starter for 10'. The headings are:

1   Recommendation and summary rationale

2   The vision and strategy

3   Current must-keep strengths

4   Current issues and case for change

5   List of design criteria

6   Options

7   Summary of value streams

8   Summary of how each option would work

9   Recommended option with rationale

10   Benefits

11   Implementation plans and costs

Your business case could be documented in different ways, whether in presentation form or full prose. Taking the latter, the above structure could translate into:

> We recommend implementing a [*the recommendation, eg a functional organization*] because we need to drive [*the summary logic, eg efficiencies and functional expertise*]. Given the strength of our current local sales and customer services, they will remain in their current country structures.
>
> Our aim is to become the leading [*the market sector you compete in*] through [*how you are going to win, eg cost competitiveness and product innovation*]. Currently, our [*state a data-driven case for change: eg our costs are 10 per cent margin points below target and our time to market for new products is 75 per cent too long, resulting in a declining market share of 25 per cent in the past five years*].
>
> The criteria we used to design the to-be organization include [*A, B, C*] which we used in evaluating the *x* main options [*list them: 1, 2, 3, 4 etc*]. The way each option works is [*show how options support the underlying value streams*].

Option 1 is [*explain it with pros and cons: how it will work*]. Given our criteria, Option [*X, eg functional org*] was selected because [*list your logic in terms of how it scored and a simple summary of the method chosen to decide, and those involved in the process to recommend the option*].

By implementing [*the recommendation, eg a functionally driven org*] we expect to achieve the following results: [*list the expected business outcomes by delivery dates*]. In order to implement this, we are going to need the following team [*list team*], for [x *months; show the high-level plan*] at a cost of [y: *show the summary cost breakdown*].

The above runs to approximately 250 words. Once you fill in all the details, you should be able to write it in 1,500–2,000 words or fewer than 20 presentation slides.

Final thoughts: Have a strong case for change

What seems easy is hard and what seems hard is easy. My view is that the micro design seems hard but is easy because it is so methodical and it just flows, but it seems hard because there is so much to it (as you will see by the length of the micro versus macro sections). The macro design probably seems easy but is actually hard. There is more ambiguity, there are no perfect answers and it is the most political of all the phases. It is about choices and trade-offs. It is about big change. It is about distilling big ideas into simple phases and pictures. The numbers are directional and can easily be questioned. The level of vested interest is high and there will be many who have a lot to lose.

If you don't have the justification behind your decisions you can be knocked off course easily. Critics of the decisions taken will probe and question to find holes in the process and logic. So be prepared for this. The key step at this stage is defining how each option will work by linking the to-be structure to the high-level processes. By doing this, most of the time the best option will become obvious. If that is not the case, then tools like multi-criteria decision analysis (MCDA) can really help drive rigorous thinking, and enable you to step through a process that is most likely to yield the right choice and justify your decision-making. Often in life it is the journey, not the destination, that matters. Doing MCDA is one of those instances. It is more about the thought process it forces you to work through: how you build your value trees, curves and weightings really helps you to define what matters most.

Having said all this, no matter whether you are doing a complex redesign of an entire organization or a smaller project involving a function or geographic area, until you detail what it really means and how it will work in practice all you have is a range of good ideas. If you want your ideas and chosen option to work, don't fall into the trap of just trying to implement the macro design without doing the detailed micro design work. The micro design is the heart of organization design, the heart of this book and the subject of Part Three.

Remember this

1 Develop a comprehensive list of options to give yourself the best possible chance of finding the right design.

2 Be wary of overprescribing the design at this stage. The decision you are making is more about narrowing possibilities and setting direction rather than specifying the details.

3 Map out your options so that you understand the look and feel of each one.

4 If there are no clear options use techniques such as multi-criteria decision-making to bring rigour to the process of decision-making.

5 Use your work throughout the macro design to tell an engaging story for change in your business case.

Notes

1 Hinssen, P (2014) *The Network Always Wins: How to survive in the age of uncertainty*, Mach Media, p 93

2 Nutt, P (2002) *Why Decisions Fail: Avoiding the blunders and traps that lead to debacles*, Berrett-Koehler, San Francisco

3 Galbraith, J R (2002) *Designing Organizations: An executive guide to strategy, structure, and process*, Jossey-Bass, San Francisco

4 Wright, G (1984) *Behavioral Decision Theory: An Introduction*, Sage, Beverly Hills, California

5 Goodwin, P and Wright, G (1991) *Decision Analysis for Management Judgment*, Wiley

PART THREE
Micro design

Introduction

3.1

Fools ignore complexity... Geniuses remove it.

ALAN PERLIS

Micro design is the real heart of the organization design process. It involves defining all the elements of the design across the organizational system so that the macro vision is implementable. A useful metaphor is that of constructing a building. First, you have to decide what the purpose of the building is. What is it going to look and feel like? The architect sets out the broad plans and high-level blueprints and options. This is the macro design. Then you have to draw the floor plans, measure the site, plan how many materials you will need, and estimate the costs and resources. This is the micro design. If macro design is top-down, micro design is more bottom-up. It is about the work people really do, day to day. It is how decisions are and should be made. If macro design is done more in the ivory tower by a small elite team, micro is done in the mud with the troops. Micro is where you have to define how all the elements depicted in Figure 1.3.1 should work in the organizational system.

Changing an organization can be terribly slow. From the moment the macro design team has determined what it wants to the system actually working can take years. The trap is the mental state of believing that because something is clear in one's mind it will just happen. My hypothesis for why so many people are confused in their roles, and why so many organizations struggle to make headway, is that the elements of the micro design are carried out infrequently. In our study of 34 organizational design practitioners with the University of Westminster in 2012–13, 87 per cent said they 'mostly or always' create the structures and 80 per cent of their designs were implemented. However, only 40 per cent build a baseline, 47 per cent mapped objectives, 46 per cent defined the required processes, 54 per cent defined how decisions should be made, 20 per cent mapped competencies, and 46 per cent went through a method-driven rightsizing exercise.

The detail of what each role is responsible for, the competencies required or how many Full-Time Equivalents (FTEs) are required to fulfil each one needs to be properly specified. However, it is far too often left to the manager to muddle through long after implementation. A further common complication is the macro pendulum swings from one extreme to another. For example, from a geographical framework with a focus on local customer closeness to a functional, centralized framework that focuses on cost reduction. The vain hope in swinging between two or more extremes seems to be that it will 'sort out the mess' and drive the right behaviour. In that process employees just become more confused and continue to do whatever it is they have always done.

Part Three is far longer than Part Two, because micro design is far more labour intensive with longer elapsed times. It is the real application of the philosophies and methodologies discussed in Chapter 1.3. Without doing the micro design properly, it is impossible to effectively communicate any change in a way that employees will understand how it applies to them personally. At the same time, this also represents a challenge. In the macro design there are fewer people involved, but those who are involved are more political and have greater impact. The micro design requires specialist knowledge, and whom you decide to include in the design process will have a big impact on both the outcome and the perception of the outcome by those not involved. To continue the building metaphor, one of the challenges for architecture is the degree of specialization. Those who do the initial concept drawings may well have nothing to do with structural engineering or the interior design finishing eye. The same is true in an organization. Often it will be your managers whom you rely on to implement your design lower down the organization and to oversee those elements of the work. They all have different expertise, drivers and ambitions. Their expertise needs to be leveraged and their biases managed. In order to do the macro design the numbers of people have to be carefully balanced. People typically find it hard to remove themselves from thinking about what it means to them and which box is theirs. Using independent external support is, therefore, a natural consequence for many programmes. The project management of the design process must be structured and tightly controlled.

If you let go of the overall design criteria and case for change, then you can be sure that the end result will not be what you expected. Someone needs to keep an eye on the entire end-to-end solution. That person is the architect. So make sure you give people time to step back to the macro design business case and to verify that detailed work is consistent with those recommendations and commitments.

Structure and logic for Part Three

Before you start to detail the design, you need to know exactly what your starting situation is. How can I get somewhere if I don't know where I'm starting from? Chapter 3.2 starts with the analytical building blocks you need to build your data baseline. Put another way, you need to know the detail before you can do the detailing! Creating a baseline is crucial because when creating and designing your future design, or what I call the to-be, you have to be able to compare it with your as-is to know where you are, where you need to go, where the gap is and what is going to change. This is crucial in developing an understanding of the impact assessment on your employees and determining the implementation plan that is outlined in Part Four. Unfortunately, it is almost always the case that the baseline data is structurally flawed and riddled with errors. Bringing together and cleaning organizational data can be a real challenge. It relies on Information Technology (IT). Much of the IT is owned by technical teams that are not involved. There is frequently a knowledge gap of practitioner core analytics skills. One of the goals is to provide an overview of the common IT terminology, how to do the data work and how to avoid silly statistical traps. It provides tips about many of the useful steps you can go through to get the organization to engage with data. It provides the analytical foundations to design the system and eventually quantify and manage the change over time.

Chapter 3.3 addresses how to make sure high-level goals and objectives are effectively cascaded through the organization and linked to the to-be positions. It puts the foundations in place so that they can be tracked over time to ensure they are delivered. The common traps and unintended bad behavioural consequences of poor objectives management are detailed too, as many SMART objectives actually drive siloed behaviour and task suboptimization.

Chapter 3.4 is the detailed process design combined with detailing of the final organizational structures. It answers the questions of what work is required and who is going to do what. To start, the key step is to get a good understanding of what people currently do, and then how that needs to change. A large part of this chapter, therefore, goes through the steps of performing an individual activity analysis and how to use the information to model the to-be process design. Process design isn't just doing the work, it is also deciding what needs to happen. Decision-making is a core part of designing a process. It goes to the heart of accountabilities and the fundamental governance question. Too often, too many people are involved in decision-making, the consequence of which can be crippling. The decision-making part of the process chapter demonstrates how to quantify this issue and gives you a set of tools to balance individuals' desire for autonomy, a corporate need for strong governance and ensuring the risk of a bad decision is traded off with the cost of the decision-making processes.

The last step in the process chapter is learning how to bundle activities and decisions into accountabilities through a matrix like the RAS framework outlined in Chapter 1.3. These bundles are done at the level of granularity of individual roles. Because of the need to have managerial control of individuals, roles are structured into boxes in a hierarchical organizational chart (org chart). Each of the boxes in the org chart is a position and eventually, as is outlined in the MiR section, you will need to fill those positions with people. The structure will be driven by the chosen macro design option and design criteria. I often say, it isn't where the box sits but what is in the box. The org chart defines where the box sits. The rest of the micro section deals with what is in the box and how many boxes are required.

Much of the work in an organization isn't captured by the fixed-value chain process design paradigm. For example, sales force optimization, project portfolio design and risk management cut across traditional functional boundaries and need different methods to design them effectively. Some organizations are entirely defined by a set of projects, so Chapter 3.5 covers how to design for these dynamic processes.

We all have different skills, knowledge bases, aptitude and behaviours or what is commonly called 'competencies'. Chapter 3.6 helps you think through what is required, where there are gaps and how to aggregate this in such a way that it can be improved. My perception is that competency management has a bad reputation because it has been too fluffy, not data-driven, too tied to performance management and reward. I therefore make the case for investing in this area and using it to improve performance.

Finally, I tackle the subject of rightsizing. Too often rightsizing is taken to mean downsizing. That is unfortunate. Rightsizing is fundamentally knowing how many FTEs in each role are required. Given the importance of this question, I find it surprising that there is a relatively modest amount of literature or thinking that has gone into answering it. It is also one of the hardest questions to answer effectively because there is no silver bullet. And the answer is often: 'it depends'. It depends on the level of productivity; the scale of the organization; the economics of the business; whether there are system dynamics such as the impact of queues and service level trade-offs.

Throughout the micro design there is a recurring theme of dealing with ambiguity. As part of the methodologies outlined in Chapter 1.3, a key part of micro design is about understanding the as-is, linking the organizational system and analysing and visualizing to understand your design. It also requires you to model scenarios and test the impact of each one. Getting the level of detail right is one of the biggest arts, and building strong analytical foundations is the greatest enabler.

The data goldmine

Introduction

There is currently a gap. A business opportunity if you will: to connect your people with business performance; to tie the crucial elements of the business together by tracking and managing drivers from across the organization, and understanding their impact. Data lies at the heart of achieving this – linking all the elements of the system together by bringing organizational and business data together.

We are living in the information age and the pace of growth in human knowledge is exponentially increasing. In 1965 Gordon Moore noted that the processing power of computer circuits had doubled every year since their invention and predicted, correctly, that this trend would continue into the future, except now the accepted time is 18 months (Moore's Law). As Buckminster Fuller predicted, new knowledge, which doubled every century until 1900, is now estimated to double every 18 months.[1]

This is a hard thing for the mind to grapple with. For example, take a piece of paper a tenth of a millimetre thick. Fold it ten times and it will be will be 102 millimetres thick; 20 times takes you to 105 metres, 30 into space at 107 kilometres, 42 to the moon, and after 51 folds you reach the sun. After 103 folds you will be outside the observable universe, which is estimated at 93 billion light years in diameter.[2] With exponential growth comes exponential value. For example, in the 1990s it cost billions to map the human genome. Today it costs less than $3,000 and that is predicted to drop even further.[3]

The most successful organizations of today are those that can harness these exponential gains of the information age. For example, when Google first indexed the internet in 1998 it found 26 million pages; it now indexes over a trillion unique URLs.[4] And Facebook gained more than a billion users in just 10 years.[5] Businesses are sitting on a goldmine of organizational data that, if used in the right way, could return exponential amounts of value by connecting the organizational system. However, many still struggle to simply track headcount.

A lot of the basic building blocks for getting the most out of organizational data are currently missing: ensuring data quality; having consistent role titles; counting FTEs by a common understanding of grade, function or geographical unit. Organizations need an end-to-end data-driven approach to process and maintain organizational data over time and connect the various elements of the system. Today we are at the beginning of this journey. A shift is emerging as organizations begin to appreciate the value of this data more. For example, Norwegian retailer Elkjøp, working with psychological testing company Cut-e, increased sales performance of new hires by 14 per cent. They identified the personality types most effective in sales roles and by screening candidates they were able to target recruitment. Then by connecting their recruitment profiling data with sales data they were able to compare the two and measure the value returned to the business.[6]

In this chapter, I set out a method for building a baseline of data and gaining an understanding of your organizational as-is. I begin by exploring four data myths, which have traditionally hindered those working with organizational data from making progress. I then provide an end-to-end seven-stage process for how to collect, understand and maintain a baseline of data. Finally, the last section investigates how to analyse your data effectively so that you are getting the answers you need and you can avoid some common statistical traps when analysing it. This chapter provides the platform for the rest of the book. Building a comprehensive and focused baseline is essential for designing and managing your organization, because if you don't know where you are, how can you know where you are going? By getting your data processes right you are setting yourself up for success throughout the rest of your design.

Data blockers and myths

A trend has emerged over the last few years that spending on technology is increasingly moving away from the IT function and towards specific digital units.[7] One of the best examples of this is the rise of digital marketing. The ease with which marketers have been able to gather and analyse data has transformed the industry: from how consumers are targeted down to the very skills considered essential to become a marketing professional. As Marketo's chief marketing officer Sanjay Dholakia commented, 'Marketing's changed more in the past five years than in the past 500 years.' It is a 'whole new learning curve for marketers, who are starting to have to be more and more technical'.[8] Indeed, in 2012, Gartner analyst Laura McLellan declared that by 2017 the Chief Marketing Officer would spend more on IT than the Chief Information Officer.[9]

People and organizational effectiveness functions are increasingly seeing the need for investment into systems that make the most of their data. However, they are lagging far behind other business functions such as marketing. Why have other organizational functions got so far ahead in their utilization of data? For a start, in contrast to functions like marketing and finance, organizational analytics are less obviously connected to business outcomes, and so by their nature it is harder to demonstrate their value. More importantly, though, I believe it comes to an approach. Unlike marketing and finance, functions typically dealing with organizational data have been slower and less eager to embrace a data-centric approach. The result is they have found it harder to substantiate arguments and demonstrate value to the business, in turn making it hard for them to get the funding required to put people at the top of the business agenda. A range of data myths has emerged over the years which have obscured, blocked and been provided as excuses for not embracing a data-centric approach. In this section I outline four of these myths to help highlight how the systematic process of building a baseline (covered in the next section) can help you make the most of your data and overcome these traditional blockers.

- Myth One: 'Data and technology are scary.'
- Myth Two: 'Organizational data is too hard to process.'
- Myth Three: 'One system fits all.'
- Myth Four: 'More data means more insight.'

Myth One: Data and technology are scary

Two years ago I worked on a project with an HR manager who was extremely competent in many aspects of HR. We were looking at a spreadsheet containing employee pay, pay increase and bonus. I asked her to calculate the total pay increase (a simple calculation of pay increase + annual bonus) and it emerged she had never learned to use the sum function in Excel. Despite holding a master's degree in HR, and five years of work experience, she had not moved beyond the stage where Excel terrified her.

Too often when working with people who have traditionally dealt with organizational data, I hear 'I don't do numbers' or 'I don't do data.' Unlike the marketing function, organizational analytics have not been made a business priority. There is a lack of urgency to appreciate and understand the value data can give to enhance people functions and employee relations. For example, how a data-driven approach to areas such as objectives or competency management can help individuals improve performance and develop by identifying specific areas for improvement. Professionals working with organizational data are going to have to transition from a soft-skill focus and combine them with hard skills, if they are to keep up with skills required for the demands of data-driven organizations. Likewise, organizations that do not invest in this area will find themselves missing out on a huge area of potential business value. To help address this myth explicitly I have put together a set of definitions for technical terms when handling data and building a baseline (see the Appendix).

Myth Two: Organizational data is too hard to process

As I highlighted in Chapter 1.3, organizational data is naturally complex and messy. It can feel impossible to process because it is stuck in numerous isolated Excel islands and systems. Data professionals have reported that cleaning and transforming their datasets are an extremely time-consuming and boring part of their analytical workflows, often comprising 80 per cent of the work.[10] When dealing with organizational data this represents a real challenge, and can often be used as an excuse to not begin to use data.

Data quality should never be used as an excuse. You have to start somewhere and it is only by using data that you will be able to understand what data is valuable, what is not, and where improvements are needed. There is no doubt that data is hard work, especially to begin with when building your baseline. This means employees need to have the benefits the data will bring to themselves and the organization as a whole communicated to them. Too often the employees handling data get little personal value from the outputs of their work. It is no wonder, therefore, that excuses are found to avoid working on what is perceived to be a thankless task.

Myth Three: One system fits all

Technology is achieving some amazing things, with a range of tools now on the market to help those working with organizational data. And yet, Excel and PowerPoint are still the main tools of choice. Excel is great for many things but it has many flaws when dealing with organizational data: it isn't that visual; links between worksheets are easily broken and hard to track;

it struggles to handle hierarchies; and it is typically used offline by one person at a time, making duplications very easy to make.

Static use of technology has meant organizations are struggling with their data, and professionals find it time consuming and uninspiring to process. As our understanding of data and its possibilities has grown, so has the refinement of the tools available to us. Depending on the data you are collecting and what you are trying to achieve with it, you may require a different tool. At this point in time, I think there are four broad options you can consider to aid your approach to your data: a data warehouse; an Enterprise Resource Planning (ERP) system; a data intermediary; and specific visualization software. A data warehouse is the standard choice, but as already mentioned in Chapter 1.3, it does not suit organizational data very well. Going down the data warehouse route is a hugely complex, long and painful journey, only solved by brute force and Herculean commitment in order to collect, structure and query the data. ERPs are a vital organizational tool because of their ability to integrate and handle flows of information from across the organization. However, they often leave you short of flexible analytics and reporting capabilities, and the ability to model and run organizational scenarios so key in organization design. As the name suggests, data intermediaries are beginning to offer a middle, more niche ground. These are software and applications designed for specific organizational events rather than overarching operations: for example, specific organizational modelling software. Finally, out-and-out visualization software allows you to perform advanced analytics on top of your data, although it may lack some of the modelling capabilities of intermediary software and have very few operational capabilities. The trick is to work out exactly what you are trying to achieve and then choose the best tool for the job. Having the right tool makes the data less scary and easier to process along every stage of the data journey. And given the potential value, the investment is certainly worth it.

Myth Four: More data means more insight

Just because organizational data represents a goldmine, much of which hasn't been exploited yet, it doesn't mean you need to collect all of it. Think of data as a value chain, starting at source systems and ending in actions and behaviours. Good Business Intelligence (BI) starts by thinking through the information needs for the highest-priority actions and decisions first, and working backwards. Too often an IT team will be told 'Give me BI' without guidance about the end requirement or output. The team then starts by building a data warehouse with the information it has from various systems and never moves beyond that point. I have seen companies with a 10-year plan to build a warehouse, and other companies spend millions to achieve little more than the insight they started with.

There is so much data around that often the challenge is actually to specify and focus on what you are trying to achieve and, therefore, which data is relevant. Too much information is no information. I've heard of consultants compiling lists of 800+ HR metrics in the belief that if you think of everything, then you will be able to answer any question. However, collecting too much data will overburden people and cripple your data collection, and analysis processes will be more difficult, running the risk of nothing getting delivered. Much better is to collect high-priority data and then add to your baseline as you go. Remember, there is nothing stopping you from collecting more and new data further down the line.

Most of these myths are due to a mindset towards data. By approaching data in the right way you can overcome many of the barriers that have traditionally 'stopped' organizational analytics being at the heart of business decisions. Much of the challenge is simply a question of discipline when building up and maintaining a reliable baseline of data to work from. The next section provides a systematic process for how to build a baseline, taking into account and tackling head on the myths addressed in this section.

Building the baseline – get ready to wrangle

As I have already highlighted, organizational data can be a nightmare to work with: incomplete, hidden in numerous systems and spreadsheets, and constantly moving. No set of organizational data will ever be absolutely perfect. So get ready to wrangle. Data wrangling is at the heart of building a baseline, and covers the steps of cleaning, converting and manipulating data into a usable, convenient format. I love the idea of wrangling with data. The word *wrangle* captures beautifully the essence of the battle with data to keep it up to date, uniform and useful. And it is a battle. Making the baseline process as simple and as accessible for employees as possible will immediately get you a great deal nearer to business-changing insights. In this section I go through seven iterative steps of how to go about building a baseline set of data as shown in Figure 3.2.1. These include the steps from deciding which data to collect, right through to the collection, visualization and analysing of that data.

FIGURE 3.2.1   Building a baseline process

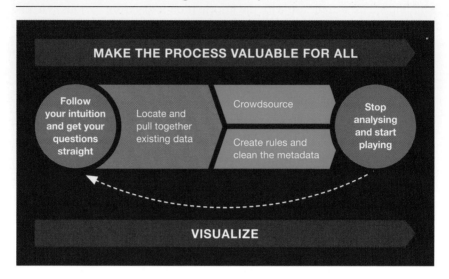

1 Follow your intuition and get your questions straight

For many years, strategy consultants have used a hypothesis-led approach to focus investigations – and it works. Data and analytics are not all about facts and figures. Often the best insights come initially from intuition, investigation and creative thinking. Therefore, when building a baseline of data think beyond the simple organizational metrics such as headcount and absence. Go back to your design criteria to help direct your focus. For example, if a key part of the design criteria is to boost productivity through centralizing the business, come up with a series of questions which will help you understand productivity throughout the business: Are some departments more productive than others? Does training affect productivity? Where do our top performers come from? These types of question will help direct the metrics you need to collect to build your baseline.

When doing a major transformation there are certain sets of metrics that you will almost certainly need, regardless of the focus of the project. A sample list is shown in Figure 3.2.2. Remember, though, your baseline is not a one-off, but an ongoing set of data which should support the ongoing development of your organization. So when tackling any problem, refer back to your intuition and the fundamental questions to guide your approach.

FIGURE 3.2.2   Example baseline properties (fields)

Category

		Must have (20)	Should have (20)	Could have (28)	Calculated (17)
Type	**Business (8)**		○ Actual sales ○ Customer satisfaction ○ Sales targets 3	○ Gross revenue ○ Net revenue ○ Revenue ○ Process level cost ○ Direct/indirect cost 5	
	Core OD (16)	○ Number of hours worked (per week) ○ FTE ○ Function/department ○ ID number ○ Manager ID ○ Title (role; post) ○ Area (geographic) ○ Vacancy ○ Country ○ Grade 10	○ Office location (City) ○ Is temporary ○ Subfunction 3		○ Is current employee ○ Span of control ○ Team potential rating 3
	Demographic (12)	○ Birthday ○ Gender ○ Leave date ○ Start date 4		○ Ethnicity ○ Role start / appointment date ○ Expected retirement age 3	○ Age ○ Tenure ○ Tenure in current role ○ Tenure in previous role ○ Years to retirement 5
	Financial (22)	○ Current salary ○ Currency ○ Currency exchange rate 3	○ Share-based payments ○ Cost centre 2	○ Cost of termination ○ Current bonus ○ Expenses ○ Healthcare costs ○ Other benefits ○ Payroll taxes ○ Pension ○ Recruitment cost ○ Relocation costs ○ Total benefits ○ Total payroll cost ○ Functional cost 12	○ Currency converted bonus ○ Currency converted employee costs ○ Currency converted salary ○ FTE salary ○ Total cost 5
	Personal (9)	○ Email address ○ First name ○ Surname 3	○ NI or tax number ○ Other unique identifier ○ Personal address ○ Photo work ○ Telephone number 5		○ Full name 1
	Talent and performance (18)		○ Absence detail ○ Employee engagement ○ Employee potential rating ○ How recruited ○ Prior period performance ranking ○ Successor information ○ Training days 7	○ Absence days ○ Absence instances ○ Absence type ○ Left voluntarily? ○ Performance ranking ○ Reason for leaving ○ Training cost ○ Target performance distribution 8	○ Bradford factor ○ Team absences ○ Performance rating category 3

Category   ▨ Must have   ▨ Should have   ▨ Could have   ▨ Calculated

2 Make the process valuable for all

As a general rule, people don't like to provide data. It costs them time and effort; it can cause embarrassment and show their shortcomings. Even if you have top-down sponsorship, your priority won't necessarily be the same as every employee. Not everyone is intimidated by authority, and those providing data can be highly creative in their delay tactics. So make the process worthwhile for them. At a high level, make sure you can answer the key questions of why you are collecting the data, how they are going to help, what the consequence of not getting the data will be, and if there is any upside for them. A good exercise is to tie the data back to the list of questions in step 1. The answers should be compelling enough to get buy-in.

At the lower data-entry levels, for those performing the day-to-day task of entering and cleaning data, you have to answer the data owner's concerns: 'If I'm going to input data, what's in it for me?' There are two methods here: first, ensure the data owner can see the value they are contributing or getting back. One way of doing this is ensuring they can see the end-to-end process. They can then understand the holistic benefits the data will lead to. Second, make the process into a game. For example, on one project, a network of hospitals wanted to clean their data. However, none of them was progressing. To incentivize them we put up a map of how each was progressing and who was top week by week. Just a week after the map went up, the progress made increased exponentially. Gamifying the process through visual feedback and competition made the process fun and part of a team effort. To get the most out of your data you have to be creative. Not just with how you analyse it, but getting it in the first place. After all, data sits with people, so you have to find ways to incentivize them and get them to buy into the process.

3 Locate and pull together existing data

It amazes me how often organizations jump straight to implementing new data collation and creation, overlooking their existing data. Often you already have in place a lot of the data you need in order to see the as-is picture; you just need to bring it all together. By trying to get insight out of your data early on in the process, you can:

- show those working hard to provide the data that they are being used and how you are using them;
- start to answer some of your hypothesis and make sure you are collecting the right data for your needs;

- gain a much better understanding of the data cleaning and further collection processes ahead.

The starting point is to be extremely clear about the data you need to collect. Figure 3.2.2 shows a sample list of properties (or fields in relationship database speak) that are frequently collected as part of an OD project. Note that I have categorized them by two dimensions. The first is the level of priority. Some properties are critical and you can't build your baseline or do an OD project without them. These nine properties fall within the critical dimensions with eight in core OD and one in financial types of data.

Once you know what data you need, the next step is to determine where to source it. In doing this, understand:

- What systems are used in the organization and where are they being used? For example, often different geographical locations will use different systems.

- How do the required properties map to the various systems and which properties currently don't exist in any system?

- Who owns which system and what is the process for getting the data extracted?

If you need to repeat the extraction process, ensure you document and test the process. Good sources to begin collecting data from include:

- Payroll – Typically this is the best source because it should contain all your people information. It is certainly a good place to start because, if you then match it up and compare it with your other sources, you can begin to see if you have a consistent view of your organization. You would be surprised how often payroll doesn't match other source systems.

- Performance management systems – Comparing this source system with payroll is a great way of testing the quality of your people data. If they are the same, then great, but if they are different you need to look at your data quality.

- Excel spreadsheets – I have not seen an organization yet that does not have Excel islands, with pockets of information siloed away. It is a problem we constantly have to tackle in my company and with our clients. However, bringing all this data together is a good chance to collect all that 'lost' data.

- HR Management Information Systems (HRIS).

- Enterprise Resource Planning (ERP) systems.

- Customer Relationship systems (CRM).
- Financial systems for customer revenue and margins, and P&L cost information.
- Applicant tracking systems.
- Learning management systems.
- Quandl for externally published sources, eg unemployment, demographic, or economic growth.

4 *Visualize*

Visualizing data is a key part of the data and analytics processes as highlighted in Chapter 1.3. When visualizing the data try to stay away from Excel, and where possible use specifically designed software that helps bring all your data together in an interactive and visual way. Visualizing the data as early as possible in the process will bring it to life and achieve buy-in from people working with it and affected by it. It may also start uncovering some basic insights to help reaffirm your hypotheses and ensure you are going in the right direction.

Think back to your original hypotheses. What are the best ways to look at the data and what stories are you trying to tell? For example, if you are interested in salary across the spans and layers of your organization, take your existing ERP data with the given reporting lines. This only requires five properties of data: Employee ID, Manager ID, function, salary and grade. Using this data you can answer dozens of questions about the organizational structure and consistency of salaries across the organization. To tell this story, think back to some of the visualizations in Chapter 1.3 such as the box grid visualizations (Figures 1.3.13 and 1.3.14). Cycle the data through these visualizations so you can see different perspectives. When looking for further insights think through the various visualization options:

- traditional statistical representations (bars, columns, lines, scatter plots, box plots, Gantt charts, tables, dashboards);
- additional analytical elements such as colouring, scaling, hierarchies;
- plotting a fourth dimension of time to highlight trends.

From this point onwards this process of visualizing data will add value throughout each stage of building your baseline. For example, visualizing data quality alone (detailed in stage 5) as demonstrated in Figure 3.2.3, helps identify where the gaps are in your data and where there may be inaccuracies. Equally, when crowdsourcing data, handing visuals back to data owners helps them identify outliers and inaccuracies in seconds (stage 6).

5 Create rules and clean the metadata centrally

Inevitably when you bring data together there will be data quality issues. So, as soon as you can, create clear rules on data structure. For example, on one project a client had a database of more than 30,000 items of IT hardware spend. The vast majority of the items were duplicates and the data could be reduced to a couple of hundred items, which accounted for well over 95 per cent of the spend. The company had made its life much harder by not having clear rules about how data was to be collected and stored.

Cleaning data is not a one-off exercise. Given that people are collecting and cleaning data in different offices or even different countries, once your data is clean you need to make rules about data collection and storage. For example, often the lowest level of data is acceptable, but it is how the data is categorized or tagged that is important. A common and easy category to grasp is gender. The male sex may appear as Male, male, m, 0 or 1, MALE... and that is just in English. Consistency is key. You have to be clear about definitions; for example, what is an FTE, or total cost of utilization? If you decide this upfront, you will save serious amounts of time later on.

Data quality can be used as a reason for not generating information. In my experience, if data is being used and presented in an understandable way, it will drive behaviour and the data quality will improve naturally. Visualizing your data will help clean data naturally for two reasons. First, it is much easier to identify inaccuracies and outliers. For example, the visualization in Figure 3.2.3 provides an overview of all the metadata and the distribution of data for each property. Second, it highlights the completeness and consistency of particular data fields (dimensions and measures) and where there are orphans in the organizational hierarchy, so you can immediately identify problem areas and where attention is needed (see Chapter 1.3 for definitions of hierarchical data).

Visualizing data in this way makes it easy to obtain the data you need from across the organization. Alongside new and intuitive connections between data and visualizations, this means you no longer have to rely on database administrators or IT to solve data issues. This is because traditional data visualization layers in software are becoming increasingly intertwined with database layers. Visualizations are no longer just a representation of data, they also link back to the data they represent. The consequence is that where previously you had to change data within a database yourself, or via a database engineer to alter the visualization, now you can alter data directly through the visualizations. You can drag and drop pieces of data to alter numbers of fields at once, making the process of cleaning data in line with

FIGURE 3.2.3   Example data types and patterns dashboard

DATA SUMMARY

Dimensions	4	Measures	4	Hierarchy		Hierarchy checks	
Text fields	4	Number fields	4	Total records	1,505	Tree roots	1
Date fields	0	Yes/No fields	0	Main structure	1,505	Duplicates	0
Image fields	0			Max depth	9	Blank IDs	0
				Orphans	0	Blank parent IDs	0
				Orphan groups	0		

82% complete

TEXT

Area	Gender	Role	Department

100% complete
13 groups

65% complete
2 groups

100% complete
38 groups

100% complete
13 groups

Area			Gender			Role			Department		
Manchester	1,138	75.6%	Female	507	33.7%	Delivery Grade 1	380	25.2%	Ops Programme Delivery	385	25.6%
Birmingham	230	15.3%	Male	474	31.5%	Delivery Grade 3	320	21.3%	Projects	282	18.7%
Head Office	60	4.0%	(Blank)	524	34.8%	Delivery Grade 2	235	15.6%	R&D	224	14.9%
West	13	0.9%				Delivery Grade 4	164	10.9%	Project Delivery	212	14.1%
East	10	0.7%				Research Level 5	50	3.3%	IT Programme Delivery	195	13.0%
North	10	0.7%				Project Manager	46	3.1%	Programme Delivery	58	3.9%
South	10	0.7%				Research Level 4	40	2.7%	Distribution	47	3.1%
Bristol	6	0.4%				Driver	38	2.5%	Sales	44	2.9%
Crawley	6	0.4%				Research Level 3	38	2.5%	Finance	22	1.5%
Liverpool	6	0.4%				Research Level 1	34	2.3%	HR	20	1.3%
3 more categories	16	1.1%				28 more categories	160	10.6%	3 more categories	16	1.1%

NUMBER

Current Salary	Engagement Index	Customer Satisfaction	Age

100% complete
6 groups

81% complete
9 groups

13% complete
7 groups

100% complete
7 groups

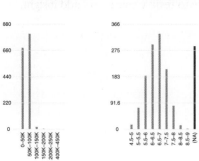

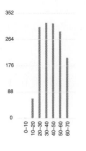

Data Key   ▨ Complete   ■ Bad values   ▨ Blank

your rules on data structure on an ongoing and ad hoc basis infinitely easier, saving time and effort in the cleaning process.

6 Crowdsource

The data you need to further improve quality or for new properties will sit in different places of the organization. Often those who are in the best position to fix data are the ones who want the maximum insight from it but do not have the time to correct it. Therefore, make it easy for people to be able to provide and alter data. Technology now allows for fast feedback, such as surveying capability, which automatically updates a person's records once completed. For example, a problem in many organizations is a simple question of organizational hierarchy. Who reports to whom? One particularly useful exercise may be to send a two-question survey to all employees asking 'Whom do you report to?' and 'Who reports to you?' Collate the data, draw an org chart and very quickly you will expose any confusion or inaccuracies. Big data is all very glamorous, but the most value is often in getting the basics right. Here are three tips to help you when crowdsourcing data:

1 **Make data easy to upload**. If the upload process is complex people will become disengaged and turn to other work instead. For example, sending out a webform that takes two minutes to complete will give you instant updates on your data.

2 **Report data back to owners**. Those who know the data should be the ones who interact with it. They will get new insights from the process. They are the ones who will identify outliers and be best placed to uncover data quality issues.

3 **Make the process mobile**. Often the best time to spend a couple of minutes uploading or analysing data is when you are in transit or a little bored. If the data is available at all times and on all devices such as smartphones and tablets, it makes it easy to review charts and add insight.

To begin with, collecting data from different areas of the organization will come down to you and your team. However, the sign that you are getting this right is when the data is seen as a business issue and function leaders come to you to drive new insights and get further data.

7 Stop analysing and start playing with your data!

As the HR Information Systems Manager at one retail client once said: 'One of the most exciting things about bringing all types of organizational data together and visualizing is that you can start to answer questions that people didn't realize they wanted the answer to.' Having built your baseline, just enjoy yourself. Start exploring, slicing and dicing the data. (The slice is the ability to split the data according to any dimension or measure. The dice is the ability to use any aggregator such as sum, standard deviation, percentile, skewness, and many more.)

When analysing your data for the first time you will be amazed what you can find. One consultant I worked with, after quickly combining two client datasets and analysing the training impact, was able to tell her client that it was wasting half of its graduate sales training budget because one group of the target audience learned nothing. By contrast, for the other group it was a great investment. The client just needed to know which graduates to target for what type of training. Simply by splitting the trainees by geographic location showed that particular office sales teams didn't increase their sales post training, while others almost doubled theirs. The underlying reasons and the action taken as a result are a separate story, but what is powerful is the insight gained by combining different datasets, in this case sales and training data.

The combination of data is frequently referred to as mash-up data. Bring together your people data with data from across the organization and see what you can find. To make sense of all the data, break down areas of insight into topics by organization or theme. For example, functional areas: HR, finance, procurement, manufacturing; or organizational areas: people, process, systems; or strategic, operational, transactional. Using these categories you can start performing advanced analytics. For instance, can you see whether sales performance links to education or recruitment channels? Do those who attend training have lower attrition? Which actions post an employee engagement review had meaningful impacts? What human factors drive profit, productivity or retention?

We have now got to into the in-depth analysis. But when analysing and drawing your insights you have to be careful. What might seem obvious in the data may be wrong statistically speaking. It is too easy to oversimplify and make errors of judgement. The next section sets out three checks to ensure you analyse your data as effectively as possible.

Performing analysis: common statistical traps

All through these practical steps you will have been building your baseline understanding. However, I have included this section because data can often be misrepresentative and insights are only as good as those who draw them. The world is full of wrong and dangerous analysis and statistics. Numbers are aggregated and conclusions erroneously drawn. Linear correlations are calculated with high correlation coefficients (R) at the wrong level and bad science is peddled as robust analysis. There are many PhD dissertations that can be written on bad analysis. Given the scope of this book, I am going to focus on the three logical statistical flaws that I see most frequently. This doesn't mean you should stop the learning here. More, I hope, that you gain an interest to want to learn more and avoid making recommendations that give the illusion of being robust but are not. The three I am going to cover are:

1 The ecological fallacy

2 Taking correlation for causation

3 Ignoring statistical significance

The ecological fallacy

In the 2004 US election George W Bush won the 15 poorest states and John Kerry won 9 of the 11 wealthiest. The conclusion: wealthy people vote Democrat and the poor Republican. And yet 62 per cent of voters with annual incomes over $200,000 voted for Bush, while only 36 per cent of voters with annual incomes of $15,000 or less voted for Bush.[11] So that conclusion is completely inaccurate.

This is a great example of the ecological fallacy in practice. 'An ecology fallacy is a logical fallacy in the interpretation of statistical data where inferences about the nature of individuals are deduced from inference for the group to which those individuals belong.'[12]

In the context of HR, an example of the ecological fallacy in practice is the likely hypothesis of a correlation between performance and absenteeism as measured through the Bradford index. The Bradford index weights the number of absence instances higher than the total duration of absence. The theory is that short, frequent and unplanned absences are more disruptive than longer absences. The formula is $B = S^2 \times D$ where S is the number of spells (instances) and D is the duration. For example, if someone was sick once for 10 days, their Bradford score would be $1^2 \times 10 = 10$. But if they were sick 10 times a day at a time, giving the same total of 10 days, their score would be $10^2 \times 10 = 1,000$. For a given group of employees, the histogram (in Figure 3.2.4) clearly shows that those with a Bradford score below 100 have an average performance of 5.6 out of 10, while those between 600 and 700 have an average of only 3.

FIGURE 3.2.4   Histogram and aggregate scatter with linear regressions of average performance rankings by average Bradford index category

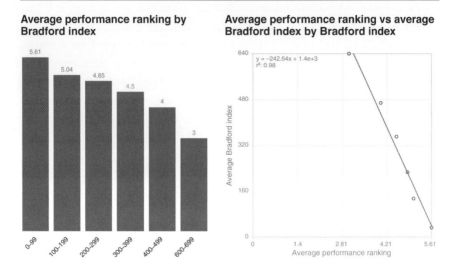

Average performance ranking by Bradford index

Average performance ranking vs average Bradford index by Bradford index

This is proven even more emphatically through the 'scientific-looking' correlation in Figure 3.2.4. The figure on the left shows the average performance for each Bradford index group while that on the right takes each of those six groups and draws a correlation between each group's performance and their average Bradford score. The same groups of employees (those with Bradford factors less than 100, between 100 and 200, and so on) are correlated with their performance ratings. Unsurprisingly, the correlation (r) is −0.97 or almost perfect (a score of $r = 1$ or −1 is perfectly correlated while a score of $r = 0$ means there is zero correlation). *Wow*, think the people reviewing these numbers. Conclusions are drawn: 'We need to sort out the poor-performing employees.' 'It's so logical that it's these people who aren't performing!' The analyst gets a pat on the back and now the management team thinks it has the proof and burning platform to take action against these low performers.

However, in this instance, they are all wrong. In fact, they are terribly wrong. They have just fallen for the ecological fallacy. In the above example, if you dig just a fraction deeper, the distribution of the 46 employees included within the analysis is shown in Figure 3.2.5.

FIGURE 3.2.5 Pivot table of performance rankings by Bradford index category

Performance Ranking

Bradford Index ＼ Performance Ranking	0–1 (2)	1–2 (4)	2–3 (3)	3–4 (4)	4–5 (18)	5–6 (16)	6–7 (12)	7–8 (4)	8–9 (6)	9–10 (5)
0–99 (43)	Jonathan Daniels	Nathan Savage Mohammad Reeves Jonathan Davis	Frank Moulton Brenda Speers	Luke Anderson	Chelsea Walsh Mark Patterson Troy Garling Melba Wilmore Chelsea Lamb Evie Dickinson	Eve Sykes Elizabeth Cox Jason Willis Bethany Banks Bailey Pugh Whitney Kowalski Ana Robinson Rosa Hall Jake Turner	Luke Hardy Daphne Sims Lara Moore Melissa Cloninger Stephanie Mercado Lauren Ray Connie Jameson Jude Whitehead George Guillemette Frank Reeve	Cory Freeman Charlie Goodwin	Natasha Hamilton Gabriel Davies Robert Sullivan Mamie Collins Inez Reed Deborah Evans	Tom Cox Fred Cole Lewis Yates
	1	3	2	1	6	9	10	2	6	3
100–199 (8)					Sophia Hopkins Christine Giddings Billy Brooks	Archie Rahman Benjamin Wall	Yuko Garcia	Gladys Powell		Scott Bird
					3	2	1	1		1
200–299 (13)	Eva Robinson				Jodie Pugh Michael Redmon Max Schofield Leo Waters Thomas Miles Jordan Bell	Sarah Cole Benito Rhoden Roy Roberts Charles Farias	Mohammed Hilton			Wendy Smith
	1				6	3	1			1
300–399 (6)		Kent Strahan		Mary Smith	Owen Oliver Ryan Savage	Matthew Warner		Dominic Gardner		
		1		1	2	4		1		
400–499 (2)			Georgina Murphy	Jonathan Cyr						
			1	1						
600–699 (2)				Dorothy Gardner	Sadie Villegas					
				1	1					

Bradford Index

FIGURE 3.2.6   Departmental and individual scatter plots of performance rankings by Bradford index category

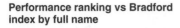

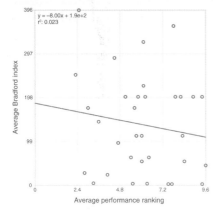
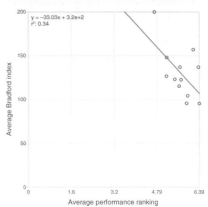

You can see, straightaway, that there are very few (four) data points of those with a Bradford score above 300. You can also see a large range of performance rankings of those with a Bradford score below 100. In fact, if you draw the scatter chart at the individual rather than group level, you can instantly see there is, in fact, no correlation (it is just 0.023).

There are only two employees with high Bradford scores and poor performance scores. This is a good example of what is officially called 'outlier analysis'. So no drastic or group action is necessary. Instead, a quick investigation into their historical performance to find out if they have always been poor performers would be advisable (if possible). Then a conversation can happen either to find out if something or someone is affecting their performance, or how the manager can help bring them back on track. This is obviously a tailored example, but it is an excellent reminder of the value of digging into statistics, questioning what you see and ensuring that you don't make sweeping conclusions which could have a negative impact.

Correlation versus causation

Did you know that it is dangerous to eat ice cream and then go swimming? There is a correlation between ice cream consumption and the likelihood of shark attacks. Sharks like people who have just eaten ice cream, right? Clearly, no. So how can they be correlated? The real correlation is that the hotter it is, the more ice creams people eat, the more they swim and the more likely it is that they are going to be attacked by sharks. This may be obvious, but every day people jump to overly simplistic and inaccurate conclusions, confusing correlation with causation.

A correlation is just a number. It happens to calculate the strength of a linear relationship between variables, but it does not carry any information about causation. Why? Because causation is far more complicated than the idea of how nicely it can fit a line to data. In general, it is very difficult to show causation. Why? Because we need to rule out all other factors that could influence the relationship. In general, showing causation is only possible in scenarios such as a laboratory environment where external factors can be controlled or at least limited and explored.

In a business context, we can show correlations are high and use these effectively for prediction. But it is important to ask why this correlation is occurring in order to examine causation. For instance, suppose that performance ratings were inversely correlated to number of absences. However, the driver of the relationship is unclear. That is, we cannot determine whether performance ratings were assigned as a penalty for absences or whether missed days actually contributed to lower performance. The causation is unclear but the correlation is still useful to drive conversation, investigate the potential drivers before acting and run relevant analysis for future conclusions to be drawn.

Statistical significance

If we are going to draw conclusions about a set of data, then we should have some understanding of how strongly we can draw those conclusions. I am going to use a simplified example to demonstrate my point. The example below shows that for a set of employees, males are higher performers than females. So does that mean that we should only hire men? The problem here is that the stats can get quite complex, so here are a couple of simple tools and thoughts. The first is to look at the variation within the dataset. The greater the standard deviation, the less likely you can draw the conclusion. Why? Standard deviation measures the average of how spread-out the data is. You can think about it this way: if female employees all have really similar performance measures, then it is possible to make better generalizations about that group. More similarity means small standard deviation. If, instead, some are performing really well, some are performing really poorly and some are doing okay, it is harder to tell a story about what is happening to the whole group. This is a situation with a large standard deviation – lots of differences, a more spread-out group.

A good way to visualize this is through the box plot diagram, which is described in Figure 3.2.7. The boxplot shows the distribution of the data.

FIGURE 3.2.7   Box plot explanation

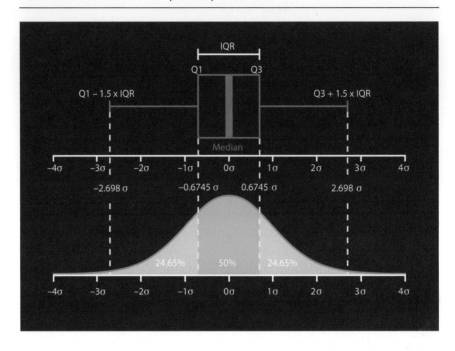

For the median, there is a thick line and a box is drawn to show the majority of the data points. This could be the upper and lower deciles (where 90 per cent of the points are above it and 10 per cent of the points below) or quartiles (the same, but 25 per cent and 75 per cent). A further set of lines shows the upper and lower limits of the data. This could be the max and min, or the 99 per cent and 1 per cent points (the percentiles). The box plot gives you a visual sense of distribution, which helps to indicate where there is more than just a simple story in the data.

The risk of using bar charts and the power of the box plot is highlighted in Figure 3.2.8. The left-hand bar chart shows the performance scores of males and females. At face value it appears males are performing far better, with an average of 6.4 out of 10 compared with the female average of 5.9. But when the same data is plotted using the box plot, another picture emerges. The median performance for females is actually 7.5. There is far more variability within the female population, with the lowest scores of '0' being 'achieved' and therefore taking the average down.

The next thing to look at when thinking about statistical significance is the sample size. The smaller the sample size, the greater the danger. This also makes sense. If you want to make a claim about the performance of women and you only measure the performance of 10 women, how confident are you

FIGURE 3.2.8 Average and box plot of gender performance levels

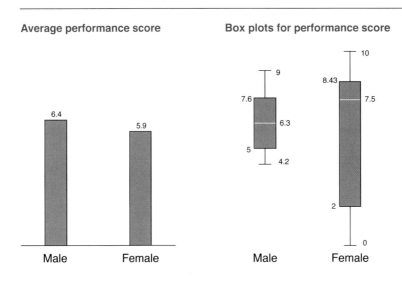

Average performance score

Box plots for performance score

that they reflect *all women* the company would ever be interested in hiring? If you get performance measures from more women, you have a clearer idea of what is happening on average. How can we make a statistical decision about whether men perform better on average? We turn to the most common statistical significance test, which is called the *t*-test. We can plug all of these numbers into the formula for a *t*-test comparing two averages. The result from such a test is a single percentage called a *p*-value.[13] (It is not in this book's scope to outline the *t*-test. For further reading on this please see the suggestions below.) In our scenario, this value is 15 per cent. Great – so how do I get any information about my employees' performance based on this number? In this scenario, the *p*-value measures the likelihood that these differences in employee performance arise completely by chance rather than due to any real average performance differences. It is standard practice to conclude that a *p*-value less than 5 per cent indicates a 'significant' difference. Here, with our value of 15 per cent we cannot make this claim. Are men performing better than women on average? Yes. But are they performing *significantly* better on average? No. So should we hire only men to boost performance scores? Not according to the data.

If you are told that a value is 'statistically significant', you should ask: 'Statistically significant compared with what?' and 'According to which statistical test?' Statistical significance is used within a section of statistical analysis called hypothesis testing and is used to infer how likely it is that we observe data by chance. Instead of using the phrase 'statistical significance', you will save a lot of energy and confusion by just explaining in words the conclusion your data leads you to. For example, it isn't (statistically) possible to conclude that men are performing better than women. It is also good practice to include details about the statistical test used to reach your conclusion and the number of data points included in the calculation.

While each of these three statistical traps is relevant, the point to take away is that data analysis isn't as much of a magic wand as many people think. Too often, people work extremely hard to build a baseline of data and leave the 'insight phase' of the work to the last minute. They then jump to erroneous conclusions because they don't think hard enough about and make too many predictable mistakes, such as the three outlined above. Unfortunately, from what I have observed from countless business presentations, most of the business world is full of terrible statistics. The bar chart is probably the most common stats tool used, yet as shown above it hides a whole range of flaws. The aim of this section isn't to make you an expert, but to improve your awareness of the dangers. If you are interested in learning more there are a couple of books I suggest you look at: *Essentials of Social Statistics for a Diverse Society*[14] and *Statistics for People Who (Think They) Hate Statistics*.[15]

Final thoughts

Data should be used to turn hindsight into insight and then foresight. While building a looking-back baseline is the logical first step in the micro stage of design, it is that dataset that you will come back to the most. In fact, it never stops being important, either through the design or afterwards. By maintaining the dataset and mashing it with other data, greater insight will be generated. You will use this data to generate scenarios and plans. With enough history, other projections will become possible and you move into helping to shape the future. The key is to make sure that you set yourself up for success by collecting, cleaning, analysing and reporting on your data consistently.

Organizational analytics have an opportunity to deal with the world as it really is: a complex, interconnected system. Consistent and focused data collection must be backed by a deep understanding of the multiple connections between people, roles, skills and activities. Too many change programmes have been overwhelmed by the sheer complexities of the organization. As you continue to build your baseline you can add more data from across the organization to really see which areas are performing well, need improvement or a downright overhaul. This is not just about a one-off design. In the future, those functions dealing with organizational data and analytics have to be able to resolve business issues before they happen by connecting the organizational system. They need to drive leaders from across the whole business to think through what their people do now, what they will do in the future and what the cost impact will be if activities change. With this, your data will become a goldmine: an invaluable resource with exponential and sometimes unpredictable benefits.

> **Remember this**
>
> 1 To get the most from your data you need to recognize potential value and communicate that value to the business.
>
> 2 Be disciplined throughout the data process. Be clear about the data you need and who or where you need to get them.
>
> 3 Make the process of collecting data valuable to everyone involved, from business owners to the employees working on the ground with the data.
>
> 4 Use the right tool for the right job. Do not try to do everything in Excel, and where possible use specialist tools to help with particular tasks. It is worth it!
>
> 5 When analysing your data, be wary of jumping too quickly to conclusions. Use analysis as guidance for further questions. It is not always a final answer and be mindful of the many hidden statistical traps.

Notes

1 Buckminster, F (1981) *Critical Path*, St Martin's, New York
2 Diaz, J [accessed 19 February 2015] Sploid, [Online] http://sploid.gizmodo.com/if-you-fold-a-paper-in-half-103-times-it-will-be-as-thi-1607632639
3 *Stratified Medicine in the NHS; An assessment of the current landscape and implementation challenges for non-cancer applications* (2014), Association of the British Pharmaceutical Industry
4 Official Google Blog [accessed 19 February 2015] We knew the web was big, Google, [Online] http://googleblog.blogspot.co.uk/2008/07/we-knew-web-was-big.html

5 Sedghi, A [accessed 28 March 2015] Facebook: 10 years of social networking in numbers, Guardian [Online] http://www.theguardian.com/news/datablog/2014/feb/04/facebook-in-numbers-statistics

6 As presented by Evensen, K and Aaserød, J, presentation to HR Recruitment Days, HR Norge, March 2015

7 Press, G [accessed 15 January 2015] Gartner Predicts Top 2015 and Beyond Trends for Technology, IT Organizations, and Consumers, Forbes [Online] http://www.forbes.com/sites/gilpress/2014/10/09/gartner-predicts-top-trends-for-technology-it-organizations-and-consumers-for-2015-and-beyond/3/

8 Koetsier, J [accessed 21 November 2014] Marketo CMO: 'Marketing has changed more in 5 years than the past 500', Venture Beat, [Online] http://venturebeat.com/2014/03/01/marketo-cmo-marketing-has-changed-more-in-5-years-than-the-past-500-interview/

9 Gartner official website [accessed 19 February 2015] Gartner [Online] http://my.gartner.com/portal/server.pt?open=512&objID=202&mode=2&PageID=5553&resId=1871515&ref=Webinar-Calendar

10 Kristi, M (204) Support the Data Enthusiast: Challenges for Next-Generation Data-Analysis Systems, Proceedings of the VLDB Endowment, **7** (6) pp 453–56

11 Gelman, A (2008) *Red State, Blue State, Rich State, Poor State*, Princeton University Press

12 Robinson, W (1950) Ecological Correlations and the Behavior of Individuals, *American Sociological Review*, **15** (3), pp 351–57

13

$$t = \frac{\bar{X}_1 - \bar{X}_2}{s\sqrt{\dfrac{1}{n_1} + \dfrac{1}{n_2}}} \qquad s = \sqrt{\frac{(n_1 - 1)s_1^2 + (n_2 - 1)s_2^2}{n_1 + n_2 - 2}}$$

For our example:

Variable	Men	Women
Mean	$\bar{X}_1 = 5.43$	$\bar{X}_2 = 4.72$
Standard deviation	$s_1 = 2.47$	$s_2 = 1.66$
Sample size	$n_1 = 29$	$n_2 = 17$

14 Leon-Guerrero, A and Frankfort-Nachmias, C (2012) *Essentials of Social Statistics for a Diverse Society*, Sage

15 Salkind, N J (2010) *Statistics for People Who (Think They) Hate Statistics*, Sage

Objectives management

*Management by objective works – if you know the objectives.
Ninety per cent of the time you don't.* PETER DRUCKER

Introduction

Objectives management (OM) is the start of detailing your to-be design. Objectives management, often referred to as strategic performance management, was defined by Bernard Marr as 'the organizational approach to define, assess, implement, and continuously refine organizational strategy'.[1] Corporate performance management is recognized as a priority and key technology investment area for businesses.[2] It is a priority for two reasons: first because companies are failing to deliver their business objectives using traditional methods; and second because they all recognize the value provided when objectives are correctly implemented and strategy is delivered. Objectives give a means of aligning everyone's effort and ensuring the most important business activities take priority.

Undertaking 'strategic corporate-wide performance management' means first defining what is the overall corporate strategy. From this, it is about defining what the objectives need to be in order to achieve the given strategy. As I outlined in Part Two, objectives are not the same as goals. Goals are directional and aspirational; they are influenced by a company's vision, and should be audacious and inspiring. Objectives are what turn these high-level visions into something meaningful and tangible; concrete, actionable steps that can be worked on and impacted immediately. The management aspect is managing the organization against meeting those objectives. I have used the term 'objectives management' instead of 'strategic corporate-wide performance management' because it speaks a lot more closely to the actual process you are doing day to day. The focus is on defining explicitly what you want to achieve, aligning this with the organization and then managing to ensure you achieve it.

A good example of objectives management in practice is the Objectives and Key Results (OKR) method, first applied by Intel and now used by companies such as Google and LinkedIn. The method defines clear Objectives (O) with each objective needing to have a set of Key Results (KR). Using Google as an example, the company reviews its OKRs every quarter with the expectation that employees will only average 0.6–0.7 for their OKR grade. If someone achieves 1.0 regularly then the OKRs are deemed to be not stretching employees enough. The benefits of this method, stated by Rick Klau of Google Ventures,[3] include:

- ensures disciplined thinking;
- facilitates clarity in communication and priorities;
- establishes indicators for measuring progress to track against plans;
- focuses effort.

These four benefits are all core goals when defining and implementing an effective organization design. In fact, the reason I have placed objectives management before detailed process, projects or competency design is because I believe that before these can be defined you need to know where you want to go and why. In this chapter I take you through a comprehensive process for objectives management. I begin by outlining some of the reasons organizations traditionally struggle with this area, before exploring how you can set and manage your objectives drawing on the methodology set out in Chapter 1.3. I then address some considerations when implementing objectives management in practice to ensure your objectives management process gives you value on an ongoing basis.

Why organizations struggle with corporate-wide performance management

If businesses recognize the value of corporate-wide performance management, why do they struggle with it in practice? I believe there are six main reasons: it is perceived as an individual performance assessment process; it is not made relevant to those lower down the organization; it is not regarded as a value-adding process; performance reviews are qualitative, not data-driven; technological issues; and inherent issues with objective methodology.

OM is perceived as purely an individual performance assessment process

Objective setting in companies typically happens as part of an individual annual performance process. This has three issues. First, there is a lack of business focus because individual objectives are not connected explicitly to the high-level business objectives set in the macro design. Second, a consequence of the first issue is that individual behaviour is driven by individuals wanting to optimize their personal balanced scorecard rather than what is right for the whole company. Thirdly, the performance assessment process is traditionally done no more often than twice a year. The result is that month to month there is no way of knowing if objectives are on track. If they are heading off target by the time the review arrives it can be a lot more difficult or even too late to address the situation.

Objectives are not communicated effectively

There is often a lack of visibility and communication about the purpose of objectives across the business. This makes it hard for employees to understand how their work fits into the direction of the overall business. In addition, employees are given few opportunities to engage with their objectives directly and give input to the objective-setting process. The result is a lack of engagement with the process of objective setting and personal objectives themselves. This situation is then exacerbated by infrequent and subjective appraisals used to inform feedback, bonuses and promotions.

Objectives management is not regarded as a value-adding process

A result of a lack of communication, the benefits of objectives management for both the business and individuals are not appreciated. Traditionally, people do not like being measured. Employees are often fearful of objectives because they believe the process of measuring them and their progress against unambiguous results will turn into a mechanism for either micromanaging them or uncovering and punishing low performance. The result is that the process is not taken seriously and can often be undermined from the top, with a lack of engagement and support from leaders, which then translates down the organization.

Performance reviews are purely qualitative and not data-driven

While most high-level objectives are tracked, invariably by financial results such as revenue or sales, objectives across the company are rarely linked to these high-level objectives and are not data-driven. Individual performance is often assessed purely on annual qualitative reviews. There is no real way of gauging quantitative and accurate performance of objectives. This is not to say qualitative reviews are not important but that you need both qualitative and quantitative reviews side by side to support each other. Currently, objectives management is implemented using old frameworks such as Management By Objectives (MBOs). This involves writing out people's objectives at the beginning of the year. However, in practice all this results in is a set of lists that quickly lose their impact and are unable to be understood in the context of the organization as a whole. Also, because appraisals are usually annual and performance is not tracked rigorously, appraisals come to represent only an employee's contribution over the few weeks or months leading up to them. In other words, objectives management stops being data-driven and a tendency to claim responsibility for company success gradually redefines the culture of a business. Office politics become unpleasant as those who shout loudest outdo those who contribute most.

How people use technology

While technology associated with performance management has moved forwards significantly, few companies have updated their technology or approach. Around 61 per cent of companies use generic tools such as Word and Excel rather than dedicated software for objectives management implementation.[4] And even when more appropriate software is used, such as Enterprise Resource Planning (ERP), the methods used are inefficient and inconsistent. To start with, traditional relational databases or Word are unsuited to linking the many-to-many links of the organization. This makes it impossible to connect objectives to people or roles and effectively analyse impact. Second, much of the process of objectives management is not done in a data-driven manner. It often involves filling in forms and providing manager or self-assessments against objectives. However, this means that those best at justifying their work are perceived to be the highest performers, rather than those who have actually had the biggest impact. Finally, the combination of the technology and the way it is used means objectives are not tracked consistently. Organizations find data maintenance near impossible with almost half of organizations having reactive rather than active data management, that is they fix problems rather than making sure that they don't occur in the first place. Ensuring ongoing quality and usefulness of objectives data is key as it is what drives agile management and intervention when objectives deviate from plans.

Improved objectives performance doesn't always mean improved business performance

While I am a big believer in measurable objectives, on an organization-wide level they have inherent conflicts of interest and they can be used as motivation for bad decision-making. Taking the first issue, often objectives associated with particular measures will be in direct competition across different organizational functions. A good example comes from the trade-offs in supply chains. A manufacturing manager's performance will often be measured on manufacturing costs. Therefore, he or she will want longer runs for each individual product to minimize set-up costs. In contrast, the person responsible for inventory management will be measured on inventory costs. Therefore, he or she will want short but frequent runs to reduce inventory costs. Their objectives and assessed performance are in direct conflict, running the risk of decisions being made for individual gain rather than what is best for the business.

This example highlights the danger of measuring and linking performance too explicitly to one measure. In one instance, again using the supply chain example, an initiative to improve productivity and machine utilization meant each manager was measured on utilization over time. However, this resulted in one manager moving a set of subcomponents to their manufacturing site. The movement cost the company money and did not result in any overall improvement for the business in terms of utilization. It only meant the shift manager could publish a higher measure for his or her site at the cost of another. I have seen this type of behaviour numerous times. The root cause is that the measures against which objectives are assessed are not connected, so no one has a holistic view of the objectives across the organization, and the knock-on effect of poor decision-making cannot be fully appreciated and addressed.

In outlining an end-to-end framework for setting and managing objectives I hope to address many of the issues highlighted above. However, a lot of these issues come down as much to attitude and communication as to methodology. As with any process you have to get buy-in from everyone across the organization, and lead by example to make it work. In the next section I will set out my data-driven process for objectives management.

Process for setting and managing objectives

A correctly and consistently implemented OM process should act as a guide for an organization to follow, not as a post mortem when things don't go to plan. A great organization is an organization in which everyone pulls in the same direction with the strategy driving desired behaviours and activities. Yet all organizations have to balance central direction with local information. How to achieve that is a key element throughout the rest of this chapter.

Summary steps

Objectives management is the process of breaking down your strategic goals (defined in your macro design) into a hierarchy of high-level objectives and sub-objectives, cascading them by linking them to people/roles in the organization, and maintaining them over time, as summarized in Figure 3.3.1. There is a debate to be had about whether objectives should be set top-down by management or bottom-up by employees. On the one hand, top-down objective setting ensures alignment and accountability, while bottom-up encourages employee buy-in and realistic objective setting based on knowledge

FIGURE 3.3.1   Goal, objective and trackable KPI pyramid

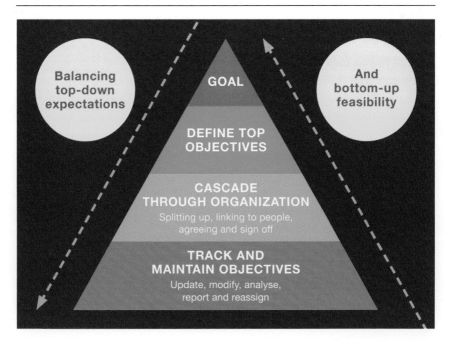

on the ground. To clarify my stance from the start, I believe that either one on its own is tricky to implement in any large organization. I therefore advocate a top-down focus but with plenty of bottom-up discussion and input, and many cycles of refinement.

Before I go into the process in detail, what does successful OM look like in practice? I believe that success can be measured by how useful the feedback is; for example, whether you can begin to answer some of the questions below:

- How are strategic goals broken down across your business?
- What progress is being made towards each of these objectives?
- How has organizational performance changed over time?
- Who is responsible for delivering key objectives?
- How many objectives are there by person and how many objectives are without a person responsible?
- Is it realistic to expect that objectives will be met in the time frames stated?
- Are the right people focused on the right things with adequate resources?

Going through an OM process helps answer these questions not only as a one-off. The real trick is setting up ongoing management, so these questions can be answered consistently. Like many aspects covered in this book, the OM process is not linear. Each area overlaps with another as iterations take place. For simplicity, I have drawn it as a three-stage linear process as shown in Figure 3.3.2.

Setting high-level goals and objectives

Setting the goals should already have been done as part of the macro phase. If those summary goals are not clear, then they need to be. Once the goals are clear, it is time to define how they are going to be achieved. What are the underlying things that need to be achieved? Developing this list is useful as a means of guiding and measuring the business as a whole. However, you need to break objectives down and structure them in a way that corresponds to the roles and people they apply to. To start off with, this means ensuring your objectives really are objectives and not goals. Objectives are Specific, Measurable, Attainable, Relevant and Time-bound (SMART). I believe in SMART objectives because they make objectives easier to measure against, and manage and track in a data-driven way. To determine whether you're

FIGURE 3.3.2   Objectives management process

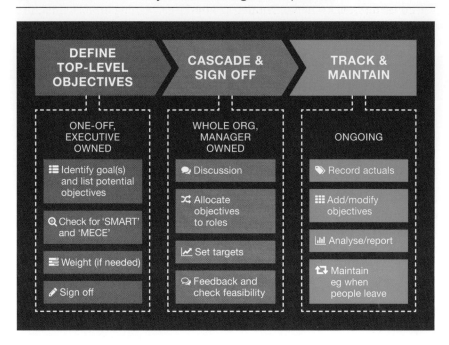

really dealing with relevant SMART objectives, throughout the objectives setting process ask yourself the following questions:

1 Is this objective directly relevant to the high-level strategy?

2 Is it achievable given the company's financial or human resources, outside regulation, or other restrictions?

3 If you agree that a company has the ability to achieve an objective, and it is one that should be achieved, has it been assigned a deadline?

4 Have you costed the implications of trying to achieve the objective? Do you have the resources to do it or should you use external support?

5 Is the objective in question appropriately specific? The objective should be explicitly targeted at an area of the organization and not too vague for actual implementation. However, you should balance this with avoiding getting bogged down in the 'nitty-gritty' of how an objective is to be achieved (for more detail, see the section on 'Cascading objectives' below).

6 How will I measure this objective? I come back to specific measures later in the chapter but, at a basic level, how will the objectives be analysed? For example, is it a KPI or a project deliverable that needs to be achieved by a certain date?

The SMART framework is a good place to begin when thinking about setting objectives but it is not the only thing to consider. Drawing on the methodologies in Chapter 1.3, objectives need to be organized and cascaded in a way that can connect them to particular roles and people through the organization.

Cascading objectives throughout the organization

Once you have clear overall goals and clear summary objectives, you need to break objectives down and structure them in a way that corresponds to the roles and people they apply to. When you break down top-level objectives they become a 'tree'. As laid out in Chapter 1.3, having the various parts of the organizational system mapped as hierarchies makes it much easier to link and see the connections across the system. The end result of the OM process is that you map your objectives tree onto your role tree by linking roles to specific objectives.

Start with your top-level goals and break them down. For example, take all the objectives that need to be achieved to reach your HR goal. Figure 3.3.3 provides an example of an objectives tree starting with a high-level aspirational goal and cascading the objectives from this.

FIGURE 3.3.3   Objectives tree example

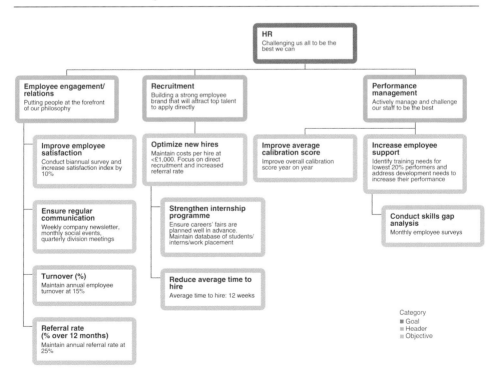

FIGURE 3.3.4   Depth and breadth sum

DEPTH		1	2	3	4	5	6	7	8
BREADTH	3	1	4	13	40	121	364	1,093	3,280
	5	1	6	31	156	781	3,906	19,531	97,656
	7	1	8	57	400	2,801	19,608	137,257	960,800
	9	1	10	91	820	7,381	66,430	597,871	5,380,840

Cascading works by starting at the top and defining only two to four levels down. Over-complexity can rapidly follow unless you are careful. To illustrate (and this applies to many of the frameworks within Part Three) the table (Figure 3.3.4) shows the potential consequences of letting hierarchies grow out of control. If each objective has five 'children' and you have three layers, you have 31 objectives. If the average number of children were nine, that would be an increase by a factor of approximately three, or a total of 91. If there are four levels (a depth of four) and an average breadth of five, then that is 156 points which need to be linked into the organizational roles and managed. If you have 50 people, then fine. If you have three, it feels like overkill.

Does the objective tree have to mirror the organizational structure tree?

There is no need for the objectives tree to stick rigidly to the reporting structure of an organization, although using the reporting structure is the most obvious way to set objectives. Another option is to cascade through the process structure of the organization. This works by the process owner defining what needs to be achieved for each step of the process, and using the R in the RAS framework to cascade the responsibilities.

Setting measures and targets

Once you have laid out your objectives you need to start detailing them to ensure you can track progress over time. When thinking through the specific wording and scope of each objective, think through what measures are attached to each objective to quantify them. I believe there are five types of objectives measures. These measures are similar to what Google calls its 'Results' within its OKR method. These groups capture fundamental differences in the way in which objectives are measured and the way in which they can be treated and analysed. Each one deals with a different type of data input, be it a date, a percentage, an absolute number or a combination of these.

1 **Milestone (event objective)** – where a target date of completion is set and progress is measured against that, either as a simple output status ('not started', 'started', 'in progress', 'completed', 'signed off') or using an RAG scale (Green = 'on target to finish', Red = 'serious concern').

2 **Recurring** – This is different from a milestone objective as it is a recurring objective rather than a one-off that needs to be achieved by a certain date. There needs to be a way of signing off if the objective is achieved or not for each period. An example is monthly financial reporting or credit control; for example, have all the invoices for this month been sent out on time? Yes or No.

3 **Averageable (KPI objective)** – where the objective is to achieve a certain level of performance (high or low) in indices such as Customer Satisfaction (CSAT) or percentage growth. It is worth noting that KPIs are probably the most commonly used measurement in OM as they make good quantitative measures for objective progress and can be either averageable or summable (see below).

4 **Summable (roll-up objective)** – where success can be measured as an absolute number (eg £ sales) and therefore values achieved can be aggregated ('rolled up') within business functions.

5 **Composite** – It is also possible that an objective is divided into sub-objectives of different types, and is therefore analysed as a 'composite'.

Weighting objectives and assigning a budget

A consideration when setting objectives and the tracking of these objectives is whether some are more important than others. Weighting each objective helps focus effort, and if tracked correctly helps direct and balance people's time and resources. Weighting objectives should not be confused with weighting people's performance scores and then dogmatically calculating a bonus or salary increase based on a mathematical formula. I don't believe there should be a direct translation of someone's objectives and how their performance is evaluated. First, individual performance is as much a function of behaviour and level of competence, as outlined in Chapter 3.6, as whether they achieve every objective. Performance management should not become purely a game of hitting a set of targets. An example of this is a story that one of my colleagues told me of a Fortune 500 company that he used to work for, where the board fired their highest-performing salesperson because that salesperson broke their contract on behaviour terms. The single pursuit of objectives above all other things resulted in him treading on other employees and engaging in inappropriate behaviour. Equally, just because you have an objective, doesn't mean you have full control over it and, as already stated, there are many instances where objectives are negatively correlated with each other. Sometimes not achieving them can be the best thing for the business and might even be expected, as in the case of Google outlined at the beginning of this chapter.

Within that further context, when deciding weighting it can be done either by top-down management, or through discussion between the employee and his or her manager (the preferred approach). Here the main focuses of the manager's objectives will be aligned with the aims and objectives of the employee to give a balanced weight to each objective. The weights can be any value so long as the same scale is used for each one of an individual's objectives, allowing them to be normalized and rolled up. Rolling up means that the relative importance of a low-level objective can be seen at higher levels of the hierarchy.

I would add the note that weighting can be complex, and its benefits should be traded off against using that time to actually work towards objectives. I like the swing method described in Chapter 2.3. If the most important objective achieves a score of 100, every other objective should be rated relative to that on a range of 1–100. The weighting helps make clear what is the real strategy. Let me explain this by way of an example. In my supply chain I can have: cost, agility, working capital and customer service. If I compete on price, then cost may score higher than service. If I am the fashion retailer Zara, then my strategy is about having an agile supply chain. In that instance I may be willing to pay more per unit. My focus changes even though my supply chain measures are the same.

If an objective is important, then you may need to ensure there are sufficient resources and/or spend allocated to each objective. It isn't always possible to deliver something through internal resources only. I have experienced a number of internal projects that were delayed or dropped because day-to-day business activities and client work got in the way. Weighting objectives gives prioritization to those working on a project and also can help you decide where budget should be put aside for external help.

Linking, checking and signing-off

Having set and cascaded your objectives, you need to link specific objectives to roles/people. This means building an accountability matrix (eg the RAS framework) in the context of objectives to ensure each objective has clear ownership, targets and tracking. The accountability linking process is iterated for each level of the organization until 100 per cent of objectives are mapped to roles or deprioritized. Once the mapping is done and you have an overview of the whole organization you can perform a sanity check to ensure that the overall strategy and the cascaded objectives align, potentially escalating objectives and targets as necessary. Make sure you check that the tree is:

1 **Coherent**: it has a clear structure with meaningful categories that don't overlap. This ensures there is no repetition or duplication of efforts. This fits with the 'mutually exclusive' part of MECE outlined in Chapter 1.3. For example, if there is more than one person linked as 'Responsible' to a certain objective has there been a duplication by mistake?

2 **Comprehensive**: it provides objectives that cover all the key areas of the business. This doesn't mean we've covered everything, but it is complete to the appropriate level of detail. This fits with the 'collectively exhaustive' part of MECE. It should be noted that achieving a true MECE tree is extremely difficult. Don't be too hard on yourself if you struggle.

3 **Simple**: objectives should not be too detailed although they should be more detailed, with less discretion, the lower the level. They should provide an overview of your focus for the coming period. The language has to be clear and unambiguous. Are the definitions of the measures clearly defined and actually possible to calculate? This makes it easy to communicate with everyone and if any confusion arises gives a clear reference point.

4 **Balanced**: are there too many objectives or too few? The chances are that the first passes of defining them will result in people having too many. Define how many objectives each person has and at what weighting. Set a limit. For example, if a role has more than 12 objectives then the employee will probably be overstretched.

Equally, does everyone have a set of objectives appropriate to the role? If the levels of effort and difficulty for objectives differ greatly between roles it can make analysis less intuitive. Also, think through how the objectives might shift and what the impact would be if priorities change.

Part of doing a sanity check is to finalize and sign off with each employee which objectives they are responsible for. When implementing OM in an NHS hospital we created objectives contracts which employees and managers physically signed. This gave employees the final say over their objectives and helped define a commitment and achieved buy-in for each objective. This ties into the mantra 'conversation is key' which I expand on in the next section.

Visualize, track, analyse and manage

In Chapter 4.8 (Sustaining the edge) I discuss the benefits and value of effective tracking: how they provide feedback loops; how you know where to focus; and when celebration is perhaps required. As a precursor to that, knowing how well you are doing against every objective over time is a crucial part of ensuring you manage the objectives. The first thing is to know what your targets and concerns are. Using the BRAG framework is useful for this. Namely:

- significantly below target (Red);
- just below target (Amber);
- on target (Green);
- significantly above target (Blue).

The first step is to define what each threshold is and how you normalize each objective so you can analyse each objective's performance against the others, enabling the focus to be effectively directed. How each objective is scored can vary. One method is to give a score of 100 for hitting the target. The target is defined by reaching the Green threshold. But there are several other thresholds. The first is going from Amber to Red. This threshold can be given a score of 50. The question then is, what does it take to get zero and should it be possible to achieve less than zero? This type of data often has outliers or data errors that, if you have an unlimited scale, skew all the aggregations. I therefore find it useful to cap the max and min of the normalized scores. I also like symmetry. Therefore, if the distance between the Green and Red is X (the threshold where you get a score of 50), then two

FIGURE 3.3.5   Objective normalization examples

	Score	EXAMPLES		
		Service levels	Cost per unit	Defects per 1,000
B	200	97%	$3.90	2.0
G	100	95%	$4.50	4.0
A	50	90%	$6.00	3.5
R	0	85%	$7.50	3.0
Actual		86%	$4.10	3.8
Normalized score		10	160	60

times X gives a score of 0. For example, imagine the measure in question was service levels, as shown in the third column of Figure 3.3.5. In this example, achieving 95 per cent means hitting the target and being Green. If the level falls below 90 per cent, then it becomes Red. A score of exactly 90 per cent is therefore given a score of 50 on our normalized points method. In this scenario, if the service levels were at or below 85 per cent, then a score of 0 is given. The inverse is true with performing better and achieving Blue. If the level is at 97 per cent it scores 150 and, therefore, 99 per cent gives the max score of 200. In the scenario below, an actual level of 86 per cent was worth 10 points. If, for whatever reason, you want to score between −100 and +100 or −1 and +1, then the same concept can apply. It doesn't matter that much as long as you are consistent.

Other examples include a cost per unit or defects per thousand, where the lower the cost or number of defects the better. What this logic, combined with weighting and cascading, results in is the ability to see every type of objective at every level of the organization in one view. The visual cue of the BRAG colour combined with the size of the node helps to visually prioritize where to focus. Figure 3.3.6 shows how this can look for a larger objectives tree where you can drill into each example.

For every objective you should then be able to track the actuals versus target as shown on the left-hand graph in Figure 3.3.6. In this example of inventory, the target is a static 94 per cent, but the actuals vary between 87.6 per cent and 96.6 per cent. It is important for the team focused on that

FIGURE 3.3.6   BRAG summary objectives tree

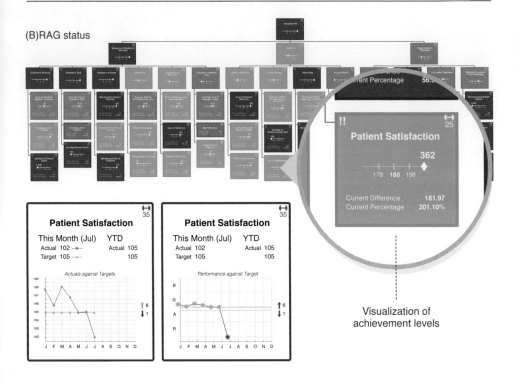

objective to know how well it is doing and if it is improving or not. However, most objectives will have different units of measure. Some will be in $000, others on a scale of 1–6 (eg CSAT), and others on percentage overruns or service levels. Therefore, it is useful to compare all the objectives in the common normalized way. The right-hand graph shows an example of how this can look.

Maintaining and improving objectives management

No framework is perfect, and it is only as good as its use in context. With that in mind, here are five things to look out for to maintain and improve your OM process.

1 **Setting objectives measures (KPIs)**: The objectives and KPIs should be strongly aligned to the strategies and goals of the organization. For instance, a growth company, division or region needs a greater

focus on revenue growth, the building of the brand and awareness versus a limited growth company that might be focused on driving profit and productivity. Getting the right measure helps. For example, in my own company we used to focus a lot on realization losses (project overruns) instead of project margins. What we really wanted was to ensure our projects reached a certain margin, and realization losses are a potential reason for not doing so. So we needed to address our objectives and measures accordingly, changing the focus to margins.

2 **Objectives are not always static:** Make sure you revisit objectives and keep asking whether each one is still relevant. It feels like a great waste of time to have these discussions only at the end-of-year annual review process.

3 **Balance the whole, not the parts:** Accountabilities are complex as there are so many interdependencies in the organization. As already highlighted in this chapter, they need to be treated with care to ensure individuals are competing with each other in as productive a way as possible. Accountabilities need to be given to those who can control the outcome but the targets have to be set within an intelligent consideration of the other elements of the organizational system and goals. Develop an understanding as to how the various KPIs impact on each other. For instance, check for negative correlations (where an increase in one KPI will lead to a decline in another) and look at groups of KPIs rather than in isolation to each other. Make the right trade-offs and work hard in ensuring that those who do the right thing for the 'whole' are not punished for their 'part'. This requires you to try to predict areas of conflict and intervene proactively.

4 **'Average is OK' trap:** Objectives analytics can lead to wrong conclusions being drawn. Remember the statistics traps in baseline? A good example for OM is the 'average issue': where each objective could be off but overall the average could be fine. For example, if you were monitoring average temperature of patients in a hospital, the average could be fine but 7.5 per cent are dead with 0 degrees and 92.5 per cent are at an extreme 40 degrees. This gives an average of the ideal 37, but that average is extremely misleading. In other words, you need to look at the range and drill into the detail.

5 **Present the right level of detail to the right groups:** Make sure the analytics and objectives are in the right hands with the right context and presented in the right way. For example, one FTSE

100 organization I worked with had a large team of highly paid people producing hundreds of KPIs each month for the global board. The person responsible for this effort told me that in all his years of putting the book together he seriously doubted if any of the board members had ever read them properly. If you publish everything in detail there will be an information overload. Also, a document gives no ability to drill into detail or slice and dice. Its use is limited when it comes to answering questions. This is where, if you use technology appropriately, you can present the most relevant analysis and drill into detail only where required on demand.

In maintaining your objectives and management process, think through how you will deal with organizational changes. For example, people coming and going or priorities being modified. I am beginning to move into the Making it Real realm of scope; Figure 3.3.7 gives some important example situations and how to deal with them.

Final thoughts

Done badly, objectives management leads to dangerous and dysfunctional behaviour. It needs a holistic end-to-end view, especially where there are negative correlations between various objectives. The term 'objectives management' might immediately make you think of individual 'performance management' associated with activities such as skills assessments and 360 reviews, but its meaning is very different. The process of doing OM starts by being clear about what you want to achieve (your goals) and then working out what tangibly needs to be achieved in order to get there (the cascading of your objectives). The transparency should result in a better balance of the level of ambition set for each person. If you develop an understanding of the relationship between the various objectives, especially those that are negatively related to each other, then you have a fighting chance of optimizing the whole. The consequence of not doing this will result in rash decisions being made and poor behaviour.

The data-driven aspect starts by quantifying the numbers of objectives and, therefore, helps you think through exactly how much work you can take on. Once defined and in live management, you will be able to track progress. This is discussed in more detail in Chapter 4.8. By knowing what you want everyone to achieve, you have started the detailed design. The next stage is to define the work required to achieve it, and that is the focus of the next two chapters.

FIGURE 3.3.7   Maintaining objectives management example 'what if' solutions

Someone leaves or changes role

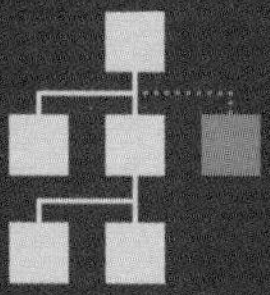

→ If objectives are handed over to their successor-in-role, these are automatically mapped across to the new owner when they are linked to the role tree

→ If objectives are retained by the person, move the link in the Objectives RAS matrix from the old role to the new role

→ If objectives are abandoned, delete the old objectives

Objective(s) change(s)

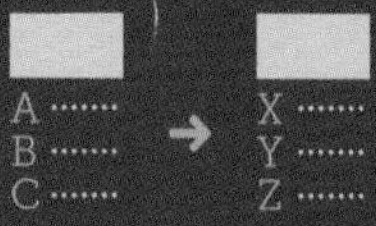

→ This is an inevitability. Know and set the process for changing them and monitor how they change during the year

→ If the change is at a larger level, consider re-drawing your objective tree

Objective/personnel hierarchy changes

→ If a change in reporting lines, then there is no change and no action required

→ If a change in responsibilities then consider reassignment

Objectives are orphaned

→ Line managers monitor orphaned objectives and bring them to the attention to the right forum on a monthly basis

It is clear someone will not achieve one of their objectives

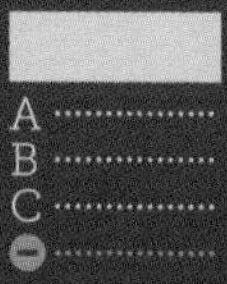

→ What is the root cause for them not achieving it? Do they have too much on? Lack the resource and/or support? There are blockers? Lack the skills or motivation?

→ It is useful to have an idea as to why with a recommended cause of action prior to escalating upwards

Remember this

1   Common performance management practices are both dangerous and drive dysfunctional behaviour, and should not be confused with objectives management.

2   An holistic end-to-end view is required to pull everything together into one picture.

3   Objectives management is both a strategic process that ties the strategy back to what each role should do, and operational process that should be maintained on a monthly basis.

4   A great organization is an organization in which everyone pulls in the same direction. You need to create systems that enable rather than hinder this.

5   Stop seeing the purpose of objectives as evaluating people, but rather as a mechanism for feedback and knowing what the business should be focused on.

Notes

1   Marr, B (2006) *Strategic Performance Management: Leveraging and measuring your intangible drivers*, Elsevier, Oxford, p 3

2   Eddy, N [accessed 28 March 2015], eweek [Online] http://www.eweek.com/small-business/business-intelligence-analytics-top-areas-of-investment-in-2014-gartner

3   Hoffman, J [accessed 15 March 2015] Slideshare [Online] http://www.slideshare.net/jaymeh13/object-25288039

4   Marr, B (2012) *Executive Summary: 20 Years of Measuring and Managing Business Performance. From KPIs and Dashboards to Performance Analytics and Big Data*, Advanced Performance Institute, Milton Keynes, p 6

Fixed process design

Indecision is debilitating; it feeds upon itself; it is, one might almost say, habit-forming. Not only that, but it is contagious; it transmits itself to others. H A HOPF

Introduction

Good process is a process that disappears seamlessly into the background. You don't need to think about it; it just happens with minimal stress and effort. All good processes are simple, repeatable and reducible. Simple does not imply unskilled. As Malcolm Gladwell puts it,[1] to perfect a set of skills requires 10,000 hours of experience. Aristotle said: 'We are what we repeatedly do. Excellence, then, is not an act, but a habit.' All this leads us to ask: What work do those within your organization repeatedly do? Are those the right things? How do you know?

If objectives are about showing where you are going, process is the basis of how you get there. A good process requires everyone to know what they are doing and to know what everyone else is doing, while making the most of each individual's specialist skills. Mapping and designing processes for a new organization can seem daunting, especially because processes translate laterally across the whole organization. It comes down to reducing the problem into small pieces, and it helps if you involve domain experts on each of the process elements. What can waste time is not knowing much about the actual content and spending too much time trying to figure it out. In addition, process design is highly related to the practice of business analysis (BA) and the myriad of tools that this involves. In mapping and designing processes, leveraging agile methods where data flows, handoffs are simple and have the minimum of ceremony, iterations can rapidly evolve, and learning is built into the method. This is preferred above trying to detail everything upfront to perfection.

In this chapter I will begin by outlining how you can map the different levels of your organizational processes, before going through the processes of collecting, building and understanding your as-is organizational processes.

The third section investigates techniques for analysing processes, setting the platform for the final section on how to create and define a to-be design and link it to your detailed organizational structure.

Types of process map

When most people think of process design, they think of process flows with 'swim lanes' representing the group responsible for the activities or decisions within that swim lane, icons to signify the type of work (for example, decision, system, sub-process), and connections showing the various flows as depicted in a simple example in Figure 3.4.1.

However, a process map does not need to fit neatly into this particular type of process map. In fact, there are five possible levels of process design with four types of visuals as depicted in Figure 3.4.2.

For the purpose of organizational design, in the vast majority of cases, Level 1 provides sufficient detail. Far too often, companies put huge amounts of detail into Level 2 and below. However, generally this is surplus to requirements when performing OD. There are two scenarios, within the context of performing OD, when delving into Level 2 design is necessary. The first is to validate that Level 1 is complete, and the second is to define how the

FIGURE 3.4.1   Example Level 2 swim-lane process map

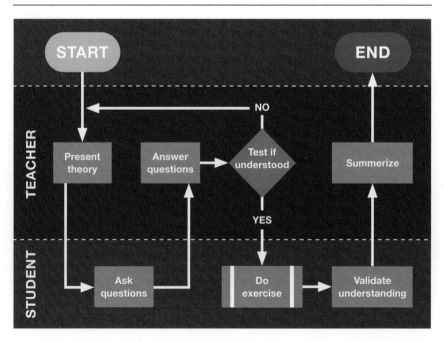

FIGURE 3.4.2   Five levels of process map and visuals

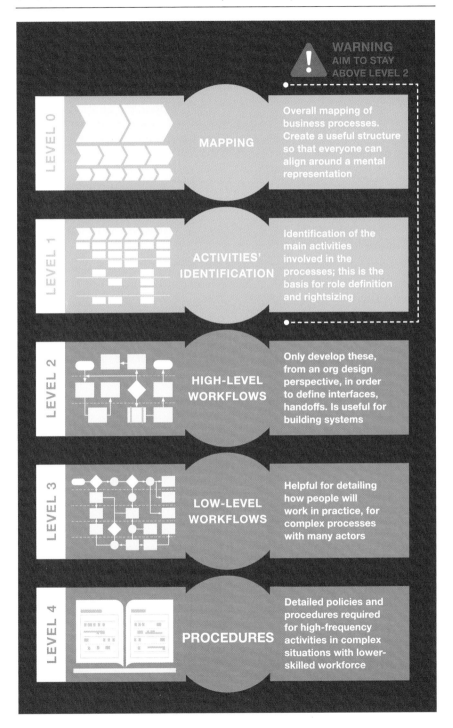

process will work in practice as defined in the HOWWIP (see Chapter 4.3). Like peeling an onion, you can always create more layers of detail, and it is tempting to do so. But hold back. The first fear that people have is that, with too little detail, the roles will not be defined in a meaningful way and everyone will be unclear about the role. The second fear is that an employee's work will be regarded as superficial and lacking quality. The first fear is legitimate and easily overcome. The second is just in someone's head and unfounded. Too much detail means too much complexity and can easily overwhelm the design process. Therefore, in this chapter I focus on top-level processes.

Level 0 value chain

The Level 0 value chain map is the summary. It is what you created and used for the macro design as described in Chapter 2.3. It covers all the core elements of the business and can fit on one page. Like the strategy map in objectives management and many other elements to come, it is crucial that it fits on one page because it represents a mental map for thinking about how 'everything' fits together. Michael Porter first described and popularized this way of thinking about value chains in his classic work *Competitive Advantage*.[2]

An example of a Level 0 process map is provided in Figure 3.4.3. It details the generic top-level processes that a product and services (delivery) company

FIGURE 3.4.3   Example Level 0 value chain map

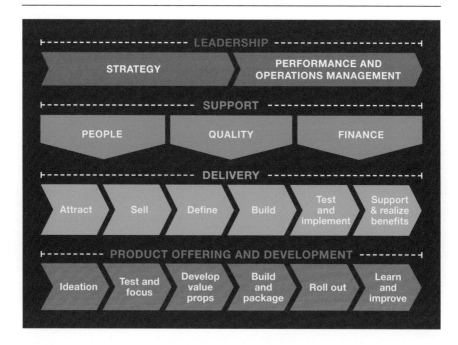

might have. Both these aspects of the business represent value chains, supported by a series of functions such as Finance and HR. While many businesses may have only one value chain, this helps show how your processes can fit together even in a more complex business.

When done well, this Level 0 value chain map should give a good sense of how the organization actually works. A natural way to think about it is: If you had to explain the business to a 'generalist journalist', how would you do it? How would you define the value that is created in a couple of steps? How would you capture all the key summary parts? It is like writing a short soundbite; it takes iterations and debate to get this right. In fact, it is the hardest bit to get right. Once you've got it, though, the rest of the process design will flow.

Level 1 activities

Level 1 breaks down the Level 0 value chain map into greater degrees of granularity and highlights the activities linked to each process. It is, therefore, still value-chain driven. You start with the high-level process and break it down into sub-processes, then top-level activities. Thinking of this level as a hierarchical tree is useful: the nodes are the processes and the leaves are activities. An example of a Level 1 map of people processes is shown in Figure 3.4.4.

FIGURE 3.4.4   Level 1 process map

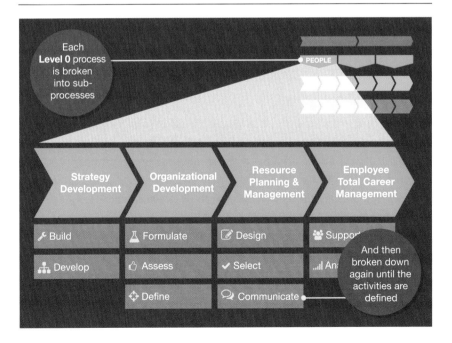

Getting the granularity of Level 1 right is more art than science. But to help, here are some rules of thumb:

- A minimum of three and maximum of eight activities should suffice for 95 per cent of roles.
- Avoid too much complexity by ensuring the maximum number of activities within the entire list is around 0.3–0.6 of the number of FTEs. For example, if you have 600 FTEs in scope, then it is a range of 180–360 total activities. I have seen organizations define 200–300 activities for organizations of fewer than 100 people; in practice it is too much detail and becomes unworkable.
- If all the activities within the parent process obviously fit into one role, then the parent detail suffices.
- The larger the organization and the more specialized the roles, the deeper one needs to go. But still start with the summary levels.

For example, if we were building a Level 1 process map for an organization that employed only two people, say Tim and Tanya, then the 'three-to-nine activities' would be enough for them to split the work. For example, Tanya might be responsible for the top-line or sales and marketing, with Tim responsible for delivery. As more people are added, the need for granularity starts to increase. If we add Bill and Bridget to the mix, Bill may do lead generation and Tanya the sales only. Bridget could do post-delivery support, letting Tim focus on the upfront delivery. There are no hard-and-fast rules about when to go into more detail, but the role of the organization designer is to ensure the processes are structured logically. Figure 3.4.5 illustrates how the level of granularity expands with the number of employees within scope. Note: the employee numbers associated with each level are examples, not strict rules.

When creating your Level 1 map, you could also think in terms of an 'RAS' accountability matrix, connecting specific roles to each process as detailed later in this chapter and in Figure 3.4.17. However, the main thing is to have a clear understanding of the standalone organizational processes required. You can think about whom they connect to and affect later when it comes to analysing the as-is versus the to-be designs, which I explore later in this chapter.

Level 2 and below

Level 2 is the high-level workflow. It shows not just the activities, but also the order in which they happen. It shows the decision paths, swim lanes and

FIGURE 3.4.5   Process depth versus number of roles

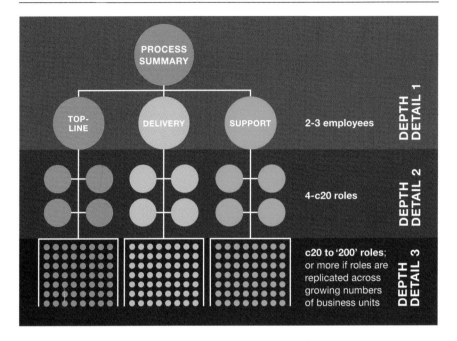

how systems might be involved in the process. Level 3 is a further detailing of these activities. Within Level 2, there may be boxes called 'Sub-process'. Level 3 includes all these sub-processes. Each of the steps, loops, systems and decision points is documented. Level 3 is needed for designing integrated systems, like the operations of an Enterprise Resource Planning (ERP) system. Finally, at Level 4 there are detailed procedures for each activity. This is likely to be captured within job manuals or detailed use cases. Examples of this might include operational procedures for multinational fast-food chains, organizations that need to reproduce the exact same product millions of times by thousands of people. For them, detailing each micro step is crucial.

Understanding the as-is

I believe you can only get to where you want to go if you know where you are starting from. So before you design your to-be processes, start by fully understanding your as-is.

Creating Level 0 and Level 1 process maps

I am a big advocate of using workshops to collect the information needed to create an as-is process map. Workshops bring people together to think through their processes and engage as a group. Have separate sessions with the relevant teams across the organization so you can ask those who know how the processes work in practice to talk through them. Start with the Level 0 processes, and then get teams to break them down. I find that while teams are exchanging ideas, writing the different levels or types of processes and activities on sticky notes of different colours is extremely useful as a quick way to start seeing a process hierarchy (as well as for documentation purposes).

Having collected the basic information, you now need to collate it so you can understand how the processes fit together in the context of the wider organization. A great way to do this is by creating process cards. These are inspired from seeing my kids play with Match Attax or Top Trumps cards. They are forever sorting the cards into groups and also seem to have an unbelievable memory for the stats. So why not do the same for your organizational processes? Take all the information you have on each process and condense it into 'process and activity' cards. An example of a card is shown in Figure 3.4.6. Each card could have:

- in large bold letters, what is the process/activity;
- how it fits within the taxonomy (ie what the parent processes and value streams are);
- colour coding and icons for the key dimensions (as described in Figure 3.4.6) such as: Daily, Weekly, Monthly, Annually;
- if it has been defined, clarity of who is responsible (which is not yet done in the scenario shown in Figure 3.4.6 because it depicts the process of actually allocating activities to teams as symbolized by the yellow sticky notes);
- a succinct description on the back of the card, if possible.

Start by taking all your process cards and lay them out on a table. Divide them into categories: for example, geographic location, sub-function, internal versus external, suppliers or role based. Very quickly you will be able to see if any processes or activities are missing. By doing this you will also be playing back information people have given you so they can fill in gaps on the cards or correct any inaccuracies. The end result will be an initial grouping of all the processes in the area you are focusing on, whether organization

FIGURE 3.4.6   Match Attax-inspired process cards

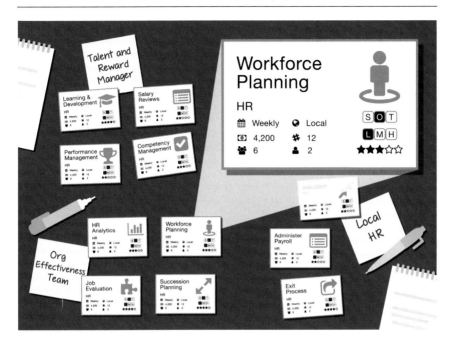

wide, departmental or project based. These can be captured and documented in a Level 1 process map.

Individual Activity Analysis (IAA)

The reason for doing Level 1 process design is to understand what work is happening. Ideally, before starting to think about a to-be design, aim to understand how much time each activity is using and which roles or people are doing what. This is how you can start spotting inefficiencies and paths to more simple ways of working. Doing this requires an Individual Activity Analysis (IAA). The question I am always asked is: 'But how do you get the data?' This section outlines three methods to answer that question: interviews and workshops; surveys; top-down estimate. These methods don't need to be mutually exclusive; in fact, using them in combination will give you the best results. Also, remember when performing an IAA you are only building on your Level 1 process map, documenting the three to eight activities done by each person. You are not trying to get everything 100 per cent perfect. The most important thing with all of these methods is to make sure the outputs are properly documented and stored for future reference.

Interview and workshops

Here you sit with the various people doing the work. They say how much time they spend doing the work with the Level 1 process map in front of them. The percentage time is written down during the interview. This is then entered and extrapolated for those doing the same roles. A great interactive exercise is to give interviewees an 'allocation of $100'. Using the Level 1 process map they split and allocate portions of that $100 according to the work they do, and how much time they spend on that activity. This works well as a physical workshop with physical coins with 4–15 people present. Have them briefly talk through their work: for example, where they spend too much time, where they are frustrated that they are not spending more time, what is working well and what isn't. This all helps improve your case for change.

Survey

Send a survey to a representative sample or everyone. Ensure those completing the survey can select the activities they do from a process taxonomy and enter their proportion of time. Ideally, have space to collect qualitative data, too. The extra information is extremely useful if you can get it, as it means once you've aggregated the data and extrapolated it you can start to assess the amount of time spent on each activity, by region and/or any other dimension that you happen to have recorded. Before doing a survey I strongly recommend that you test the Level 1 map for completeness and ease of compression through interviews or workshops as above, and phase the rollout of the survey. Otherwise the survey will cause more questions than answers and be ineffective. Make the surveying process into ongoing learning, making small iterations and constant refinements to your Level 1 map.

Top-down estimate

This method is used if you don't have the time or remit to engage with all those doing the work. It is, therefore, less accurate, but sometimes 'needs must'. In this method, you start by listing all the activities in an '$n\ n$' grid. One axis is the frequency in which the activities are done while the other is the duration of the activity. By multiplying duration and frequency, you get the amount of effort required for each activity. The total effort won't equal the total supply of hours by the employees, so you pro-rata the time to supply. You then look at the numbers of people and hours of work and use this to allocate people's time to the total. You still have to define who does what through accountability mapping (for example, use the RAS matrix). Although less accurate, this method gives valuable additional information that can be used in dimension creation described below. In other words, knowing the frequency and effort per unit is useful. I explain why this is relevant within the dimensions subsection below.

Running an IAA is a non-trivial exercise. Employees often push back on why they are being asked about what they are doing, scared of the implications of what they share. This is why facilitated workshops, while more resource intensive, are a much more effective method to start with. This is the only realistic way of overcoming people's naturally defensive position in the beginning. Equally, creating a survey, defining who should complete it and deciding whether it should be a sample is not simple. For more information on techniques to understanding the as-is, Cadle, Paul and Turner's *Business Analysis Techniques*[3] is a good source.

Analysing the as-is

Having mapped your as-is organizational processes and activities, the key is to slice and dice it further to get insight into how the organization really works. You should be able to start answering questions like:

- How many people and FTEs are involved in each process?
- What is the average cost and range of grades working on each activity?
- How many, and which, functions or sub-functions are working on each process?
- What percentage of time or cost is going into particular processes or types of process?

For example, with the information now at your disposal you will have a perspective on cost that no one has ever seen before. Based on the number of people who work on a process and the amount of time they put into it, you can see your people costs rolled up in the context of your processes. Figure 3.4.7 shows what this looks like, visualizing your processes as a hierarchical tree. The size of the circle shows the relative cost of a process based on a roll-up of all the costs of the processes or activities underneath it. For instance, Reward costs £98.5k and it consists of four sub-activities.

From this type of analysis you can start to work out where a resource is being used in unexpected and undesirable areas, and use that as a platform to find out why, and how you can reallocate your resource effectively. A good example of this analysis in practice is referenced in the introduction to the methods section of Chapter 1.3. In that scenario the cost of 'Client

FIGURE 3.4.7   Example HR Level 1 cost breakdown

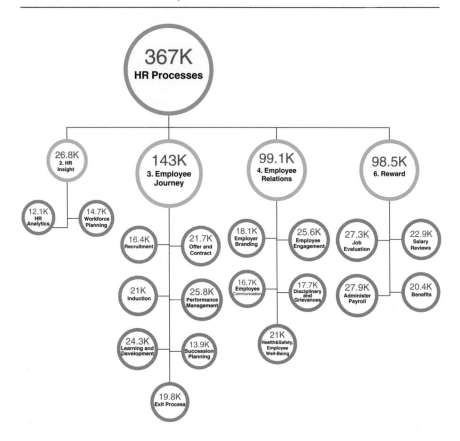

Support' activities was four times greater than expected. It turned out that a large proportion of the account manager's and sales teams' time was spent doing reactive client-facing support work. Although there was a team dedicated to this, it wasn't equipped to deal with quantity of work. This depth of insight tells you where to focus your to-be design and know what the impact on your people will be. To do this requires dimensional analysis and segmentation.

Performing dimensional analysis and segmentation

Having performed your IAA, you will have a huge amount of information at your disposal. To help organize and analyse it in a way that provides useful outputs to feed into design improvements and decisions it is useful to segment similar activities into categories. These categories can be defined

FIGURE 3.4.8   Segmenting processes example

Degree of specialization

		Low (12)	Medium (8)	High (8)
Economies of scale	Low (4)	○ Employee engagement ○ Vacation management 2	○ Recruitment ○ Benefits 2	
	High (8)	○ Work time recording ○ Employee communication ◉ Administer payroll ○ Induction ○ Health & safety, employee well-being 5	○ Learning and development 1	○ Workforce planning ○ Succession planning 2
	Neutral (16)	○ Offer and contract ◉ Absence management ◉ Flexible working ○ Minor establishment changes ○ Exit process 5	○ Job evaluation ○ Employer branding ○ HR policies ○ Salary reviews ○ Disciplinary and grievances 5	○ HR strategy ○ HR analytics ○ Macro design ○ Micro design ○ Performance management ○ Org Design – making it Real 6

Category   ▨ Core   ▨ Semi-core   ■ Non-core

by creating a set of activity dimensions based on the design criteria you set out in Part Two. For example, your design criteria might be to: 1) drive a greater focus on core business activities; 2) increase customer responsiveness. From these you can categorize processes into activity dimensions, 'core' or 'non-core' business activities and 'customer facing' or 'non-customer facing' activities. By grouping them you can plot these dimensions against each other on a graph as shown in Figure 3.4.8. Using this analysis you can see which activities are high priority (that is, those which are core and customer facing), and if they need more investment or a change in structure. You can also plot them separately against other dimensions to answer other questions such as resourcing. For example, by plotting core activities versus economies of scale you can see which is non-core and has high economies of scale and so would be more efficient if it was outsourced.

Depending on your design criteria they may demand different dimensional analysis. For example:

● reason for the work;

● nature of the work;

● fixed or variable;

● economies of scale;

- customer facing;
- time horizon – Strategic–Operational–Transactional (SOT);
- geographical;
- current (excellent, okay, poor) or new (currently not done).

Not all of these dimensions need to be used for every analysis. Think through your key questions and use the dimensional analysis to support your analysis.

Reason for the work

What is the reason for doing the particular activity? Or another way of thinking about it: if you were asked to stop doing it, what argument would you use to keep doing it? Examples include health and safety procedures for legal/compliance reasons, sales and marketing activities to drive top-line growth, operations such as procurement to drive delivery as part of the business value chain or training to support capability building in the organization.

Nature of the work

If you look at a process flow chart there is a range of different types of activity. There are high-level value streams, processes that form these value streams, activities that sit within these processes, decisions that input into these activities, and outputs produced by the activities or processes. You could also include who is doing the work, for example system versus supplier versus outsourced. However, I typically leave this out as it is often too early to decide or worry about where the work is being done. If you are looking at the outsource option, you may consider including the already outsourced processes and costs within your baseline.

Fixed or variable

A cost is fixed if it doesn't increase with an increase in volume. For example, the annual salary of a CEO is fixed, while his or her bonus, because it is dependent on performance, might be variable. This is not necessarily as clear-cut as this, because your CEO might demand higher pay if sales double. In fact, in the extreme you could argue that nothing is fixed – you never really know what might happen. However, I still think it is useful to think of activities as fixed or variable. If you wish, you could add in semi-fixed to the list and define the range of volume changes that drive fixed, semi-fixed and variable measures. For example, you could define your dimensions as follows:

- **Fixed**: No change in cost if volume increases by up to 50 per cent.

- **Linear variable**: For a 10 per cent increase in volume there is a 10 per cent increase in total cost. Put another way, the unit cost remains the same.

- **Semi-fixed**: Costs will increase by 2 per cent for each 10 per cent jump increase and only once that 10 per cent threshold is met. So if the costs were $1 million and volume increased by 5 per cent, then the cost remains $1 million. However, if the volume increases by 10 per cent or even 19.9 per cent, then the cost would increase by 2 per cent of $1 million or $20,000.

- **Non-linear variable**: For a 10 per cent increase in volume the cost increases but by more or less than the 10 per cent. For example, the unit cost of the additional 10 per cent volume may reduce by 5 per cent due to economies of scale. Without economies of scale the cost would increase by $100,000 (assume $1 million is the base cost again) but with it, the increase is $5,000 less or an increase of $95,000 to a total of $1,095,000.

The reason for defining whether something is fixed or variable is to support the thinking when doing scenario modelling as part of a rightsizing exercise, as explained in Chapter 3.7, or strategic workforce planning as explained in Chapter 4.5. For instance, if running a scenario where I expect my volume to increase by 30 per cent, which activities are going to increase by 30 per cent and, therefore, require 30 per cent more people to be recruited to do that work? Equally, which activities are not impacted, or may vary but do not have immediate consequences?

Economies of scale

Building on the idea of fixed versus variable dimensions, you can nuance your analysis further by defining what the economies of scale are. An economy of scale means that the level of scale affects the unit cost. For example, the more of a particular product you sell, the more the cost is reduced. By aggregating processes or activities that have high economies of scale, then the efficiency from those can be realized. Possible dimensions might be:

- high: eg >15 per cent decrease in unit cost or better per doubling of output;

- low: eg between 2.5 per cent and 15 per cent decrease in unit cost per doubling of output;

- neutral: eg between –2.5 per cent and +2.5 per cent change in unit cost per doubling of output;

- negative: eg <–2.5 per cent increase in unit cost per doubling of output.

This type of analysis is particularly relevant if your hypothesis is that work should be pulled together: for example, by creating a centre of excellence, consolidation into one team, or outsourcing. It gives you a way to understand the range of benefits by making top-down assumptions as to percentage savings through consolidation.

Time horizon or SOT – Strategic, Operational, Tactical

The time horizon is the length of time into the future that you need to think when doing the activity. For instance, when establishing a brand, the group doing this activity has a multiyear time horizon in mind. They are thinking what will work in the coming years and probably as far into the future as they can realistically imagine. At the other extreme, if a credit controller is chasing payment or sending invoices, they are thinking within the time horizon of a month. What needs to be done by month-end? I often define three or four dimensions here:

- strategic: eg greater than 1.5-year impact;

- operational: eg between 1 month and 1.5 years;

- tactical: eg less than 1 month;

- transactional: eg less than 1 day.

This framework is used in other parts of the book. For example, in workforce planning there are three categories or levels of planning following the exact same lines. The type of person doing the strategic workforce planning and the nature of the strategic planning are fundamentally different from the tactical one. Another use is in checking whether the job levels (grades) reflect the time horizons. For example, your senior executives shouldn't be doing transactional work. I come back to this in Chapter 4.6.

Customer facing

Is the end customer or client engaged directly through the activity? A simple example is that a waiter in a restaurant is engaging with customers when taking their orders, while counting the cash at the end of the night is not engaging with customers. If you wanted, you could have a third 'indirect' group. For instance, 'cooking the food' has an indirect impact on the customer.

Geography

One of the common macro design trade-offs is the geographical design. What gets done locally, regionally or globally? For me, the question is really about what happens at what level. And to a large extent that really depends on the detailed activity. If you are setting your brand, it will likely be a global activity whereas recruiting agency admin support staff is more likely to be local. What is the geographical scope of the activity? For example, global, regional (Americas, EAME, Asia), country, sub-country (physical states or sub-regions within the country) and physical location of each office or business activity centre. The scale you go to obviously depends on the size and reach of your organization.

'Current' or 'new' with level of excellence

At one level, this can be extremely simple. Are you currently doing the activity in question or not? From there, you can add a value judgement on how well you are doing it. You may be 'theoretically' doing something, but it is so 'hopeless' that it isn't really being done in a meaningful way. Alternatively, you may be world-class. When using this sort of dimensional analysis be realistic and set your expectations and priorities. You cannot be world-class in everything and, in fact, it isn't necessary to be. So think through the processes in which you genuinely need to be world-class and which you don't – the emphasis will come from your design criteria and priorities. Having done this, identify areas of misalignment. How good are you versus how good do you need to be? If you need to be world-class at something but aren't currently doing it, then it is likely to be one of the big drivers of change. A good example is the need for organizations to increasingly change their operating model to incorporate more digital ways of working. The types of work and talent required to succeed in these transformations are new, and a real source of competitive advantage. Therefore, they take priority. I explore the nature of implementing a digital transformation later, in Chapter 4.5.

Dimensional analysis in practice

Performing dimensional analysis is not a one-off exercise, but one which should be performed both to analyse the as-is and to-be designs while comparing the two once that to-be design is in place. I am jumping ahead here, but an example of how to do this would be to investigate what percentage of time client-facing people spend on non-client facing and non-core activities. When you then get to the to-be process design you can look at how to ensure roles have a group of similar types of activities within a process area. Before going back to your dimensional analysis you need to use your understanding and the analysis of the as-is to design your to-be processes and to-be structures.

Design the to-be process and structures

Using the insights you have got from your analysis work you can create your to-be process design and then bundle that work into roles, positions and reporting hierarchies. However, before you even start detailing your to-be processes, start by establishing the principles for the kinds of improvements that you want to achieve. Your design criteria and, if you have set them already, your objectives should feed explicitly into this. Define specific improvements. For example:

- Improving efficiency:
  - Consolidating effort by aggregating work done by many people to achieve the same output with less input.
  - Moving work from high-cost resources to lower-cost work. This does not just mean off- or near-shoring. Examples that I have seen include upskilling highly trained nurses to do more of the work of the clinicians.
  - Process change through automation, fewer and/or better steps.
  - Do the same but faster through improved execution. This is doing the same with less time. For example, by increasing training and upskilling employees.
- Cost savings:
  - Think through which activities you could and should stop doing.
  - Which activities could you outsource? Are there activities which are high risk or outside the core skills of the resource available to you? Having a strong understanding of your IAA should give you a solid foundation for quantifying the value of outsourcing.
- New business priorities:
  - What are you not doing that you should be doing in order to meet your business goals?
  - What are the key things within the case for change that need to be prioritized?

Defining your to-be processes

In defining your to-be processes you are creating your to-be Level 0 and Level 1 process maps, just as you did when mapping the organizational as-is. A good starting place to do this is your as-is baseline. Using the analysis performed you can get key stakeholders to clarify their thoughts and reflect on what works well, what can be improved, what they believe they and their teams shouldn't be doing, and what should be stopped. Here, running tight workshops alongside two or three experts in a similar style to the process outlined when creating your high-level process maps is extremely useful. The reason I advocate using outside support is that it will give focused energy and provide a neutral voice for debates. Often how a process is defined can be a contentious issue, so it is helpful to have them as intermediaries to balance and guide the debate to find the best course. The skills required to do Level 1 design may not reside in your organization or those with the capability of running the process may be either too busy or biased. However, if you do use outside help, leverage those who are genuine subject matter experts, whether in process design or that particular function, so that they can bring real business value to the table and add to the content you are discussing.

Another useful exercise for workshops or the design process is to use templates for generic functional processes such as HR, Finance or Procurement. They are extremely useful because quite often when creating a to-be design you are not trying to reinvent the wheel, but are actually trying to simplify things. Having a generic template can really help focus people on the basics. Having a draft template pre-prepared saves time and gives everyone something to react to. Getting a subset of people to modify or create a 'starter for ten' makes the contribution from everyone else far more productive. It doesn't have to be perfect. In fact, it helps if it isn't perfect.

When coming up with your to-be processes remember that you don't need 100 per cent perfection. Don't try to achieve this because it will be too costly. Get enough granularity to be useful and answer the design questions. This is not necessarily a business process optimization exercise. If you want to optimize your processes then you should do Level 2 and Level 3 design. Level 1 design is about developing an understanding of what work is being done and what work should be done.

Defining strong processes with clear improvements

Just because you have defined a set of processes doesn't mean they are any good or even workable. Like so many elements of effective organizational design, it is important to think through the unintended consequences of the design. Think about the underlying cost and practicalities. A little bit of thought can save a huge amount of effort and frustration later in the day, otherwise the size of the organization or complexity of the stakeholders involved can halt the success of the design. Design for success, design for simplicity and – to adapt the old carpenter's saying – 'measure twice before deciding'.

To help ensure the strength of your process design, the five CUWIE tests and checks as shown in Figure 3.4.9 should really help. Many of these tests come to life in Chapter 4.3 and this section is closely related to that chapter.

Gap test or is it Complete?

A large part of this is checking how MECE the process is, as already explained in Chapter 1.3. It is also a question of scope. Is the work of contractors or suppliers in or out? Most fundamentally, will it deliver the strategy and meet the requirements of the design criteria?

Visual test or is it Understandable?

Visualization techniques reduce the effort and time required to understand, learn and internalize. They make issues more likely to jump out at you. There is not one single or optimal way to visualize processes. So use a range of techniques. Each will support the other. For example, think about using swim lanes of the various dimensions for each of the activities, hierarchical scaled cards, chevrons, Match Attax-inspired cards or graph network layouts. The important thing is to use colour and icons of differing sizes to signify variation and provide focus.

Practicality test or is it Workable?

Lots of things are great in theory. Anyone can design a process but will it work in practice? Are there too many moving parts? During handoffs, balls will be dropped, information lost, actions or decisions stuck, progress stalled. The more complex and the more roles involved in a process, the greater the risk things will fall between the cracks. Do we have the skills to do it? For example, you may have health and safety processes, but how do you know if people follow them properly or know what they are? This test is about once it is implemented: how it will work in practice (HOWWIP) as explained in Chapter 4.3.

FIGURE 3.4.9   CUWIE process design tests and checks

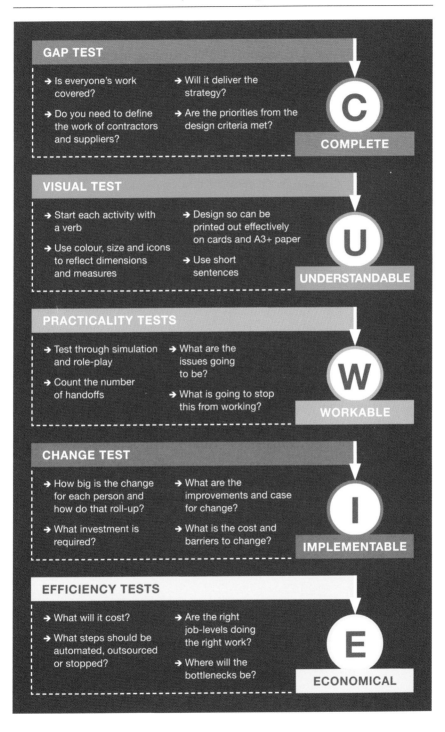

Change test or is it Implementable?

Change can be costly and hard to manage, so make sure you know what is changing. Starting with the actual processes: What is new, different, improved, going to be outsourced or stopped? Is this change going to require investment or significant cultural change? Who is impacted by the change and to what level? Given your time frames, is it realistic to expect the organization to absorb this change and do you have the competencies needed?

Efficiency test of is it Economical?

How much is it going to cost? Is it affordable? Imagine you weren't doing this activity; what would be the business case be for doing it? For example: legally required; needed to improve customer services; drive top-line growth; or to improve talent. By segmenting the processes and activities as described below with the dimensions, you will begin to be able to break the problem down.

Decision-making

Having set out your to-be processes you then need to organize which roles are connected to which processes and how decisions are going to be made. This is an area that, if not thought through, can significantly hinder organizational performance. For example, a few years ago, my uncle moved from being a senior partner in a law firm to an executive with a global insurance firm. Having served large institutions in their M&A for over 30 years, he thought he knew how corporations worked. He was wrong. One of the biggest shocks was the number of meetings and endless global conference calls, the number of people involved in any number of decisions and the sheer magnitude of the 'politics' and 'noise' involved to decide on seemingly obvious things. Large organizations are rife with lobbying; aligning large numbers of stakeholders prior to meetings; and lack of clarity on how to actually get decisions through. One study of 500 office workers in the UK found that 'the average office worker spends around 16 hours in meetings each week'.[4] That is, 40 per cent of the time. And how much of that time is to coordinate decision-making? My guess is a significant proportion.

Are you playing like a pro or a team of six-year-old children?

Decision-making in most organizations isn't too dissimilar to the insurance firm in the example above. Lots of people feel they need to be part of the

Decision-Making Process (DMP). This is, in part, because often the actual process isn't even defined nor are the accountabilities for making the decisions. Those needing to have a decision made can waste large amounts of time navigating through the power players in the search for what the DMP is, let alone actually get a decision made. One of the real drains on the organization is the seniority and cost of those involved.

I have coached children playing rugby for a couple of years. I started with 6–7-year-olds and am now busy with 9–10-year-olds. The hardest thing to get the kids to understand is playing in a field position: to learn how to pass into space and maintain a position to receive a pass. The sight of kids running around in a large group like bees around the honey pot is all too familiar and not dissimilar to many of the ways in which organizational decisions are made.

Sports teams demonstrate, when everyone knows their role, what everyone else is doing around them and exactly what they are trying to do, the result can be beautiful and appear to be effortless (Figure 3.4.10). Defining the DMP is pretty simple: define the decisions; define the accountability matrix for each one; and reflect on the practicality of the structure. Then ask yourself if it will lead to good, timely decisions.

FIGURE 3.4.10   Playing like novices or pros

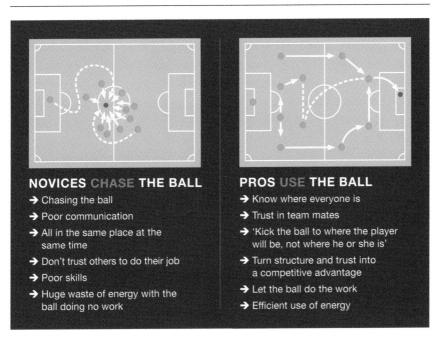

NOVICES CHASE THE BALL
→ Chasing the ball
→ Poor communication
→ All in the same place at the same time
→ Don't trust others to do their job
→ Poor skills
→ Huge waste of energy with the ball doing no work

PROS USE THE BALL
→ Know where everyone is
→ Trust in team mates
→ 'Kick the ball to where the player will be, not where he or she is'
→ Turn structure and trust into a competitive advantage
→ Let the ball do the work
→ Efficient use of energy

FIGURE 3.4.11   Decision-making combinations

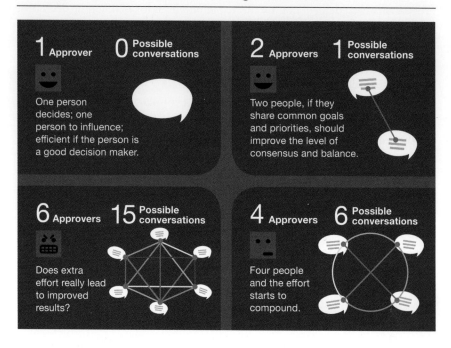

One of the elements to define here is who has veto power or must approve the decisions. Figure 3.4.11 highlights how the number of conversations and politics rapidly increase as approvers are added. Imagine a world where there is only ever one approver. In that world, there is only one person to influence or lobby. That one person doesn't need to lobby anyone else. That person 'just' needs to do his or her best to make the right call. The downside, however, might be that that one person doesn't have all the right perspectives and motives to make the right decisions. So, you add another person into the mix. Now there are two minds at work, but also two people who need to attend a meeting or be part of a process to agree the decision. As you add more approvers, the number of possible 1-2-1 conversations grows factorially as shown in Figure 3.4.11.

Then think through what happens if people don't agree. Does nothing happen, does it get escalated or is there endless horse trading of decisions? The question you have to ask is whether the increase in decision-making quality is worth the extra cost. Equally, the assumption that the more people involved means the better the decision isn't always true either. Committees don't always do the best thing and will as a rule of thumb be more risk averse. Therefore, quantify the numbers of those involved in the DMP.

FIGURE 3.4.12   Decision-making quantification

Scenario 1

Number	Area	Decision	Chairman	NEDs	Managing Director	Finance Director	Marketing Director	HR Director	Director of area X	Manager of X
1	Strategy	Launch a new product	A	A	R	A	S			
2	Strategy	New launch plan	A	S	A	A	R		S	S
3	Strategy	Pricing of a new product		S	A	S	R		S	S
4	People	Set senior exec compensation	R	A	S	S	S	S		
5	People	Hire new role X	A	S	A	A		S		S
6	People	Recruit candidate X		S	A	S	R	S	S	S
7	People	Agree X holiday				S	A	A	R	

KPIs

Average number of	
Approvers	2.0
Stakeholders, excluding those informed after the fact	3.0
Total people involved	6.0

Scenario 2

Decision	Chairman	NEDs	Managing Director	Finance Director	Marketing Director	HR Director	Director of area X	Manager of X
‸duct	A	A	R	A	S			
	S	S	S	S	R		S	S
‸oduct		S			R		S	S
‸mpensation	R	A	S	S	S	S		
			A			S	R	S
‸X		S	S	S	S	S	S	R
					S	S	R	

	0.7
after the fact	1.7
	5.0

Think through whether the increase in the number of approvers will lead to better results.

Figure 3.4.12 shows how you can quantify the numbers involved in each decision if you use the RAS accountability framework outlined in Chapter 1.3 and drive complexity out of your organization. Given that efficient processes are predicated on trust, you need to ensure alignment to common objectives as outlined in Chapter 3.3. Inherent conflict over what each role is trying to optimize is extremely common. In such conflicts, having more people involved in DMP makes sense, as does involving more senior executives than those within the conflict.

Furthermore, not all decisions are equal. Most have insubstantial impacts and occur on a weekly basis. They are part of the standard day-to-day routine. Others set the direction of the entire business and could have terminal implications. So in overlaying the number and seniority of those making the decisions, it is worthwhile thinking through the frequency and impact of the decision when building your RAS matrix.

Figure 3.4.13 highlights five segments of increasing criticality and seniority required to make the decisions. The senior executives or board should be making those decisions with the greatest strategic impact, which by their nature happen infrequently. At the other end of the spectrum, those decisions with low impact that are infrequent should be made by a single person. If the frequency is high, then the data required to make the decision should be prepopulated with decision rules. I've included a couple of marketing

FIGURE 3.4.13   Organizational level of decision-making matrix

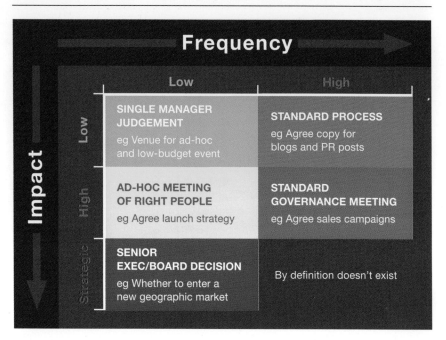

examples as a further guide. Depending on the level of detail of your detailed design, stop at defining your RAS matrix at either stage 3 or 2. I don't see the point in defining all the Level 1 decisions. There will just be too many. The Level 5 and to some extent a sample of the Level 4 decisions could be defined as part of the macro design phase.

Just like the 'dimensionalization' and segmentation of the processes earlier in this chapter, you are doing the same for the decisions here. If you then overlay the numbers and seniority of those involved in the decision, you can list the proportionality of the resource you are dedicating to each one.

Link the to-be work to to-be positions and hierarchical structure

Now that you have defined what work needs to happen and given that you should have decided (reference the macro design and Chapter 2.3) in what fundamental way your organization will be structured, it is time to link the two. In defining the detailed organization, you move into role and position definitions. A position is a role that reports to the same position in the same geography. The reason for the geography distinction is because the

FIGURE 3.4.14   Roles versus position example

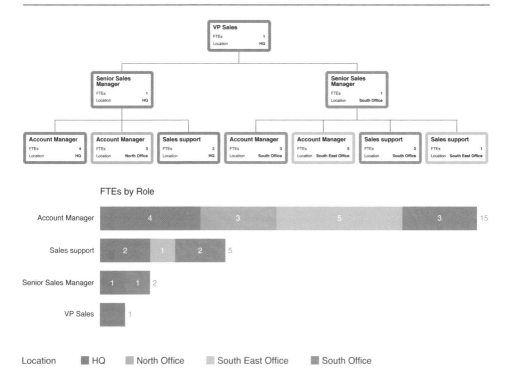

geographical location impacts workforce planning and recruiting. There is a many-to-one relationship between positions and roles. A role has the same job title, accountabilities and competencies. It is possible to have more than one FTE and person per position. As an example, imagine your sales organization had 23 FTEs across four roles in four different locations as shown in Figure 3.4.14. What this shows is the four roles divided across 10 positions. Each box on the to-be org chart is a separate position. Some positions require one full-time person (for example, VP Sales), while others require more than one (for example, the five account managers in the South East Office).

Having defined the work and your macro level design, you should be ready to iterate your way through the entire detailed design. The first iteration was done in the macro design phase where you chose your depth 1 and 2 org charts. The meanings of the positions in those org charts were defined by what they were responsible for. The summary value chain elements were defined (to a max of 50 process elements or depth 2 of your Level 1 process map).

Figure 3.4.15 shows how each of the process steps iterates. For each iteration, you define the position hierarchies and link those through an RAS accountability matrix to the Level 1 process map. If you wish you could decide that

FIGURE 3.4.15   Iterative process and position design method

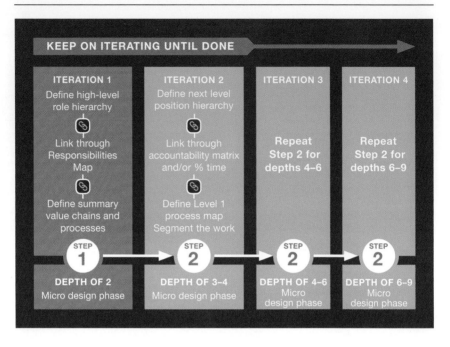

the link is the percentage of time in addition to or instead of using the RAS matrix. The reason for the iterations is you need to define each level of detail together. Only once you know what the summary elements look like can you define the next level down. You keep on iterating until all the required work is allocated to a position. The number of FTEs required is not defined at this stage but during the rightsizing step, as defined in Chapter 3.7.

Working this through in more detail, again, the starting point is the over-arching structure from the macro to-be design phase. With that chosen option, start to add the obvious senior roles: the senior executives and managers. Figure 3.4.16 shows an example of a manufacturing plant. The first step is to define the top (Level 1) structure. If you have the metaphor of a tree, you are adding in the big branches. The senior roles tend to be roles that have predominately fixed activities with a strategic and operational focus. By fixed, I mean those where the number of FTEs required doesn't vary by a volume driver like the number of customers or revenue. These sorts of roles tend to have a greater number of activities they are accountable for. From a design perspective, they are harder to define because the work is more complex. I am using a dense layout so that I can see more of the roles on a page. And then I add the variable roles, coloured here in orange.

FIGURE 3.4.16 Detailing the org chart with fixed and variable positions

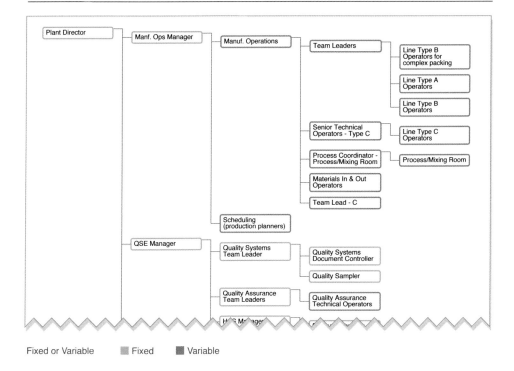

Fixed or Variable ■ Fixed ■ Variable

Defining the draft to-be position structure should be about getting the key roles down. Start with your gut feeling as to where they report based on your design criteria. Don't worry too much to start with, as this isn't the final version. As you go through the process you will continuously add roles and take them away. As explained in Chapter 1.3, the main step is defining what each role does. What are they responsible for? You have two angles to think from: the org chart view with the positions; and the work view with the processes, activities and decisions. By flipping your view to the work perspective, you can see what each role and position is going to be doing, as shown in Figure 3.4.17.

There are many questions that you need to ensure are answered at this stage:

- Does each activity have the right job level (grade) of role working on it?

- Are all the activities at a similar level? For example, using the SOT framework, if the role is predominately 'Strategic', does it also have lots of 'Transactional' work? If it does, is that likely to be an issue?

FIGURE 3.4.17 Detailing the work with the process and position views

Position View

Process View

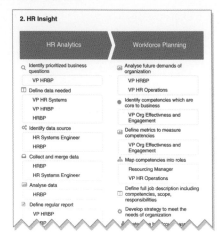

- Is it complete? Have all activities been linked to a position and do all positions have clear accountabilities?

- In your judgement, do all roles that are not variable add up to a balance of effort that is equal to one FTE?

- Will you be able to recruit such a person do to the role? The types of competencies defined in Chapter 3.6 will further help you answer this question.

- Test that similar work dimensions and segments map effectively. For example, are client-facing activities clearly done by client-facing types of roles?

- How many handoffs will there be and/or are too many people involved in any given process? You can see this by counting the number of roles in the process. Heat-map the processes by the number of roles involved and use this as a sanity check.

So, from the position perspective, you can see all the activities plus:

- number of activities;

- the percentage of a given dimension, for example client-facing time;

- given the as-is IAA, the current number of FTEs that would be required. Chapter 3.7 takes this analysis further.

I find this sort of mapping and structural design work is best done in small teams in a workshop style. What kills energy and open discussion is a group of people sitting around someone presenting the information (for example, org charts; process maps) on a screen with one person driving the mouse. An exercise, therefore, is to go back to the 'process cards'. Have sheets of flipchart paper laid out on a large table. With marker pens or sticky notes, write out draft roles. Then physically place each process card into the role box. Some things will be obvious. Again, use the segmentation thinking and dimensions described as a way to help sort the thinking. Build momentum by sorting the easy decisions first. As you go, you will end up creating new roles and/or merging two or more roles into one. You may realize that you need to break some of the activities into a bit more detail or that the to-be process isn't really clear enough. While doing this, have someone create the to-be org charts and project that on the screen. Iterate until you are happy and then ensure your information is appropriately documented (ideally in a dynamic system and not hundreds of PowerPoint slides). Remember my saying 'It's what in the box and not where the box sits'? I hope that is now ringing true. Once you have the accountabilities and structures clear, then it is time to think about how many FTEs are needed for each role. That is a question of rightsizing and is fully covered in Chapter 3.7.

Final thoughts

Good process design and analysis are core to doing good micro design. Once you have a taxonomy of processes and a knowledge of who does what, then you have a base of understanding on which to build meaningful change. By slicing the analysis in different ways as described by the dimension analysis, you can answer many of the significant detailed design questions. For example, what should be outsourced, centralized, stopped or refactored or started as a new investment. Equally, you can drive complexity out by quantifying how many people are involved in the same decision or work. Think about how many handoffs there are or the cost of making low-impact, but frequently made decisions.

Once you understand the current work and how to improve it at the process level, you can also start to think through the future role design. What roles should be doing what work? Where should that work be done? The first step is to agree the content of the roles. Where a role reports to, in my view, is of secondary importance. It is the stuff of egos and power plays. Not everyone of major strategic importance should need armies of people reporting to him or her to show their power or how important they are.

By linking the work to roles you are defining exactly what each role does, how it connects to other roles and, therefore, how it fits within the whole. This enables you to understand your cost base in a way totally different from the traditional financial view. Once you have done your process analysis, you have broken the back of your micro design. Having done your process design you are on your way to rightsizing the organization and providing huge clarity on how the new organization will work in practice. However, not all positions can be defined by these repeatable and predictable value chain processes, for example project work, and in other cases the detailed drivers need to be analysed, for example the sales force and how they best map to customers. This dynamic process design is the focus of Chapter 3.5.

> ### Remember this
>
> 1 Understand your process maps and keep them simple.
>
> 2 Get an understanding of the as-is through information capture.
>
> 3 Analyse the as-is and your to-be design through dimensional analysis.
>
> 4 Create your role hierarchy and connect it to your to-be process design.
>
> 5 Ensure decision-making is simple and you avoid having too many approvers.

Notes

1 Gladwell, M (2008) *Outliers*, Penguin

2 Porter, M (1985) *Competitive Advantage: Creating and sustaining superior performance*, The Free Press, New York

3 Cadle, J, Paul, D and Turner, P (2010) *Business Analysis Techniques*, BCS The Charted Institute for IT

4 Burn-Callander, R [accessed 18 March 2015] Management Today [Online] http://www.managementtoday.co.uk/news/1175002/

Dynamic process design

Time is the scarcest resource and unless it is managed nothing else can be managed. **PETER DRUCKER**

Introduction

When doing organization design there are many work areas that don't fit neatly into the method described in the previous value-chain-driven fixed process design chapter. Unfortunately, not all work can be captured in repeatable process maps. Areas that are more dynamic in their nature include:

- portfolio management and project work;
- risk and compliance maintenance;
- sales force effectiveness;
- procurement optimization;
- software product development.

Each of the above examples could easily be significant chapters in their own right, if not their own books! I think it is extremely important to address these areas, even if not in such detail, as they are so often the focus of design work. I have positioned all these areas under the term 'dynamic' process design because of the variable and constantly changing nature of their drivers. They demand a flexible and continuous approach to their design. Each area has its own nuances and related drivers, but you can approach them, if not with exactly the same methods, with some shared principles for designing each one.

In this chapter I begin by defining the impact of having variable drivers. I set out how you can generically approach dynamic design before detailing a specific data-driven approach to portfolio management and project work. I finish by covering the high-level drivers and points that you should consider when designing other dynamic areas of an organization.

Dynamic process design methodologies

The nature of work within dynamic process design requires greater agility, is less formulaic and cuts across more functions than in fixed process design. Fixed processes are stable for long periods until conscious changes such as process engineering or system automation are implemented. Otherwise, they are subject only to limited change through relatively small tweaks where efficiencies can be realized or handovers improved.

By contrast, dynamic processes have a range of drivers that strongly impact how the work should be organized. In the context of sales these include drivers such as the number of potential customers, how much profit can be generated, what the cost of sale is, the geographic dispersion, the number of products you are selling and much more. Procurement drivers include the nature of what is being purchased, the nature of the supply market and which categories are global, regional, local; which categories have a strategic impact or not; your degree of market power, and much more. These drivers change with time and can often change rapidly.

There are two main consequences of having variable drivers. First, you have to continuously assess what and where opportunities for improved performance are, second you have to design the organization around how much resource you allocate to make the most of a particular opportunity. For example, a sales force could be impacted by the launch of a new product. To make the most of the sales opportunity this may require the sales force to be reallocated or increased in a particular market. In procurement, the organization may be impacted because the supply market is evolving with new technologies, entrants, aggregators or disaggregators, or the decision to buy rather than make a new product. Each time one of these drivers changes, you will have to assess whether that area of the organization needs to be altered to make the most of opportunities or head off risks.

To deal with dynamic processes, there are some generic approaches you can use by adapting methods used in other areas of design work (and covered elsewhere in the book). I briefly touch on each one and refer you to where to read (or reread) further.

Treat each dynamic process design as a mini-macro design project

Each dynamic process can be thought of as its own mini end-to-end design project. The place to start, therefore, is with the macro design. The same steps outlined in Chapters 2.2 and in particular 2.3 can be applied. What are the goals for that part of the organization and how do they fit with the vision of the organization as a whole? Within the area, what are the strategy, growth potential and economics? Then for each area of dynamic process create a list of drivers and build them into a taxonomy. This will give you a comprehensive understanding of your value chains and areas of potential impact. For example, for procurement, you need to understand spend, number of suppliers, complexity, and supply market dynamics. Based on these dimensions you will be able to come up with a set of design criteria and options, and analyse them to choose the best one to deliver your strategy.

Rightsize based on demand drivers and economics

Having understood the value drivers and defined the dimensions you can start to rightsize the organization. If there is a change in one of the drivers such as launching a new product for sales, or a change in the supply market for procurement, you need to know how that will impact the number and nature of the employees. Taking the example of sales force further, if the cost of sale halves for a given product, for example because market acceptance means it has become significantly less complex, what does that mean for the sales model, numbers and ability to reallocate resources to other opportunities, as detailed in Chapter 3.7?

Treat as a dynamic system

The drivers for each area will be constantly changing. It is useful to track these changes so that you can assess the performance of your dynamic design over time, keep the design up to date and model organizational scenarios to prepare for change. For this you need to define the system so that you can track actuals against plans whether those are objectives, headcount or competencies so that you can react with focus and agility when required.

Having said this, you have to rely on your workforce on the ground to adapt to a certain amount of granular change. There is no doubt dynamic processes require a highly skilled workforce with a greater level of autonomy so that they can adapt to the small changes that will inevitably occur without requiring unnecessary attention on redesigning the whole area. In a beautiful example, the US retailer Nordstrom's Employee Handbook says: 'Use good judgement in all situations. There will be no more rules.' Nordstrom relies on its employees to deliver famously good service – a dynamic requirement – and does so while paying the second-highest wages in US fashion retail.[1]

Finally, do not assume that one model for dynamic design will work in another context. For instance, a sales model that works brilliantly for one region could be a disaster in another owing to different drivers. For example, this was experienced by a high-growth US tech firm. In the United States, their sales organization was centred on industry verticals. It worked brilliantly because each market was large and the sales force could easily travel. However, when this model was applied to Europe, it dramatically failed. Each vertical was too small within its national market.

Detailed example: project-driven organizations

Kenichi Ommae, a Japanese organizational theorist, once famously said: 'Nobody knows how Honda is organized, except that it uses lots of project teams and is quite flexible.' Many organizations are project driven and I have spent a good 75 per cent of my professional career sitting within projects. When I talk about projects I am referring both to external projects such as services delivered by professionals, technology and engineering firms, and internal projects such as change programmes, technology implementations and product development.

We don't live in a world of certainty and when it comes to programmes and projects, you have to bring these uncertainties into your design process. As Bent Flyvbjerg, Professor of Major Programme Management at the University of Oxford's Saïd Business School, says, overruns in the order of 50 per cent in real terms are common for major infrastructure projects.[2] He says this is because it is not uncommon for demand and benefit forecasts to be wrong by 20–70 per cent compared with actual development. Public passenger rail and urban projects tend to have especially big overruns. A study of more than 5,400 IT projects found the average overspend of the starting budget can top 45 per cent. The average budget overrun for producing the Olympic Games since 1976 has been around 200 per cent.[3] Projects might be uncertain, but the uncertainty is predictable. So you need methods for effectively dealing with and designing for that. The first step is to agree which projects should be prioritized and allocate the right resources to them.

In many organizations there will be a large number of projects planned or in progress. In one extreme case I worked with an organization that had 12,000 projects. When we arrived to do a 'procurement transformation', we had to identify any existing projects with which our scope would overlap. The number turned out to be a whopping 6,000. We then had a lot of questions about who would get credit for what savings. It was a dream day for financial controllers; a nightmare for anyone who had to get stuff done.

I am all for projects that sit outside the ongoing business-as-usual structures to drive any range of improvements or to move strategic goals forwards, but they need to be controlled. It helps to have a list of all the projects with the key pieces of information about each one quantified; for example, start and finish dates, resources required, cost and benefits summary.

For me, this has to be integrated with your workforce planning and how you manage resource, as described in Chapter 4.5. Also, many of the visual aids as described in Chapter 3.3 are extremely useful and the projects should, in a perfect world, be linked to specific objectives in the objectives map. Just like with the rest of the micro design, when it comes to projects a whole host of questions are raised: Do you have the right skills working on the right projects? Are all the experienced people on the same projects and those with less experience on others? Do you have the right resource allocated to the right type of project? Do people have the time to commit to the project? And my personal bugbear: How many projects is each person on and how does this work with all their other 'day-job' commitments? If you add up all the commitments you will see that many people are frequently overly committed, with most of their time dedicated to a range of projects. This falls into one of the common traps I describe in Chapter 4.2: having too many initiatives. However, getting things done on time and in budget also requires planning at the detailed level.

Three levels of project planning

Most project managers I know start their planning by creating a plan in Microsoft Project. They are keen to define start and finish dates, capture the dependencies and work out the critical path. This is all good practice. But plans can quickly become unwieldy. In one example (which discuss in detail below), the programme ended up with six MS Project files, each having 1,000 rows. Like a lot of other aspects covered in micro design, when it comes to project planning I find three stages useful:

1 the milestone map and project summary;
2 the integrated plan;
3 the detailed actions.

As in the rest of micro design, there are many more facets within each stage, and I think these parallels should be drawn. For example, there are:

- stakeholders;
- objectives;
- deliverables;

- competencies;
- positions and people who need to fulfil those.

Project planning is based on assumptions. So there needs to be a great deal of scenario planning and rigorous risk management. Implementing a project requires fluid feedback loops to ensure learning, improvement and tracking along the project life cycle. These plans are where you start.

The milestone map and project summary

The milestone map is a one pager, similar to the strategy map or the target operating model. It has swim lanes with the key areas down the left side, and time along the top. For each area, the key milestones will be clearly noted. They will show start and/or finish dates. The swim lanes will be the key organizational and delivery elements. Although this milestone level should be relatively static, it does require iteration with the bottom-up detail from the two lower levels. As you move down the levels of detail, each should act as a sense check for the level above. The other key elements of the project brief are: a summary of the overall goal and objectives; key stakeholders; and costs and benefits. The milestones should be seen in the context of this crucial summary information.

Integrated plan

The next level is the integrated plan. The milestone map is an extract from the integrated plan. For this, I think a Gantt chart is the most useful visual (see Figure 3.5.1). The chart was created by the mechanical engineer and management consultant Henry Gantt in the 1910s. Gantt worked on major infrastructure projects like the Hoover Dam and the US Interstate System. The Gantt chart is in reality just another hierarchical breakdown structure. What is clever is how the relationships between a whole range of activities or deliverables are captured.

To create a Gantt chart like the one below you need to define:

- Start and finish dates.
- The amount of effort required (eg how many days or FTE months of work).
- Who is responsible for doing the work (use the RAS framework in Chapter 1.3).
- Dependency relationships.
  - A **start–finish** where a given activity can start only once a particular activity or set of activities has been completed.

FIGURE 3.5.1　Example Gantt chart

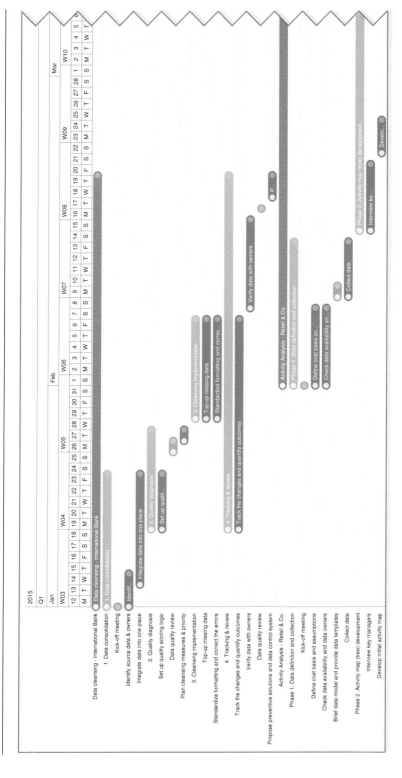

Category　▓ Activity　▓ Meeting　▓ Phase　▓ Project

- – A **start–start** where two or more activities have to start together or one activity can start only once another one has.
- – A **finish–finish** relationship where two or more activities have to finish together.

- Types of node and dimension (for a detailed explanation of how to build a taxonomy see Chapter 1.3):
  - – Milestone: A key event that needs executive monitoring. For example, a 'go-live date'.
  - – Work stream: A contained set of actions that can be grouped together. Will often have substreams and list of activities. For example, 'training'.
  - – Activity: An activity has inputs and uses resources to turn those inputs into outputs. Will always start with a verb. For example, 'Develop training materials for logging on'.
  - – Dimensions: A way of categorizing elements of the work. Examples include: grouping particular activities by the geographic location in which they will be done; the phase; whether it is done internally or externally; or if it is on or near the critical path.

The risk in developing your Gantt chart is going into too much detail. I think it becomes too much of an administrative burden to define every action in this format. Action plans need a different mindset and method. The Gantt chart is for the integrated plan, to define the interfaces and the critical path. My rule of thumb is that the integrated plan shouldn't be longer than 100 rows.

Action plans

Once you have those key elements, you then break down all the actions that are required to deliver it. These are task-level items. Because of the number of tasks and the management routines necessary to manage them, don't try to manage these in a centralized way or capture the dependencies with all other tasks. The person responsible for each task should know what he or she needs to do. In many projects this list of actions is likely to be a living, evolving backlog of activities whose delivery is measured in a higher-level meta-process such as Scrum or Kanban. The process of managing these tasks and getting the work done is covered in Chapter 4.7.

Estimating the resources and impact of risk

The scope of the micro design is to determine not just what needs to happen, but the resources and cost required. Within projects and programmes this is often far more complex than with the business-as-usual processes. I will highlight this with an example. A number of years ago I was brought in to review a large multi-year, £350 million government programme being delivered by a large systems firm. What we found exemplified why data-driven project design is so essential. On the surface everything seemed in place with all the classical elements: detailed project plans, risk and assumption logs; cost estimates and budgets; governance meetings; a change plan. After a couple of weeks' reviewing the detail, it was clear the programme was going to miss its budget and target dates that had already been announced publicly. The key questions were: 'Will it deliver?' 'At what cost?' 'By when?' In this section I outline the case study, bringing out the key questions that need to be asked when doing project planning.

Does everyone understand the plan?

This programme had 6,000 rows of project tasks in six files on Microsoft Project. But no one knew what the overall milestones were, as they were hidden in the detail. So we created a one-page milestone map and an 80-row integrated plan of all the key elements. The milestone map was printed out and put on the wall. The milestones had clear owners and an RAG status as to the likelihood of meeting the dates and budgets.

Is the resourcing plan realistic?

What was interesting was that the detailed project plans had not only start dates and end dates, but also the number of days' effort by task – a wealth of information. We took those numbers and turned them into a resource profile. It showed that the number of FTEs would need to grow from a team of 150 to 400 in a matter of months and then it would drop almost as rapidly – an impossibility to implement. Figure 3.5.2 shows what the profile looked like before and after we had planned out the work.

Are the cost estimates realistic?

Cost is a major area of risk when it comes to projects. In this example the cost estimates were provided by around 15 stream owners for 25+ major work streams. They had a spreadsheet showing each deliverable, the amount of time per resource type per deliverable and a three-point estimate to give the range of that time. In total, this resulted in more than 500 separate spreadsheets. A master spreadsheet took all this data in, providing a summary of all the costs. The problem was that no one understood the numbers in totality nor had confidence in them. When the senior government stakeholders asked which levers could be pulled to reduce cost, no one could provide an answer. When asked if they could be certain that everything was captured

FIGURE 3.5.2   Before-and-after project resource profile

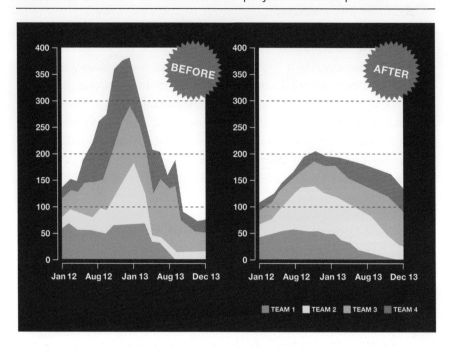

or they were not double counting costs, again, no one could answer. So we built a single integrated costing model with all the assumptions fully linked in it.

How do we factor in risk and uncertainty?

There was an assumption log with over 1,000 assumptions. But it was just a log. What the impact was of an assumption change or the probability of that happening wasn't clear. It was just a long list. There was a risk log, but each risk just had a high-, medium- and low-impact and probability rating. So we defined how each risk would specifically impact both cost and time, using a simulation model to quantify the impact.

What management tools should we implement?

At face value, all the elements were in place but in reality none were. The interconnections between the teams were not well defined, nor were the means to control cost, risk, resourcing levels or any of the other basics. The reason for this was that the programme data was all in unconnected Excel islands. Scenario modelling, visual analysis and effective tracking simply weren't practical, even for a project office of at least 10 people. An integrated plan, as described above, was developed, but with a difference. Each risk was linked to the plan (and cost model), so that we could quantify the impact on the plan if that risk would happen. By assuming risk probabilities, we ran a Monte Carlo simulation that gave a distribution of the probability that each of the key milestones was going to deliver on time. A Monte Carlo simulation runs a model through a large number of iterations. For each iteration, the assumptions and risks are randomly selected based on their distribution (and sometimes their correlation matrix). What it showed was that the chance of one of the key dates being met was only 6 per cent. A sanitized version of the curve is shown in Figure 3.5.3 below.

It is always possible to make models more accurate and sophisticated, but bear in mind the famous words of the mathematician George E P Box: 'All models are wrong but some are useful.' The complexity and size of the programme made it worth investing in a more complex model and it turned out to be extremely useful. With this information, we managed to identify what the critical path was and what the likely impacts of each risk happening were going to be. From this base, it was relatively easy to de-scope, taking large areas of work off the critical path, and build effective buffers into the plan. For example, the number of extensions that were going to be built was reduced from 429 to 280, interfaces for the first go-live date reduced from 23 to five, and the number of data items required to be migrated

FIGURE 3.5.3   Milestone delivery distribution curves

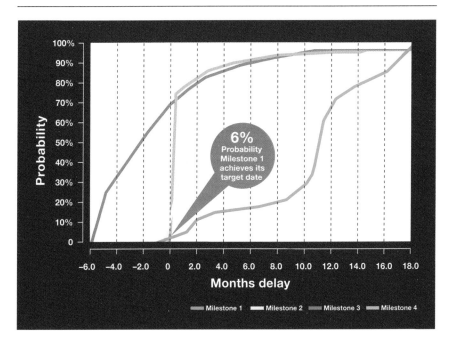

was reduced by 45 per cent. It enabled the programme office to pull the right levers, using information rather than just opinion and conjecture in their arguments. We significantly increased the probability of on-time delivery and in the end the programme was saved. We would never have got there without data-driven methods.

Mini-examples

The generic approaches applied at the beginning of this chapter are a useful way of thinking through how to approach different areas of dynamic process design. Combined with these approaches there is a certain amount of specialization and focus required for each area. This section briefly highlights the key opportunity drivers and design trade-offs to be made for each of the dynamic processes mentioned in the introduction.

Risk management

- **What is it?** Risk management is the process of analysing, prioritizing and addressing (where possible) risks to ensure organizational performance is sustained. Risk management cuts right through every aspect and function of the organization. Each risk is defined by: its impact; the probability it will impact; when it might impact; and how controllable it is. Over time, all of these will change depending on various drivers. To reduce each risk there will typically be a set of actions you can take. Often these actions will impact more than one risk. For example, for a law firm high-level risks could include losing top talent and failing to follow compliance laws. Implementing the necessary training will impact both of these risks.

- **Doing dynamic risk management:** Risk management is often done in a manner that doesn't truly reflect the dynamic nature of risks. Risks are constantly changing but the standard process is that risks are listed and defined by a small group, attributed a level of priority and mitigating actions. The risk scores don't change much and all the details get held in static spreadsheets. How these risks evolve over time and what the impact of mitigating actions has been isn't made clear. To deal with this, you can set an operating measure to act as an early warning when an area needs attention (an approach often used in preventive maintenance in oil refineries). For example, in sales you might track leads generated and if they drop below a certain level it triggers an alert. See more on measuring in Chapter 4.7. An alternative approach is to improve risk identification by periodic crowdsourcing and scoring perceived risks across the workforce. Often those on the ground will have a much better idea than management of potential risks.

Salesforce effectiveness

- **What is it?** Salesforce effectiveness refers to the process of ensuring your sales force is converting clients at each buying stage of the sales cycle. Salesforce is one of the most common areas addressed in organization design because of its importance to many businesses. Owing to the way sales fits with with the target market according to customer profile, ambition and cost of sale, the sales force requires constant analysis, redesign and structuring to ensure it is performing to its optimum potential. In essence, what is the maximum return you can get from a limited set of resources? There is process within designing sales force, but the dynamism comes from the flexibility and continual adjustments you have to make to adapt to the market. Examples of the key questions that need to be answered include:

  - How big and concentrated is the market with how many potential customers?

  - Is there a particular demographic, function or sector I should target?

  - What am I promoting and what is my value proposition?

  - What type of people am I talking to and what messages will be most effective?

  Dimensions you may consider include: geographical focus, product mix per sales team, stage and use of presales support, vertical market segmentation and what the sales process is. This last point relates to where sales stops and starts. What is the handoff with marketing and operations? Defining this should be done using the techniques described in Chapter 3.4.

- **Doing dynamic sales force effectiveness**: A simple way of segmenting a customer population is by looking at the *concentration* of a product or market across all potential customers. First, compare your customers in terms of potential for your product and the market. Note that the scale of value for the product is smaller than the total market sales, so absolute comparisons will be misleading. A method is to segment the customer population into *deciles* for the product and market sales, to make them comparable. Customers in decile 1 are those who contribute to the top 10 per cent of business, decile 2

FIGURE 3.5.4   Analysing product and customer deciles

MY PRODUCT DECILE	MARKET DECILE 10	9	8	7	6	5	4	3	2	1	Total
1									2	8	10
2								2	7	7	16
3							4	10	7	1	22
4					1	8	7	5	5		26
5					1	6	12	9	6		34
6			1	5	11	9	10	3	4		43
7		1	7	16	15	9	5	2			55
8	5	9	25	28	11	5	4	2	1		90
9	23	44	32	18	10	4	1	1		1	134
10	427	85	34	8	7	4	2	3			570
	455	139	99	76	61	51	42	34	26	17	1,000

customers contribute the next 10 per cent of business, and so on. Once we establish which decile each customer resides in for both my product and market, we can cross-tabulate their positions. This is shown in Figure 3.5.4.

You will want to avoid placing resource on the low-value customers (red shaded), as any effort made to these customers will not result in sufficient benefit. Once you know whom to target, then you can align this with your team capacity to build up an answer to the level and frequency of contact.

Procurement optimization

- **What is it?** Just like the sales force needs to be managed to best align with the market, the procurement function needs to align with the supply market. The first step is to define what the overall procurement process is using the fixed process design methods explained in Chapter 3.4. What is the category manager responsible for relative to the buyers, technical specifiers and finance? Procurement functions typically break down into various roles including what are commonly called category or sourcing managers who are responsible for defining which suppliers to buy from and on what commercial terms. It is this role that I will do a deep dive into.

There are several drivers that determine how to design the category managers. Examples include: the impact of each category in terms of spend and business impact; the savings potential; the technical and supply market complexity; how global or local each category is; and any contractual constraints. The driver for how you best organize category managers is to design them around how the supply market is organized. If it is a global supply market, then have a global category team. If it is a local supply market then have a local category team. The other element is the level of knowledge required in understanding exactly how that category works. What complexities should the category manager be aware of and what are the additional value drivers? The level of knowledge required is so great a whole industry of procurement outsourcing and category management consultants has emerged!

- **Doing dynamic procurement optimization**: Too many procurement teams struggle to understand the true business impact of what they are sourcing and struggle when there isn't a true competitive market so that they can run their bids and simply pick the lowest price. The ability for many teams to quantify the value suppliers can bring is missed. The idea of value-adding resourcing is an opportunity being missed. The techniques of multi-criteria decision-making, as described in Chapter 2.3, can be applied in the sourcing decision-making process to help make these decisions. Lastly, the decision as to whether you make something yourself or buy it in is an organizational design decision. It requires a good understanding of which competencies are core and how much the area in question currently costs. Doing an IAA, as described in Chapter 3.4, can help with this. The IAA quantifies how much each activity costs, who is doing it and where it is done. By providing this information to an outsourcing firm, they have a basis to provide a proper quote. You can then effectively decide whether outsourcing or not is right.

Software product development

- **What is it?** Some of the most valuable and fastest-growing companies in the world are software development firms. Many other firms need to create digital teams to take advantage of new market opportunities like e-commerce in the retail sector or the level of software integration in the automotive sector. Software development is a complex intellectual process. Often, the idea at the beginning of the requirements definition evolves into something radically different. The process of design, develop, test, release, maintain is pretty standard. But how that is done does not always reflect the linear structure you would expect. There are constant feedback loops, new ways of solving old problems and changing requirements. Sometimes, it is only when you see the solutions that you understand what was wrong with the design and how it should change. It can be extremely onerous to actually detail the design; the fact is, it needs to evolve is a core part of the process. There is a large range of competencies and computer languages to write the code for.

Therefore, I think it is best to base the organization around competency areas and common elements of the product or solution that is being developed. At Spotify, to enable agile software development, there are teams of eight called 'squads' that focus on specific features of the product.[4] These are interlinked flexibly throughout the company so that small releases to the software can happen often and with minimal bureaucracy. This is similar to the way my current company is structured, with each team organized into technology capability pods. Each pod has a project manager, a designer, three to five developers and a quality engineer. Each discipline, for example quality, has a manager who forms skills groups, provides a career path down that competency and, therefore, co-manages the person. Other considerations to factor into the design include: the product roadmap; future capability needs; how agile or fixed is the development process including how the design–develop–test set of iterations is done; the cost and complexity which can help define whether the teams should be either onshore or offshore.

- **Dynamic software product development:** I have learnt so much from my seven years of managing a software firm that applies beyond the scope of just software. How to be truly 'agile' and what that word means are illuminating for many outside the industry. Chapter 4.7 provides an overview of this agile approach that many leading software teams use.

Final thoughts

There are many examples of organizational elements that require dynamic design. Fortunately, many of the techniques described throughout this book apply to these areas. Like the rest of the micro design, there are well-established methods for designing these areas and linking them into the overall org system. Chapter 3.4 dealt with those more repeatable and predictable activities, that is those that can be mapped onto traditional value chain process maps. This chapter is no less method driven, but because of the uncertainty and more rapidly evolving nature of these areas, a more agile risk-based approach is required.

You should also note how organization design cuts right across all elements of the organization and needs to bring in broad levels of non-traditional HR data. The best example from this chapter is the sales, customer and marketing data needed to support the design of the sales force. But this is also true in other areas that I haven't detailed like procurement and spend data or R&D pipeline or product roadmap ambitions. The other principles in the remaining chapters apply equally here. Given you need people to manage your projects, risk and to make your sales, you also need to determine how many people are required, with what skills, experiences and behaviours. The added insight is that you are using other business drivers to determine how the work is defined and organization designed. I hope the examples in this chapter serve as a practical reminder as to how holistic your thinking, and therefore data to support it, need to be.

Remember this

1 A large proportion of the work is not defined by fixed value chain processes as described in Chapter 3.4, but by more dynamic variable drivers.

2 When doing portfolio and project management design, break up your plans into three levels.

3 The redesign of each dynamic area can been seen as end-to-end OD projects where the steps within macro design are required.

4 For each area, for example sales, procurement or software development, you have to think through what the fundamental driver is. For sales it is the customer, for procurement the supply market, and for software the combination of competency with the roadmap.

5 Because of the dynamic nature of these areas, there will be faster change and more need for continuous assessment and redesign.

Notes

1 Peterson, H [accessed 26 January 2015] Business Insider [Online] http://www.businessinsider.com/the-10-top-jobs-in-fashion-retail-2013-10?

2 Chartered Institute of Management Accountants [accessed 26 January 2015] Financial Management [Online] http://www.fm-magazine.com/infographic/prime-number/15-world%E2%80%99s-biggest-cost-overrun-projects#

3 Sources: CIMA, Centre for Major Programme Management, University of Oxford's Saïd Business School; McKinsey and the London School of Economics

4 https://dl.dropboxusercontent.com/u/1018963/Articles/SpotifyScaling.pdf

Competency management

Every artist was first an amateur. RALPH WALDO EMERSON

Introduction

There is a lot of noise made about 'talent management'. I have lost count of the number of talent management speeches I have heard at every HR conference I have ever attended, references in the papers to the 'war for talent', let alone the vast number of articles, blogs and tweets on the subject. The HR profession is obsessed by talent and rightfully so. However, the debate has to move on from the recruitment and retention 'war' to a constant development of the core competencies. Strategy professionals talk about how organizations need to focus on their core competencies while talent professionals talk about learning and development, performance versus potential, and retention strategies. Data-driven competency management can bring these two perspectives together and put it at the heart of the organizational design debate. I believe it can also drive an increase in employee engagement, productivity and retention together with transforming the way people are reviewed.

The tool of choice for most HR professionals for talent management is the nine-box grid. Developed by the consulting firm McKinsey in the 1970s, HR has embraced it as a simple and effective way to carry out talent management. The nine-box grid locates an individual's talent by mapping performance on the x-axis against potential on the y-axis in three columns and rows: for example, low; medium; high. Depending on the two scores, an individual can be in position 9 – 'Underperformer' – all the way up to position 1 – 'Future Leader'. HR has utilized the nine-box grid too much as a solution for talent management, resulting in a debate that hasn't moved on. The profession hasn't challenged itself to find something better, and this is a problem as the nine-box grid, for all its usefulness, has some significant gaps:

- **It is opinion-based**. More often than not it is just a manager's judgement at a point in time.

- **It lacks clarity of measurement**. So you are talking about performance, but what does that mean? Before even getting on to which metrics it is linked to, does performance mean performance in relation to objectives or competencies? For example, if you are talking about achieving objectives, then lack of achievement may not necessarily mean someone is not top talent, but that he or she needs more support in developing competencies.

- **It lacks clarity of purpose**. The nine-box grid helps you think through potential, but what potential are we talking about? Potential for what sort of role – one level up, or a role in another area of the business that is in critical need of new blood? Particularly, when thinking about succession planning you are thinking at two levels: 'What is the full potential for an employee?' and 'Are they ready for role change?' (See more in Chapter 4.6.)

Managers sit down to review the performance of their team members approximately every six–12 months and the decisions made off the back of this process include bonuses, salary increases, promotions and, in some instances, who gets to keep their jobs and who doesn't – not trivial matters. If I asked you: 'What and where are the talent pools in your organization where a 20 per cent improvement in quality or availability would make the biggest difference to organizational success?' could you answer the question for certain? It's likely that while intuitive knowledge of strengths, gaps and talented individuals exists in most organizations, there may be little logic or data to hand to answer this fundamental question. If this is the case, then how can we systematically identify the pivotal resources needed for organizational development and sustainability? The idea of competency management isn't new. It has been around since at least Roman times and still adds value when done well. But too often it isn't done well. Many of the root causes of implementation failure include:

- a confusion between objectives and competency management;
- a linear rather than holistic approach to appraisal and management;
- a strong link to progression and reward, therefore taking away from development and an improvement focus;
- an isolated view rather than part of the organizational system;
- a lack of emphasis in ensuring employees and managers receive genuine added-value information.

Competency frameworks need to be seen in context of making an organization fit, not just lean, to sustain performance for the long term. Frameworks need to be linked to what motivates employees; language used must be meaningful and relevant; they need to be visual and interactive. Competencies are important for individuals to track their development and should be seen first and foremost as a development rather than performance tool. In this chapter I put to you the business case for data-driven competency management. First, I define my interpretation of competency management in relation to objectives management. I explore the value of competency management and the benefits it can bring to the organization as a whole and to individual employees. Finally, I will present a framework for implementing a thorough and data-driven approach to competency management, connecting it to the other aspects of the organizational system.

Objectives versus competency management

Both objectives and competencies need to be discussed, measured and managed, but in different ways. When measuring anything, the first thing is to get your definitions straight. Having sat through several thousand performance reviews, I reflect that a large proportion of the objectives listed next to someone's 'MBOs' are really competencies. (MBO stands for Management By Objectives. The process requires each person to list his or her objectives and that person is then judged against them at the end of the year. This is most typically a form-filling process.) For example, I often see evaluation areas such as 'How well do they communicate?' 'How good at building rapport are they?' 'What are their technical knowledge and expertise?' or 'How resilient are they are in achieving sales or delivering CSAT (Customer Satisfaction Score)?' As discussed in Chapter 3.2, objectives management is the process of setting, measuring and tracking specific, time-bound and measurable outcomes. Achieving an objective can be the result of an individual or set of activities using a range of resources that produces an outcome. It is an output measure and normally not fully in the control of the person held to account for achieving it. In contrast, competencies are linked specifically to individual people and are not the product of a team or set of resources. They are a set of behaviours, experiences and skills. It is an input measure. Competency management, therefore, is the process of setting, measuring and tracking these.

Competencies can be a mix of soft and hard attributes. The soft side is the cultural fit, attitude and aptitude. It is the kind of stuff that is innate. It is the sort of thing that one already sees in a five-year-old child: the ability to empathize; learn quickly; be open-minded; be tenacious; or have a high pain threshold. It is also much harder to quantify and measure. When CV screening, it shows itself in the extracurricular activities. In an interview, it is the answers to the personal questions, the rapport that is developed, and the answer to the airport test (If I was delayed at an airport for seven hours with this person, how happy would I be given it is this person versus another? Would he or she make the delay much easier or harder to endure?). The hard side is the technical ability, the official certifications, the expertise. Both are important, and the emphasis on either one depends on the type of role you are looking at, as I explore later in the chapter.

Both objectives and competencies are intrinsically linked, given that competencies are attributes that allow a resource to effectively complete a set of activities or have the judgement to make good decisions. By default, therefore, achieving certain objectives requires having or building the right competencies. Competencies are inputs into the value chain and not the outputs. From that perspective, they are easier to manage because they are more controllable. It is relatively harder to control the outcomes and relatively easier to control the inputs and what work is done by whom, as defined in Chapter 3.4.

The business case for competency management

Competency management has a bad name. It is regarded as old-fashioned. My clients don't ask for it and it is not on many senior managers' to-do lists. Clearly the business case isn't compelling enough for managers and employees to go through the effort of putting a competency framework in place, let alone populating it. And that is understandable. Competency management is advanced. It requires a level of granular analysis that can be put in place only once the other basic foundations are in place. But that doesn't mean it shouldn't be an ambition or isn't the right way to do things. So let me put the business case to you.

The management perspective

Consistency

For the Human Resource (HR) and management functions, competency frameworks can help to improve consistency in HR processes such as:

recruitment and selection; performance management; workforce and succession planning; and the learning and development function. For example, competency-based role specification and interview techniques can help to make the recruitment and selection processes fairer, and help recruiters adhere to legal requirements. Appraisals become more transparent and differences in role levels and job titles become more meaningful.

Effective talent management

Competency management can act as one of the foundations of your workforce and succession plan. After all, if you can map role-specific competencies against people's competencies and connect them, you can identify future successors or gaps in talent. On the one hand, you can predict with a lot more certainty whether a potential successor is ready or will fit well into a role. On the other, by identifying the gaps you can start to build an idea of your recruitment strategy going forward, and where the focus will need to be (read more in Part Four).

Close the gap

You can define which competencies are crucial and quantify your strengths and weaknesses. By identifying key gaps, you can focus on closing them. By measuring you can keep on track and focus on improving. Having an overview of which competencies need to be developed means you can target learning and development resources more effectively. You can define performance standards and provide clear guidelines to employees regarding what the organization expects.

The employee perspective

Employee engagement

An accurate and thorough competency framework can help boost engagement in everyday work. By matching people's skills more effectively to specific job requirements you can build an individual's competence through appropriate utilization of skills. If people are involved in activities that both reward and stretch their capacity to perform they will achieve 'flow'. As Mihaly Csikszentmihalyi writes in in his book *Flow*: 'The best moments in our lives are not the passive, receptive, relaxing times. The best moments usually occur if a person's body or mind is stretched to its limits in a voluntary effort to accomplish something difficult and worthwhile.'[1] Flow is achieved (and is defined as) when an activity is goal directed so that there are direction and purpose to action; when perceived challenges are balanced by a perception and self-confidence in individual levels of competence; and where there is immediate feedback in order to support continuation or adjustment of current actions and behaviour.[2] It becomes an intrinsically rewarding experience that both supports and is enhanced by successful goal achievement (for example, closing a sale) and skills development (for example, communicating more effectively and succinctly in the sales process).[3]

While anyone can experience flow, there needs to be a specific challenge for an individual's particular skill set to promote efficacy and achievement, and to increase motivation to perform at a high level. Good organizational design and thinking about competencies across the organization can directly support the development of two out of the three preconditions above in achieving this: clarifying and identifying stretch goals, and achieving balance between challenges and skills.

According to the flow model, the correspondence of the appropriate level of challenge together with a positive self-concept of capability can encourage persistence and active engagement because of the intrinsic rewards and experience of achievement. This is depicted in Figure 3.6.1. Flow also supports the development of skills and expertise in a relatively short period of time. According to Csikszentmihalyi, in order to achieve flow, nine conditions

FIGURE 3.6.1   Flow Channel (adapted from Nakamura and Csikszentmihalyi, 2002)

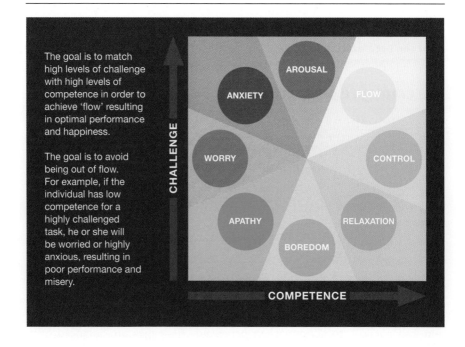

FIGURE 3.6.2   The nine conditions of flow

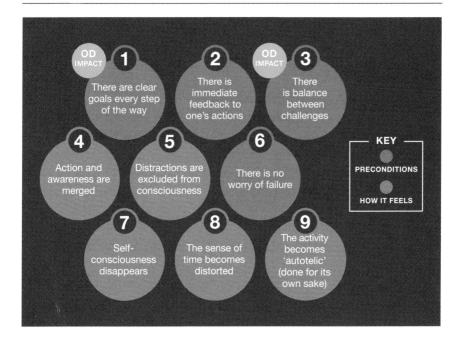

must be met (Figure 3.6.2). Of these nine, four are preconditions and five are how you feel while doing an activity. Of those four preconditions, I believe the micro design sets the first and third conditions. The second condition is also a large part of the data-driven method described in this book.

The challenge is how an organized set of challenges and a corresponding set of skills result in optimal experience. This is where, I believe, the concept of 'flow' and helping individuals to achieve positive 'flow' reaps benefits for organizations. Individuals who are happy, have a positive outlook and are engaged in their work are more productive than those who are negative, neutral or stressed.[4] By putting emphasis on achieving excellence rather than identifying deficiencies[5] it helps to create an environment that nurtures individuals and supports organizations that 'flourish'.[6,7,8] If they can see the competencies they need to progress, and can personally track their progress then they are going to engage more in their personal development.

It is supportive

If someone isn't achieving their objectives it is either because they don't have the time/resource to do so OR they don't have the competencies required. Assuming it is the latter and they have the will and aptitude to learn, then what better conversation to have than working out together how to overcome whatever competency needs to be developed? Helping the team succeed is a crucial role of management and one of the nicest parts of the role.

Career progression

Competency management can help individuals to map their careers. Where competencies are mapped clearly to roles within the organization, and this information is available to all employees, then it is possible for individuals to identify routes for possible development or job specialization, and become aware of specific skills and competencies required or roles to which they may aspire. This supports a transparent approach to career progression.

Developing and putting the framework to work

Like all frameworks, there is a process for defining, designing, measuring and driving improvements over time. With competency management, there are six steps:

1 Create the framework and descriptors.

2 Create targets for the roles (and/or activities).

3 Populate actuals.

4 Calculate competency gaps.

5 Improve over time.

You will note we are creating a framework that is ready to be data-driven. The framework should enable you to answer:

- Who has what competency?
- How many people have them?
- What is the average level for each competency?
- What and where are the gaps?
- Who is above or below where they need to be?
- Who is improving and by how much over time?
- Where would our training budget get its biggest return?

Create a framework

The first step is to define your competency map framework. As with all of the 'micro system datasets', we follow a process of making a taxonomy that is as intuitive as possible, as explained in Chapter 1.3. It is common practice for each competence to have a list of levels. Figure 3.6.3 is a four-stage example of this.

In this example I have given an even number to each level so that there is no middle ground and have chosen four categories above two in order to give that extra nuance. However, there will be certain competencies that are binary: you have it or you don't. This is particularly true when it comes to needing certification in regulated environments like healthcare. In those cases, you could choose to either not score it (so a zero) or give it a 'Competent' level. If you want to define greater levels of competence, you could document them separately. This would result in having a larger list of competencies (the number of nodes or rows in your framework) but less work needed to define four descriptors for each one. Because of my data-driven ethos, I believe it is useful to turn each level of competency into a number. That helps with analysis and aggregation. The simplest is to score 1, 2, 3, 4. But that assumes a purely linear progression in something that isn't linear. It is much harder to become 'World Class' in one thing than a 'Novice' in four things. So why not use an exponential scoring sequence with the implicit logic it is twice as hard to move up a level again? For example, 1, 2, 4, 8 (or 16).

FIGURE 3.6.3   A four-stage competency framework

NOVICE

Is demonstrating early signs of getting to grips with the competency. Is able to understand the basic concepts. Still needs support to do it.

COMPETENT

Needs occasional guidance but is generally self-sufficient. Performance is improving with practice.

EXPERT

Highly skilled and completely self-sufficient. Can support, advise and coach others.

WORLD CLASS

Has mastered the competency. Quickly recognizes patterns; executes all aspects of the competence; is recognized as an expert; is a leader and example to be followed.

The next stage is to really define what you mean by each level. For each state, you need to describe what the specific competency is. For each level, an additive set of skills that depict reaching that increasing level is detailed. It takes a great deal of effort to create descriptors. The key is to ensure everyone understands the same thing when they read the descriptors and it is easy to judge whether or not someone has reached that given level. The list of all competencies can be quite large. Just as with Google Maps, it is useful to be able to zoom in and out, to be able to see the whole and then dive into the detail. A good taxonomy is useful to support navigation and is a key part of the framework. Figure 3.6.4 shows a heat map of 15 competency areas with a total of 56 separate competencies. The colour represents the count of people with a competency at each level.

Create targets

There are two sets of competencies. The first is the required competencies or the demand. The second is the competencies that your employees actually hold or the supply of competencies. This subsection starts with defining the required targets before moving to actuals in the subsection following. For the target competencies, you have three options:

1 **At the activity level:** Here you are defining what competencies each element of the process map needs.

2 **At the role level:** Here you are making the jump to assuming what competencies are needed for each of the activities for which that role is responsible.

3 **At the workforce planning group level:** A workforce planning group is a group of roles that have broadly fungible skills *Fungible* means that the the employees can be easily be substituted or replaced with each other, as their skills, experiences and behaviours are sufficiently similar. This is the level at which strategic workforce planning is done (Chapter 4.5) and ideally the level you think about your transition management (Chapter 4.4).

If you do your target creation at the activity level, assuming you have defined who is responsible for each activity, then by defining the accountability matrix, you can by definition list the competencies required for each role. If you have IAA information, then you can calculate exactly the percentage of time each competency is required, leading to real prioritization. The downside is the number of elements that need to be defined and maintained. I doubt many will have the resources to do this. If you define competencies

FIGURE 3.6.4   Heat map example of 26 generic competency frameworks

HR Competencies

Category

■ 1–3 people   16–30 people

▨ 4–7 people   ■ 31–100 people

▨ 7–15 people   ■ 101–300 people

at the role level, then you can still define a subjective level of importance. That will be far simpler and require less work. If you define competencies at the workforce planning level, the number of links and data entry will be minimized. No matter what, it is extremely useful to define workforce planning groups because it is at this level that you will do so much of the Making it Real work. If you define the target competencies at either the activity or role level, it is useful to then determine which roles have broadly the same set of competencies and, therefore, are by definition within the same group. Some additional practical advice:

- When linking competencies to roles to create target competencies, don't give in to the temptation of linking large numbers of competencies to each role. Keep the numbers small and manageable. Be realistic when creating this target. My rule of thumb is an average of 15 and maximum of 20.

- You may want to define the target competencies as Must Have or Desirable. This relates to the prioritization point above. But, be careful: it will mean creating and maintaining more and more data. If it is Must Have, then it is a strong reason not to give someone the role if he or she doesn't have the competency.

- The descriptors need to be clear and tightly written. Words matter a great deal here and ambiguity will come back to haunt you.

- When recruiting to fill the role, think through how you are going to test for each competence. For technical competencies, run technical tests. It is easy for some people to blag their way through an interview. After CV screening and a brief HR lead phone interview, we put our candidates through a range of job-specific technical tests. It saves a lot of recruitment time and significantly improves our decision-making process.

Populate actuals

Populating actuals is the hardest step, especially if the scores directly affect pay and promotion chances. So, as with objectives, try not to make the competency score link dogmatically with pay. For example, don't say: 'If you meet all your target competencies you will get a bonus of £x and if you overachieve them by 10 per cent then you get a further £y.' This isn't physics or engineering with precision in measurement or direct predictable cause and effect. Just because you give stuff numbers, it doesn't mean they are 100 per cent precise. They are directional. Be mindful and careful. Once you have reassured everyone about the sort of thing that will be done with the information, go through a scoring process. This can include any combination of:

- a self-assessment;
- a manager assessment;
- calibration reviews by a committee;

- peer-to-peer 360 assessments;
- outside assessment centres.

Once done, you can start to see not only who has achieved what score, but also how each team scores. Figure 3.6.5 shows where a group of employees sit. Amber Hutch is a Level 1 for deploying IR. The colour of the dot against each employee's name represents how far off or ahead of the target employees are: blue is ahead, green on target, amber is one below and red is two below. The colour on each descriptor is the heat map of the number of people with that competence.

One of the issues here is grade inflation. Grade inflation is increasing the scores for the same level of competence over time. That is why the descriptors need to be so precise. It is also why a group of people should be validating the scores as part of a calibration exercise. I believe that whatever the mechanism is for generating the first draft of the actual scores, having a group that both understands the framework and each of the people being assessed is a crucial step. This group validates the scores and ensures both fairness and completeness. This is a timely process and requires significant management commitment.

FIGURE 3.6.5 Example scores

Employee Relations

Deploying IR

Level 1	Level 2	Level 3	Level 4
Informs and advises managers and staff about employee relations policies and practices	Supports and coaches managers in understanding employee relations policies and practices, ensuring understanding of compliance imperatives	Ensures that policies and practices cover the full employee relationship and industrial relations strategy	Leads the development of the employee relations strategy and plan that delivers and supports the organization's objectives

Amber Hutch	Charlie Goodwin	Declan Reid	Barbara Gray	Tylor Swift
Fran Daniels	Denise Towner	Sarah Cole	Michael Reed	Wendy Smith
Frances Bush	Cameron Lane	Connor Mann	Greg Johns	
Thomas Lee	Barbara Stultz	Joseph Mack		
	Jack Little	Logan Price		
	Sarah Flynn			

COUNT: **20** AVG TARGET: **2.3** AVG ACTUAL: **2.2** AVG GAP: **–0.1**

Shaping Employee Relations

Level 1	Level 2	Level 3	Level 4
Ensures that staff and managers receive new information and updated literature when policies and procedures change or are updated	Ensures that employee handbooks, contracts and the intranet site are consistent, up to date and in line with the organization's ER/IR principles and policies	Leads the development of employee relations policies and practices	Shapes culture by ensuring the appropriate ER/IR principles and tools, policies and practices are well executed

Amber Hutch	Frances Bush	Charlie Goodwin	Declan Reid	Wendy Smith
Fran Daniels	Thomas Lee	Denise Towner	Sarah Cole	Tylor Swift
Sarah Flynn	Logan Price	Greg Johns	Michael Reed	
Barbara Stultz	Joseph Mack			
Jack Little	Cameron Lane			
Barbara Gray	Connor Mann			

COUNT: **20** AVG TARGET: **2.3** AVG ACTUAL: **1.5** AVG GAP: **–0.8**

Calculating competency gaps

Now that you have defined the actuals and target competencies, then you can calculate the gaps. The sort of questions you can answer and points to reflect on include:

- Does the person in a particular role have all the competencies required?

- When an individual exceeds the target, what does this mean? You may want to think about how to use this person's expertise and skills in another area. Should the person be promoted? Maybe the person can design and deliver a training course and share his or her knowledge with colleagues? Will the person get bored and do you need to challenge him or her in a new way? That is, add to their responsibilities and required competencies.

- When an individual falls short of the target, identify the areas that require improvement (that is, the gaps). Then encourage the individual to suggest ways of addressing these gaps and support him or her through this process.

But having this information makes organizations think about competencies in new and different ways. You can start to utilize individuals' skills and capabilities more effectively and, ultimately, it supports the entire succession planning, development and talent agenda. The ability to aggregate this data in the context of the organization then becomes possible. Figure 3.6.6 shows the status of each role or you could drill down to a summary for each employee, for example Tasha Allred.

We can see the competence target for each role and person. At a group or organizational level we can start to see hotspots for development and map concentrations of high-level skills. This can support strategic thinking and risk assessment in relation to managing change, defining the learning and development plan, ensuring the core strategic competencies are given sufficient attention or recruiting to fill key gaps.

Improve over time

Competency management isn't just about auditing today. It is about development and progress. Figure 3.6.7 shows the target competencies for a given employee, but this could equally be for a team, function OR a given competency and those who need to have it. Each colour represents a different area of competency while each line a specific competency. For this employee,

FIGURE 3.6.6   Example summary results for a series of roles and individuals

FIGURE 3.6.7   Individual example of tracking competency gaps over time

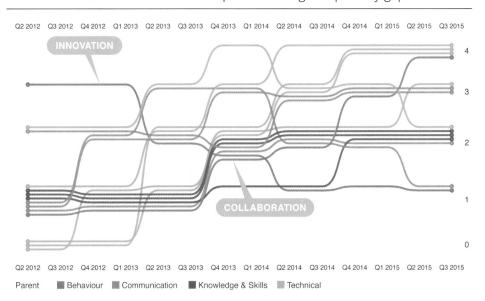

the two orange lines represent behaviours. The Innovation behaviour is deemed to have significantly decreased while Collaboration has increased over the 14 quarters. This highlights the fact that not all competencies increase in a linear fashion. For instance, my personal Excel skills have eroded over the past eight years as I have stopped using that as my primary tool for analysis.

As another example, every six months a snapshot of everyone's competencies could be taken for biannual review meetings. Each line would represent a competency. The colour could also represent how far off target each one is with the frequently used BRAG status. This example could be aggregated to a team, function or geographical level. When you flip to a team view, the patterns change. As members of the team come and go, so too does the average score. There will be more volatility. It is likely that, as highly skilled people move on, the averages drop. Other visual additions that could be made include changing the thickness of the lines to represent the number of team members who actually have that competency or to aggregate the lines by competency areas rather than specific ones.

Final thoughts

The reality I observe is that the pervasive way of reviewing people's performance muddles objectives and competencies. The first is an output and not fully under someone's control while the latter is an input and it is broadly under someone's control, though that person will need time and sometimes investment in training to move his or her levels forward. My observation is that the lack of this competency management theory being practised or even desired has to be a result of the perception that it will not add enough value to either the managers, individuals, L&D departments, OD practitioners or leaders. Because the competencies are looked at only on a biannual or annual basis and owing to their strong if not direct link to reward, they are not properly used as a tool to either manage the business or drive improvements. More often than not I observe that the actual competencies defined are too flaky and subjectively measured. I have, therefore, mostly witnessed these as a box-ticking exercise with limited business value. If you make the required competencies challenging enough and provide continuous feedback, with good role design, you have a chance to create roles that provide 'flow' for all your employees. When in flow, work doesn't feel like work. Engagement, happiness, productivity and superior business performance will soar.

> ### Remember this
>
> 1 The debate has to move on from the recruitment and retention 'war for talent' by using competency management as a key management tool.
>
> 2 Carrying out competency management effectively will drive employee productivity and happiness through flow.
>
> 3 Objectives are an output measure while competencies are an input.
>
> 4 Capture the demand and supply within a competency taxonomy so that gaps can be identified and performance improved.
>
> 5 Create workforce planning groups so that broadly fungible roles can be grouped together (this supports several processes, such as workforce planning and transition management).

Notes

1 Csikszentmihalyi, M (1990) *Flow: The Psychology of Optimal Experience*, Harper & Row, New York, p 5

2 Csikszentmihalyi, M, Abuhamdeh, S and Nakamura, J (2005) Flow, in Elliot, A J and Dweck, C S (eds), pp 598–608, *Handbook of Competence and Motivation*, The Guilford Press, New York

3 Nakamura, J and Csikszentmihalyi, M (2002) The Concept of Flow, in Snyder, C R and Lopez, S J (eds), pp 89–105, p 90, *Handbook of Positive Psychology*, Oxford University Press, Oxford

4 Anchor, S (2010) *The Happiness Advantage: the seven principles that fuel success and performance at work*, Virgin Books, New York

5 Searle, T P and Barbuto, J E (2011) 'Servant Leadership, Hope, and Organizational Virtuousness: a framework for exploring positive micro and macro behaviours and performance impact', *Journal of Leadership & Organizational Studies*, 18 (1), pp 107–117, p 107

6 McLean, J and Wells, S (2010) 'Flourishing at the edge of chaos: leading purposeful change and loving it, *Journal of Spirituality, Leadership and Management*, 4 (1), pp 53–61

7 Ghaye, T (2010) 'In what ways can reflective practice enhance human flourishing', *Reflective Practice: international and multidisciplinary perspectives*, 11 (1), pp 1–7

8 Bakker, B and Schaufeli, W (2008) 'Editorial: Positive organizational behaviour: engaged employees in flourishing organizations', *Journal of Organizational Behaviour*, 29, pp 147–154

Rightsizing

> *The Ringelmann effect, also known as 'social loafing', was discovered by the French professor of agricultural engineering Maximilien Ringelmann. Ringelmann had his students, individually and in groups, pull on a rope. He noticed that the effort exerted by a group was less than the sum of the efforts exerted by the students acting individually.*
>
> **BERNARD SIMON**[1]

Introduction

Although the two are often confused, rightsizing is different from downsizing. Rightsizing is the decision on how many people and how much effort to invest against any set of activities. The outcome is a resource profile allocating talent within the organization to a particular area. In my experience rightsizing has not been data-driven and so has lacked focus when it comes to ensuring you have the right amount of people doing the right activities and processes to deliver your objectives and strategy.

There is not much literature on the subject, so in this chapter I provide four data-driven methods to help take you through the process of rightsizing your organization. Before exploring these methods I begin by highlighting how most rightsizing is typically done. I then go through each rightsizing method in turn: ratio analysis, activity analysis, driver analysis and mathematical analysis. There are case studies throughout to demonstrate the application of these methods and bring them to life. This is the final stage of the micro design and will be the foundation for delivering and implementing your organization design successfully.

FIGURE 3.7.1   Most common organizational sizing methods

Common currently used flawed methods

Before we get into the solution, it is worth reflecting on how rightsizing currently is often carried out. I observe four broad methods, shown in Figure 3.7.1.

1 It just evolves

This is the most common. Ask employees why their organization or department looks like it does and often the answer will be 'It just is.' Decisions are made for one reason or another and a shape is created. Natural evolution is not a problem in itself, but the lack of control is.

2 Who shouts loudest

The evolution of a team is often driven by who shouts the loudest – by managers who are adept at getting their way and ensuring they have resources. This is what makes rightsizing so fraught. It defines people's empires, and that is an emotional subject. You can be sure that in a discussion about rightsizing, egos will be challenged and dented.

3 Across the board cut

Just as wages have 'stickiness' (a term economists use to mean basically that once people are given a set wage, they don't take pay cuts), so does headcount. Last year's budget is the basis for this year's budget. Which works until there is a shock. When that shock happens, Finance demands cuts. Because it is so hard to work out exactly where those cuts should be, they are made across the board and unilaterally, for example '20 per cent reduction no matter what'.

4 Magic number

There is no magic number to rightsizing. Using any one number for it is dangerous. Benchmarks are rarely direct comparisons, and too often based on a tiny sample. Proper thought is required. For example, your marketing department should not necessarily look the same as your finance department. Or the group of companies from which the benchmark is drawn may have different priorities. What works in one company may not work in another.

Four methods for rightsizing your organization

In a balanced system, the 'right' size is the size that delivers the desired business outputs most effectively. Rightsizing naturally follows on from all the work done in the rest of the micro design. Without fully understanding your organizational as-is, objectives, processes and competencies, you are simply shooting in the dark. Given both how important and political rightsizing is, it often scares executives. It is a political hot potato. So when you start the estimation process of the number of FTEs required, ensure you discuss the methods you are going to use first. Ideally, sign off the method; even if you end up changing it, you have protected yourself. You are going to need to take all the key stakeholders on a journey. Everyone needs to understand that no matter what, there will be ambiguity. If a frank and honest debate is not had you will likely sleepwalk into making bad decisions.

This chapter outlines four rightsizing methods, as shown in Figure 3.7.2. The first method is the simplest and the one that should be most frequently used. As you deal with more complex sizing situations you will need to include more of the methods from further down the list. The more complexity, the

FIGURE 3.7.2 Recommended rightsizing methods

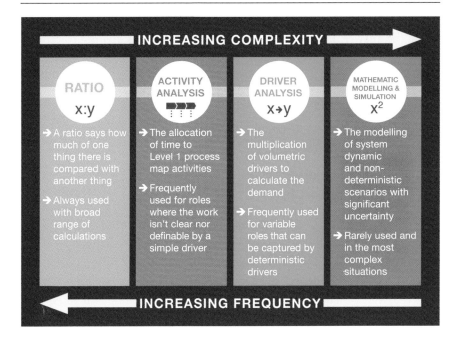

more of the four techniques you should use. To be clear, as you use the more sophisticated techniques, this doesn't mean you stop leveraging the others; that is, you will always use ratio analysis.

Method 1: Ratio analysis

When designing or creating something new you want to create comparisons. In an organizational context this often means asking: 'How do I compare?'; 'Where are we relatively lean or fat?'. The answers to these questions are typically found through ratios. A ratio in this context is the number or cost of one group relative to another. For example, the number of direct reports that each manager has is a ratio and is called the 'span of control'. Another common ratio is the number of FTEs divided by the total number of HR professionals. Each time you calculate a ratio, you are defining a numerator and denominator, for example Total FTEs/HR FTEs or Direct Reports/1 (the manager). The numbers used don't need to be headcount numbers either; they could be the Total Revenue or Profit/FTEs.

Example: Salesforce ratios

Ratio analysis helps identify opportunities for investigation. It does not define the answer. The trick is to define a series of ratios and not to rely on just one. For example, if you are trying to size a sales team, the following ratios could be used:

- average revenue per sales person;
- sales cost as a proportion of revenue;
- number of clients per person;
- number of leads per person;
- sales force to presales support.

The goal here is not to be blinded by one number. For instance, it might be possible to sell £1 million per person, but is it possible to manage 30 client relationships per person? What if the deal size is £20,000 versus £200,000? When dealing with people as the agents, there is a huge variability in performance by individual and by time. A team cannot be composed of equally performing people, and you cannot model around the best performer. For this, you need to look at availability of resource, not optimal resource, since optimal resource will very likely not be available.

As the number and nature of the sales vary, so too do the ratios. For example, if the deals average £20,000 each, then the ratio of leads and clients per person will be much higher. The type of person who can transact that flow will be quite different from someone who has two to five key clients and sells deals worth £500,000–£5 million+. As the deal size increases, then the ratio of salespeople to presales support will probably change. For more on optimizing your sales force, refer back to dynamic process design in Chapter 3.5.

The problem with benchmarking

Benchmarks are dangerous. To be applied, benchmarks have to be an exact comparison within a comparable context. For example, are the benchmarks from similar industries, geographies, scale and maturity (to name a few of the context drivers)? Because of this, always start benchmarking with an internal focus. You can see how business units or regions compare with each other and how these ratios may have changed over time. However, even with internal benchmarks there are dangers. An example is one of my clients, which operated in 180 different markets. But these markets (they were countries) were radically different. How can you compare Ivory Coast and the United States? There are a number of drivers making comparison dangerous: the rate of GDP growth, GDP per capita, market share, regulatory environment, number of years' presence, the labour market conditions. My client's market share varied significantly for a range of historical reasons owing to all the factors I mentioned. The regulatory environment was a big driver of cost for the company, as was its strategy for determining whether the market had a high growth potential or was declining. So in order to compare meaningful ratios, the markets needed to be clustered into similar groups. The purpose of calculating the ratios was to see if there were productivity opportunities and we didn't want the entire analysis to be nullified by logical differences. The political complication was the fact that this company was regionally organized with powerful regional owners sitting on the main board. So to suddenly compare markets across regions required a new mindset. All of a sudden Canada was being compared with Australia while many of the South East Asian countries were being compared with some from Africa.

Generic ratios

Another way to think about ratios is to take a financial lens. For example, review the top-down annual budget as a set of ratios. The simplest example is percentage of revenue or cost. In financial budget terms this includes ratios such as:

- What percentage of the total cost is labour?
- What is and should be the operating margin?
- How much of the cost of goods sold should people represent?
- What percentage of labour should be indirect?

A note worth mentioning here is that for the public sector, revenue is less of a driver, so when it comes to budgeting the questions focus on trade-offs required in each department to achieve the quality and quantity of work required. Other examples of ratios include comparing the headcount or cost of one function, or even set of roles with another. For example:

- How many HR FTEs:Total FTEs.
- The number of 'software developers' to 'technical project managers' to 'quality engineers' or to generalize this: Role X:Role Y.
- The number of marketing managers to marketing spend or marketing projects, or to generalize this: Role X:KPI or financial number.

- Ratio of grades. For instance, billable staff per partner for a whole range of professional service firms.

- Average number of people being managed per manager (ie the span of control).

- Comparing ratios over time makes them even more useful; for instance, what is the number of caseworkers to total cases per month? This is an example of a productivity ratio.

Each industry and function will have its own set of useful ratios. Some ratios can be interpreted as a productivity number (for example, revenue per consultant in a consultancy firm) while others are about balance (number of software developers per quality assurance engineer in a software development firm). The danger comes when some are thought of as productivity ratios but are not, or are fraught with danger when taken out of context. The most famous organizational design ratio is the span of control. Given the obsession with span of control, I believe it is worthy of special attention.

Example: Span of control

One of the questions most often asked in rightsizing is: 'What is the ideal span of control?' Span of control is the number of people that each manager has reporting to him or her. There is a famous example of a consultancy firm marketing a blanket 88 approach: never more than eight layers and no fewer than eight in the span of control. I am sure there are situations where eight is the ideal figure, but realistically there is no such thing as an ideal span of control. It depends on a large number of factors and dogma is incredibly dangerous. Numerical rules neglect the realities of different work complexity in specific areas of the organization. In call centres, typical spans will be 12–15 people while in executive teams Neilson and Wulf report a median of eight people in the CEO's span of control.[2] As I have said, there is no magic number. For example:

- A highly technical role might just have two or three people reporting to one senior manager.

- A pool of support staff might be managed with 30 people reporting to one manager.

- If the manager of four people spends half of his or her time actually doing technical work, should we count it as one manager, or actually only half a manager, giving a span of control of 0.5:4? A smaller span means a technical resource can dedicate a greater percentage of their time to technical work. Given that a more senior resource may be a more productive one in these roles, smaller spans could lead to greater productivity.

The questions people often want to answer are:

- How can I calculate the span of control? (Sum the number of direct reports for each manager.)
- What is the average span of control for my whole organization? (Take the above sum and aggregate it.)
- What is the average span of control at each level? (Slide by job grade or depth.)
- What is the average span of control for each of the top 10 roles? (Filter to those top 10 roles and calculate it.)
- Where are the outliers in span of control for each of the top 10 roles? (Develop a leader board by ranking each manager by his or her span.)
- If we set a minimum span of control, how many people would be affected? How much money would we save? (Take all people with that minimum and sum their costs.)
- Where are managers dangerously overstretched? Finally, we are getting somewhere interesting: this isn't so easy to answer. It's a point I aim to address below.

The problem with many of these questions is they focus too much on averages. What is more interesting is the spread and seeing where the possible outliers are. Figure 3.7.3 shows, by department, how many managers have what span of control within a new design. In HR there are four managers: three with a span of four and one with five. In this view, you can quickly see where there might be issues across the 230 managers you have designed. Iterate the design in areas that don't make sense. The big question in discussing spans of control is: 'What number makes sense?'

A framework for thinking through an ideal span of control

There are three factors that drive what the span of control should ideally be, as shown in in Figure 3.7.4. These are: the nature of the subordinates, nature of the boss and the overall context of the organization. Each of these has various sub-drivers, and understanding these drivers should help to answer what the span of control ought to be.

FIGURE 3.7.3 Average span of control by department

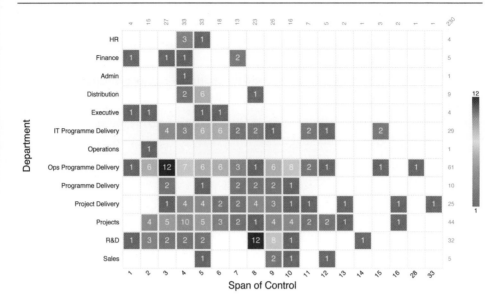

FIGURE 3.7.4 Span of control drivers

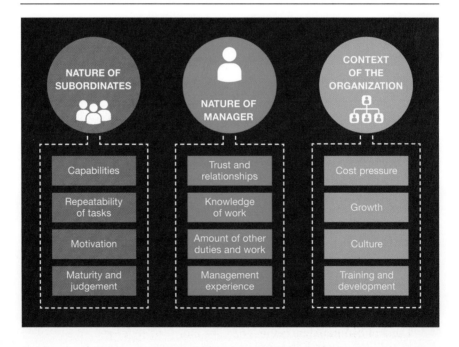

Nature of the subordinates

Level of self-direction of work and amount of supervision required:

- **Capability of workers**. If highly capable they will need relatively less supervision.
- **Degree of repeatability of task**. The more similar the tasks are, the easier it is to manage more people because I can manage by a process and become more numbers-driven in that management.
- **Motivation, judgement and maturity, autonomy of workers**. Are they self-starters? Are they prepared and allowed to make mistakes? Do they know when to escalate and is real trust given? If the answer is yes, then less supervision is required.

Nature of the managers

- **Capability of managers**. Do the managers have a good understanding and knowledge of the required work? How technical are they and have they fulfilled the role they are supervising or not? What is the average time in grade of the average manager? Think of those new to managing or those who are more junior. Management is a competency like many others and takes time to develop.
- **Trust and relationships**. The greater the trust, the better the relationships and the easier it is to supervise more people. How long have the core members of the team been working together?

These factors are driven more by the nature of the people. When designing a group when you don't know who is in what role, assumptions will need to be made about competence and strength of relationships.

'Task activity' versus 'management activity'

- **Level of content and technical work required from the manager**. If the role has technical deliverables and is required to produce output and not 'just manage'.
- **Volume of other tasks**. Tasks such as membership of committees, involvement in project work and need to liaise with stakeholders are all factors which make the ability to manage larger teams more difficult.

Context of the organization

- **Level of geographical dispersion**. The more widely dispersed a business is, the harder it is to supervise, resulting in a smaller span of control. It is easier to manage face to face.

- **Training and development.** How much training and development needs to come from the manager? Is it an apprenticeship or a providing-direction-only model?
- Need for cost savings and perspective on the maximum number of layers.
- **Culture:** How autocratic versus democratic? The more autocratic the greater the span of control can be.
- **Administrative management.** Amount of administrative management tasks and the maturity of the organization's systems to make those tasks efficient. Examples include: appraisal and development plans process, input to remuneration plans, need to explain employment policy changes, time required in recruitment, time to specify and manage the objectives.
- **Amount of change.** The greater the change, the lower the span of control.

Thinking from a drivers perspective demonstrates the holistic approach needed. You should segment each management role using the above span of control drivers. To do this practically, use proxies where possible like the number of different roles (specific job titles) reporting to the manager or the percentage of time allocated to specifically managing. (This is the type of information you will have if you have done an IAA – see below.) Develop rules of the expected span of control by clustering similar roles and then do a gap analysis for each manager against that cluster.

Method 2: Activity analysis

Chapter 3.4 detailed how to build an Individual Activity Analysis (IAA). To recap, the activity analysis quantifies the amount of time that each person spends on his or her main activities. It answers what people actually do rather than what their job descriptions say they do. It is worth pointing out that this type of IAA analysis is not appropriate for everyone. For rightsizing people in roles involving highly repetitive basic activities, such as working on a manufacturing line or taking calls as first line support, the third method of driver analysis is more appropriate.

In my experience, simply seeing the cost of every process and activity produces incredibly valuable insights. It immediately shows where there are likely to be inefficiencies or a lack of investment. Figure 3.7.5 shows the cost

FIGURE 3.7.5   Process cost coloured by number of FTEs involved

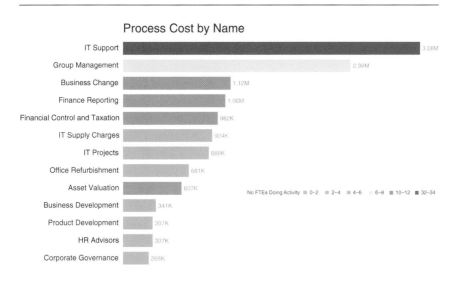

broken down by a given number of processes. The chart is heat-mapped to show the number of different people involved in that process. The more green, the fewer people involved. For the organization in this example, we can start to ask valuable questions such as: does it really make sense for 'Finance Reporting' and 'Financial Control and Taxation' to be the fourth and fifth greatest cost areas?

Example: Building a new product commercialization team

On one project, I worked with a fast-moving consumer goods company to improve how it took new products to market. We had no idea who was involved with this process because no one had a job title referring to new product introductions, innovation or commercialization of the new products. Adding to the complexity, lots of functions were heavily involved at different stages of the process. By performing an IAA we were able to see that of the 1,000 people who were not directly involved in manufacturing and distribution elements of the process, approximately 40 FTEs-worth of effort was involved in the planning and liaising of new product introductions. Broken down, this represented 50 per cent of 50 people's time and 10 per cent of another 30 people's time. Knowing the current effort from an activity perspective gave us a starting point for sizing a new team focused purely on a large number of these activities.

We noticed a large amount of duplication across the countries. Each country had a group of engineers and buyers doing exactly the same work. By centralizing, we could save redundant effort. We created an area of expertise or what is commonly referred to a centre of excellence and we consolidated the new team to 25 permanent roles by prioritizing and reallocating certain activities. A further four FTEs were added to do new activities, which had previously been missing, such as project managing and coordinating product launches, which required new competencies that didn't previously exist in the organization.

Further activity analysis

By doing activity analysis you are providing the basis for a robust and detailed business case. To add insight and rigour to your analysis you can use internal benchmarks. For example, compare the amount of time across different organizations (countries, divisions, products) for the same activity in the same way you do ratio analysis. I have seen 300 per cent more time spent on the same activity from one site to another in situations where the scope, order of magnitude of complexity and underlying work were fundamentally the same. The dimension categories explained in Chapter 3.4 now become extremely useful. For instance:

- By using each of the chosen dimensions from Chapter 3.4, you can group them into logical areas and optimize how they are delivered. For instance, are the 'transactional activities' in the SOT dimension being done by appropriate job levels (grades)?
- What percentage of people are customer-facing by function, and are customer-facing roles spending enough customer-facing time?
- What are the highly variable activities? Once you know which ones are significant, you can then use this information as an input for driver analysis (where FTE required is directly related to the volume of production).

From this you can ask and try to answer:

- Are there economies of scale by aggregating activities?
- Should a more junior grade be doing the work?
- How much duplication is there?

- Could this activity be outsourced? If it could:
  - What kind of cost saving would that deliver?
  - Would it mean losing a core competence?
- Should we even be doing it? What would be the impact if we just stopped the work?
- Given our goals, objectives and issues/case for change, are we doing enough in our key focus areas?
- What impact would automation or streamlining have?

Because you know who is involved in every single activity, if you make changes to who does what and how much of that time you are expecting then you can complete a responsibility impact analysis, often the hardest element of an impact analysis to quantify. It means defining the percentage of each person's work time that will change. Will only one or two small responsibilities (5 per cent to 10 per cent of their work) change or more than 50 per cent? The impact analysis outlined in Chapter 4.4 shows how you can further use this information as part of the implementation process. The process of doing all this analysis will probably highlight data flaws. Socialize your analysis to those who have a feeling for the work and the sorts of improvements required. Sit down with them and gauge their reaction on where you are under- or over-investing. A great deal of this is a reflective process. It is about asking: 'Does it look and feel right?' At the end of the day, your experts' intuition is the final arbitrator. Although this book is about data-driven organization design, gut feeling is always important in assessing results and analysis. A large part of using your gut feeling is thinking of possible explanations why there may be differences and testing them. The next example explains how.

Example: Testing why different areas have performance variances

Just knowing one area performs better than another doesn't help you that much in closing the gap. Good analytics aims to help you understand why so that the right positive actions can be taken. For an example of applying internal benchmarking think of six manufacturing sites. The six sites all produce similar products and volume of outputs but are in different geographic locations. Figure 3.7.6 represents the results of an IAA for employees doing a particular 'activity X'. The results suggest that sites 2 and 3 are extremely inefficient compared with sites 4 and 6. But why? What is the secret of the high-performing sites that can help me understand what actions

FIGURE 3.7.6   Activity of multi-potential drivers

Activity Analysis								
	Site 1	Site 2	Site 3	Site 4	Site 5	Site 6	Total	Correlation
Activity 'X' hours worked pm	2,077	3,876	3,461	1,661	2,769	1,800	15,644	
FTEs doing 'X'	1.5	2.8	2.5	1.2	2.0	1.3	11.3	
Number of people that do 'X'	2	6	8	2	4	2	24	0.91
Average % dedication	75%	47%	31%	60%	50%	65%	47%	−0.78
Quality: Defects per thousand	65	61	49	110	83	75	55	−0.68
Avg Grade (1 = CEO; 10 = Lowest)	5	5	6	6	6	6	6	−0.31
Performance (5 = Excellent; 1 = Poor)	4	3	4	3	3	4	3	−0.33
Competence in skill 'Y' (4 = Expert; 1 = Novice)	4	3	4	4	2	4	4	−0.63
Avg years experience	7	5	7	6	5	6	6	−0.22
Average Salary Cost	$49,000	$36,490	$51,935	$44,201	$35,558	$39,842	$42,607	−0.12
Total cost for activity X	$73,500	$102,172	$129,838	$53,041	$71,116	$51,795	$481,462	0.87

I need to take to make those unproductive sites productive? Use additional information captured from a series of potential explanations (hypotheses) together with more input and output measures. An example where the IAA can help is by quantifying the percentage time that each person doing the given activity is focusing on it. With site 4 it was 60 per cent versus 31 per cent for site 3, or twice as much dedication.

To analyse the data further, start visualizing it. The scatter plot on the left of Figure 3.7.7 shows the six sites' percentage dedication versus number of FTEs. The colour is the competency score, where green is excellent. The size of the bubble is the average number of defects. From this I can see that the most productive sites have far greater dedication of time and are far greener, but the quality doesn't seem to be better. The plot on the left shows visually, however, that neither the average number of years' experience nor the performance scores seem to have much of an impact. But looking at the scatter plots alone is a bit dangerous. Take a look at the data table (Figure 3.7.6) again and see the correlations in the right-hand column (to build a correlation in Excel, enter =CORREL (first row or column of data, second row or column of data), for example =CORREL(B15:G15,$B$14:$G$14). I fixed the second row so that I could drag the formula down and it fixed on the dataset in question. This shows which factors statistically explain the most. There does seem to be a fairly high correlation between quality and productivity after all. The main decision based on this data would be to increase the

FIGURE 3.7.7 Activity of multi-potential drivers

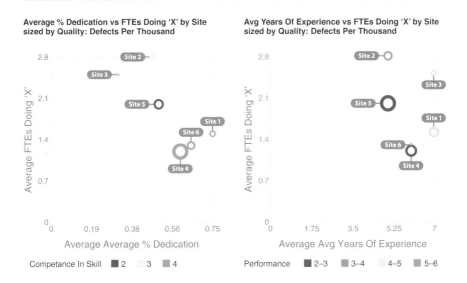

Average % Dedication vs FTEs Doing 'X' by Site
sized by Quality: Defects Per Thousand

Avg Years Of Experience vs FTEs Doing 'X' by Site
sized by Quality: Defects Per Thousand

focus and train the team to improve its competency levels. If unsure, pick one of the sites and run a pilot to see if the interventions work.

Clearly, the sample size is small and there might be other factors at play (refer back to Chapter 3.2 for the dangers of drawing conclusions from small datasets). The point of this analysis is to try to find patterns and insights. Be careful in drawing any definitive conclusions. However, the analysis should give sufficient evidence to allow us to probe further into the reasons for a site's performance and run a pilot at the site. What I hope the above example demonstrates is:

1 **The risk of over simplicity.** If only one measure was used, then insights could and most certainly will be missed. I should also point out that this analysis is far from being statistically significant: the sample size is so tiny it could just be random. What I'm looking for is signs of patterns, of hypotheses that may be interesting to test.

2 **The power of supporting statistical analysis with visuals.** The way you see the world defines how you understand it. Most minds find it hard to look at a table and draw from it all the relevant conclusions.

3 **The power of using activity analysis combined with other measures.** The value one can gain should far outweigh the activity analysis on its own. For instance, the relationship between the various measures could be totally different from the above example. What if time in grade was the main reason for variation in efficiency?

4 **It doesn't need to take much more effort.** Collecting the activity data is the hardest bit. Collecting other measures like output or quality should be easy. Your baseline information should already contain collected data items like start date, tenure and, hopefully, time in grade/role information.

Example: Step change in cost structure

If the goal is to dramatically reduce the costs through headcount reduction, the activity analysis is an excellent starting point. Improvements in efficiency, that is doing the same thing with less, will only take you so far. What if you need a dramatic reduction of approximately 20 per cent to 50 per cent? Then you need to start thinking about what you are going to stop doing. In order to continue with a certain activity, the answers to the questions below have to be an *emphatic* Yes:

1 Do we need to do X for legal or compliance reasons?

2 If we stopped doing X, would it cost us significantly more?

3 Is X best done in house, because it is core and outsourcing it would affect our competitive position negatively?

4 Is the cost of automating X far too high, risky or impossible?

Another thought process to go through is to ask the specialization question: 'If the activity was the only thing that someone did with the optimal skills and operational settings, then how many FTEs at what level would be required?' For these activities, flag them as such (create dimensions against them) and then review the number of different people who do the activity and what percentage of their time this takes. If the answer is lots of people with a small percentage of their time doing these sorts of 'high economies' activities (economics of scale were explained in Chapter 3.4), then think through radically changing the delivery model. This kind of analysis includes answering the following questions:

- Is it regular enough to fill someone's time?
- Would it be too risky for having only one person/role dedicated to it?
- If you created a role that only focused on it, is there a sufficient pool of candidates to be able to staff this job?

Method 3: Driver analysis

Driver analysis is an extension of ratio and activity analysis. It is only really relevant for variable roles or activities. The questions asked in driver analysis are: 'What is the driver and if that driver changes, what is the impact?' For instance, drivers for a call centre are the number of calls, flow of calls, service levels demanded, skills needed, time in grade and, therefore, time to resolve a case. In other words, there are numerous influences. The fact you can have multiple drivers is one of the reasons having a magic number for rightsizing can be so dangerous. However, by doing such in-depth analysis you are mitigating the risk of applying one number too soon.

Driver analysis is effectively a subset of ratio analysis but for variable roles and, ideally, activities. For example, if the main ratio for sizing the account management team is the number of clients, then if the number of clients doubles, we would expect the number of account managers to double, all things remaining equal. This type of analysis is used in 'what if' scenario building, or where there is an expectation of significant change. Only use this method if:

1 there is one or a number of variable drivers that impact on the demand for FTEs;

2 there is more than one FTE in the role;

3 the driver(s) is measurable.

Another tip is to start simple, for example one linear driver, and then build in complexity if the cost of that additional complexity is worth the cost of the measuring and maths. Use the driver analysis as a rule of thumb, not scientific certainty. By doing this sort of analysis, one is simplifying the universe so that decisions can be made. Once the analysis is completed, think through how to factor in the complexities. For example:

● other relevant ratios;

● economies of scale;

● the option to apply a more complex group of roles.

Example: Multi-plant driver analysis

I once carried out driver analysis for a group of 20 manufacturing plants. Each plant had grown independently from a design perspective. Having done the role ratio and activity analysis, we found that, correcting for scale, some plants had eight people fulfilling a given role while others only had two. It was a stark difference, even when corrected for the level of automation and age of the plants. The 400 per cent difference was replicated across many other roles. Another issue was that different plants had subtly (and not so subtly) different structures: orders-of-magnitude differences in investments in core processes and large ranges in the percentage cost of supporting functions. Each plant was different in terms of its volume, mix of lines and to some extent the level of technological capability. But they all had a broadly similar process and were all making exactly the same product.

The goal was to define a generic organizational chart that would work for each plant. The roles were broken into fixed or variable dimensions, as explained in Chapter 3.4. If the role was fixed, it typically required only one FTE. If the role was variable, we then determined what the driver was and how that driver impacted on the number of FTEs required. Building the model included defining: driver assumptions for each plant; calculations; and output reports. The mechanism and logic were then sense-checked by several acting and former plant managers.

Define the standard org chart blueprint

The standard org structure was defined with the focus on whether the role was fixed or variable, represented by the blue colour for variable as shown in Figure 3.7.8. In total there were 39 roles shown of which 'only' 16 were variable (the figure doesn't show all the roles).

FIGURE 3.7.8   Role tree coloured by fixed or variable

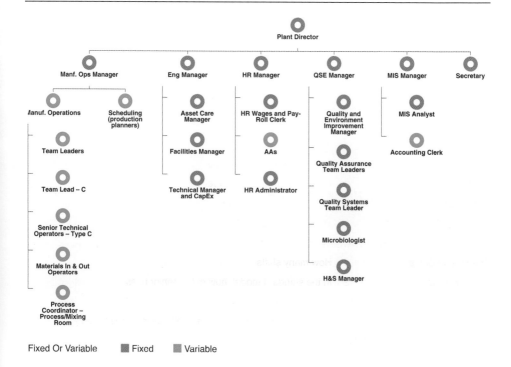

Define the list of drivers

After much discussion, it turned out there were only five basic drivers for the volume of people required:

1 **The number of lines by types of line.** Each line has a number of operators per line. Not all lines are the same in their nature.

2 **Number of shifts.** There are shift workers and non-shift workers. The number of shift workers needs to be multiplied by the number of shifts.

3 **The presence or absence of a technology.** Not all plants have the same technology. By having a 'yes' or 'no' response to a type of technology, then the accuracy of the model can be improved. This can also lead to the easy development of a business case.

4 **Senior roles.** The number of admin staff is driven by the number of senior roles as one admin role looks after x executives.

5 **The volume.** In the end, volume wasn't treated as a driver in this model. But it was useful for sense-checking the scale and economics by doing ratio analysis with volume as the denominator.

The drivers and the volume of each driver for each plant were then added to an assumption lookup table. Figure 3.7.9 is an example. A lookup table is used to capture the key assumptions and it is connected to the main calculation table. Using assumption lookup tables allows you not only to be clear about your assumptions, but also to run automated sensitivity analysis.

FIGURE 3.7.9 List of drivers

Plant Driver	Num	Notes
Num lines – A	3	How many lines of this type
Num lines – B	4	How many lines of this type
Num lines – C	3	How many lines of this type
Volume – A	11,500,000	What volume of this type
Volume – B	17,600,000	What volume of this type
Volume – C	8,600,000	What volume of this type
Number of Shifts	4	How many shifts
Senior Roles	12	In the standard model, how many senior roles
Total Line	10	How many total lines are there?
Has tech X	Yes	Does the plant have Technology 'X', which enables the n[
XYZ	4,234	Dummy driver

Build the model and populate it

Figure 3.7.10 highlights most of the calculations. For each role, there is a driver. Take the example of 'Line Type B Operators'. The driver was the number of lines being operated, the number of FTEs per line and the number of shifts. In this case there were 2.5 FTEs per line and four shifts with four lines = 2.5×4×4 = 40.

The calculation numbers for Line Type B Operators are highlighted in Figure 3.7.10. The other calculations are the sum of FTEs and the FTE Roll-up. The FTE Roll-up at the Plant Director level is the total number of FTEs required for the entire plant. This worksheet shows each of the roles in their reporting hierarchy, so you can see the numbers as you cascade down the organization. The Function and Senior Role dimensions are used for additional analysis. The number of FTEs for that given role is determined by the driver. It should be easy to change the drivers in order to see what impact other assumptions have, as explained in 'Method 4: Mathematical modelling' below. The 'Num' is from the lookup table in Figure 3.7.9. For instance, in this example, there were four Line Type Bs (that means four different manufacturing lines of a given type). The 2.5 FTEs per line is shown in the right-hand column. The productivity assumption is one of the critical assumptions or 'driver ratios'. Once this has been set, you can start to analyse it. From this example you can roll up the total number of FTEs, as shown in column 6. In this case, there is a demand for 272 FTEs. This data can be seen visually in the scaled org chart view for the manufacturing roles in Figure 3.7.11.

FIGURE 3.7.10   FTEs calculation for each role

Role Title	Function	FTE Actual	FTE Demand	FTE Gap	FTE Roll-up	Fixed or Variable	Driver
▼ O Plant Director	GM	1	1	0	272.75	Fixed	
▼ O Manf. Ops Manager	Make	1	1	0	210.75	Fixed	
▼ O Manuf. Operations	Make	6	5	1	204.75	Variable	Total Line
▼ O Team leaders	Make	17	20	-3	130	Variable	Total Line
O Line Type A Operators	Make	65	54	11	54	Variable	Num lines - A
O Line Type B Operators	Make	35	40	-5	40	Variable	Num lines - B
O Line Type B Operators for complex packing	Make	15	16	-1	16	Variable	Num lines - B
O Team Lead - C	Make	1	0.75	0.25	0.75	Variable	Num lines - A
▼ O Senior Technical Operators - Type C	Make	3	3	0	15	Variable	Num lines - A
O Line Type C Operators	Make	11	12	.1	12	Variable	Num lines - C
O Materials In & Out Operators	Make	46	40	6	40	Variable	Total Line
▼ O Process Coordinator - Process/Mixing Room	Make	4	4	0	14	Variable	Number of Shifts
O Process/Mixing Room	Make	10	10	0	10	Variable	Total Line
O Scheduling (production planners)	Make	5	5	0	5	Variable	Total Line
▼ O Eng Manager	Engineering	0	1	-1	22	Fixed	
▼ O Asset Care Manager	Engineering	1	1	0	16	Fixed	
O Engineers (Asset Care)	Engineering	14	12	2	12	Variable	Total Line
O Storeman	Make	3	3	0	3	Fixed	Total Volume
▼ O Facilities Manager	Engineering	1	1	0	2	Fixed	
O Site Services Support	Engineering	1	1	0	1	Fixed	

Fixed Or Variable   ■ Fixed   ■ Variable

FIGURE 3.7.11   Required FTEs by role and by depth

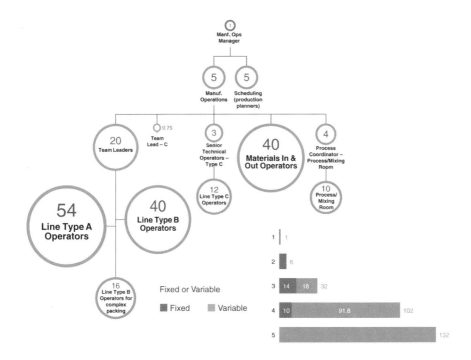

I like the scaled org chart because it helps to give a sense of proportion within the familiar org chart picture. The bar chart shows the same information, but this time how many FTEs are required by organizational depth.

Once the driver model blueprint has been developed, it is crucial to test the thinking and results. The best way to test is for a group of stakeholders to review many of the conclusions in graphical format and to see the organization in different ways. Each way is likely to raise a different question, building both confidence and refinement in the recommendations. For example, the split of the roles can be seen by depth. In Figure 3.7.11, depth 1 is the Plant Manager, who has a team of six. Again, the blue and yellow are showing the number of fixed and variable FTEs required according to driver analysis. In this example, although there were only 16 variable roles, those roles accounted for 93 per cent of the total FTEs. For the highlighted plant, the calculated FTE demand was 273 compared with the as-is number of 314, implying a potential saving of 41 or 13 per cent.

Scaling the analysis for all plants

Once the model works for one plant, the next step is to run it for all of them. In this example, the 20 plants had a total of 4,400 as-is FTEs. The driver

FIGURE 3.7.12   Scatter plot of plants FTE difference by as-is
FTEs

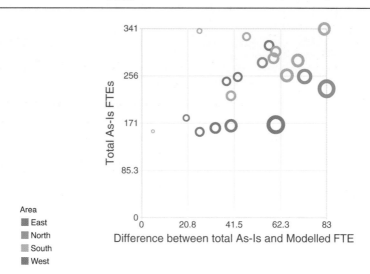

Area
- East
- North
- South
- West

model based on a standard plant org model reduced this to 3,800 or 600 fewer. The scatter plot (Figure 3.7.12) shows each plant as a circle, coloured by its geographical region. The x-axis is the difference in number of FTEs between the as-is and to-be scenarios. The y-axis is the number of current FTEs. The size of the circle (or what is often referred to as the bubble) can be any other measure: for example, the quality score, average tenure, productivity or service measures like line fill rate or a measure of the overall equipment efficiency (OEE) which is a percentage measure of the actual output versus the potential output.

Further analysis was conducted at both a function and a role level. What transpired was that some plants have significant variances at the function and role levels. Additional elements of analysis and testing included:

- Spans of control – have a max and min for each role type.
- Output measures versus the numbers; for example, revenue or units produced versus the number of FTEs, and broken down by plant clusters, for example:
  - large plants and modern;
  - large plants and old;
  - small plants.
- Quality scores for those with a higher ratio of staff in a function (for example, quality FTEs).

- Other possible drivers that are harder to quantify, but might have an impact. For instance:
  - age of the plant;
  - level of capital investment.
- Items like level of automation should be captured within the model. However, if they are not, consider this as a way of explaining the variances in the number of FTEs. If automation is a big driver, then this sort of analysis should support your business case for increasing the level of automation.

These sorts of exercises don't mean that each plant has to suddenly reduce its numbers in some sort of dogmatic way, hence the recommendation for additional analysis. There may be robust reasons for why some plants need more people relatively. For example, capital investment is required to increase the numbers of operators on Line Type B from 2.5 to 4 in many plants and the ROI from that investment might be below the minimum hurdle rate (the minimum rate of return on a project or investment required). The quality of the analysis is based on the robustness of the standard org design and the drivers selected. That requires a good understanding of many of the as-is current designs through interviews and workshops with those who manage and understand the plants.

Method 4: Mathematical modelling

In scenarios where there are system dynamics impacts, such as trying to size complex pathways where the demand and productivity are variable or when the drivers are not linear or deterministic in nature, then mathematical modelling is useful. The number of times you come across the need to understand this sort of complexity is rare. You should only use this last technique when there are system dynamics at play. An example includes queuing effects or variability in demand with target service levels that need to be achieved. Modelling is a fantastic way of testing hypotheses and scenarios in complex situations, but it is not always straightforward, and it comes with a price tag and a number of risks, for example:

- Getting lost in the detail.
- Over-complexity. The modeller becomes fixated on everything that can be done rather than what should be done. Keeping it as simple as possible is the name of the game and is really hard to do.

> Each added bit of complexity has an exponential impact on the
> modelling task.

- Poor communication. The model needs to be structured to facilitate
  communication. Assumptions need to be separated, and it should be
  easy to see the impact of changing an assumption on the key output
  parameters. The logic of the model should be structured so that
  others can understand it.

A mathematical model is a description of a system using mathematical concepts and language. Mathematical models can take many forms, including
but not limited to dynamical systems, statistical models, differential equations,
or game theoretic models. A deterministic model is one in which every set of
variable states is uniquely determined by parameters in the model and by
sets of previous states of these variables. Deterministic models perform the
same way for a given set of initial conditions. By contrast, in a stochastic
model, randomness is present. Variable assumptions have probability distri-
butions rather than just being a single number. Model complexity involves
a trade-off between simplicity and accuracy. Often it is best to start simple
and add complexity with time. It is equally important to think through the
exact questions which need to be answered first and only add complexity as
that complexity supports improving the accuracy and ability to answer
those questions. A model should have the six modules described below.

About

This should summarize the objective of the model: aims; scope; context;
history; team; versions; functionality.

Inputs

This essentially comes down to data. Start with the solid facts, and if external
data sources are used ensure it is easy to take further extracts from the
sources. Ensure that it is easy to update data loads, if you rely on external
sources. The other crucial point is to manage your metadata effectively in
separate tables. With Excel models avoid hard-coding meta tags as it will be
impossible for you to dynamically add new elements to the model. In particular, avoid hard-coding numbers to cells as these may well change over time.

Assumptions

Assumptions are also data, but they are variable and, as the term suggests,
assumed. What is important to understand about each assumption is how
changing it will impact the outputs and which ones require the greatest focus.
An example of an assumption might be how long it takes to do a certain

task on average. As explained in Chapter 3.5, it is useful to specify the minimum expected and maximum possible numbers for each assumption in order to get a sense of volatility. Equally, for each assumption, understand what the impact would be on your key output measures so that you can categorize each assumption by its Volatility Impact Category (VIC). Furthermore, with this information, it is possible to run an automated Monte Carlo analysis. By automating the sensitivity analysis and creating structure around it, you can focus management attention and you will rapidly improve the insight generated.

Working pages

Inputs and assumptions once entered into the model get manipulated to produce output calculations. A good example of this is what happens in a budget, taking past results and making assumptions about future work to create a forecast. Working pages demonstrate the manipulations so you know what is happening beneath the data; it is the logic of the model. The key is to structure these logically so that the calculations can be checked. Build flexible structures so that if you add new categories of data the model can easily accommodate them.

Outputs

The results of the calculations of the inputs and assumptions form a set of output tables or files. The key thing is to structure these so that the analysis can be flexible with slicing and dicing along any of the metadata tags.

Visuals and analysis

Develop visuals that answer the key questions the model was designed to answer. The model should feel like a presentation and help the users walk through a story.

There is a variety of tools that can help with modelling. I am going to give a brief overview of three types: Excel, Monte Carlo simulation packages and bespoke solutions. For each one I will give an overview, the advantages and disadvantages. The aim of this section is to give an introduction and help you decide which approach works best. It is not intended to teach you how to do the modelling.

Excel

- **Description/summary of approach.** When dealing with a simple model and a relatively small amount of data, Excel is probably the best tool for the job.

- **Advantage.** Excel is highly flexible and allows you to insert plugins such as the software Monte Carlo plug-in @risk, which further enhances modelling capability.
- **Disadvantage.** The visualization functionality is poor and it doesn't do discrete event simulation. The fact that it is offline makes it difficult to share with people and it is hard to maintain if you want to repeat the model – something you will often want to do.

Simul8/Monte Carlo simulation package

- **Description/summary of approach.** This off-the-shelf product helps define process and simulation rules, built for discrete event simulation.
- **Advantage.** It is more accurate than Excel and can handle more complexity.
- **Disadvantage.** It is a reasonably technical tool and will often require a third party to implement it. It can become a black hole.

Bespoke solution

- **Description/summary of approach.** There is a range of technologies: .Net, SQL, Scala and Python. You will need a range of resources to design, build and test the system. The crucial piece is the upfront definition of the method. Rapid prototyping is a must.
- **Advantage.** You can answer all possible questions and complexities.
- **Disadvantage.** Expensive and once built hard to change. Extremely difficult and expensive to build a highly usable front-end interface.

I have built a number of models over the years using all three types of approaches. I have had my share of successes and failures. You will need a range of highly specialized skills, potentially from outside your organization. If you do go down this route, be sure:

- the business case is significant;
- you have the budget and resources allocated to it;
- you allow enough time.

The process of developing your models is a learning process. As you write them you think about the nature of the problem you are trying to solve in new and deeper ways. Because of this intellectual journey, prototyping can be invaluable.

Final thoughts

Be sensitive in determining the final numbers required. The outcome of this analysis is going to lead to decisions about hiring and firing. The ability of your organization to meet its goals requires channelling the right number of resources into the key pieces of work in an optimal balance. Achieving that is no mean feat. Unfortunately, the world isn't static. The numbers of FTEs required will change and managing that ongoing demand forecasting is a central part of doing workforce planning as I will explain in Chapter 4.5.

I believe that it is time to stop leaving to chance an issue as important as the number of FTEs that should be in each role. Too often the answer comes from a combination of the four dangerous methods, namely: 1) who shouts loudest; 2) it just evolves; 3) blanket cuts across the board; 4) the magic number. I fully appreciate that the four methods you should use require investment in time and effort. These four methods (ratio analysis, activity analysis, driver analysis and mathematical modelling) don't all have to be used all the time. Mathematical modelling will rarely be used and driver analysis only in certain scenarios. I'm a big believer in activity analysis and how it can provide such a deep and rich understanding that it will transform how you think about your organization. But again, you don't need to do activity analysis for everyone. For example, certain variable roles with lots of FTEs in them can be sampled and if roles are similar, ratio and driver analysis are better tools.

The key to doing good rightsizing analysis is to use the right tools for the right set of roles. Start with the simple and add complexity if the cost of the additional robustness is worth it. Although this is very analytical, it is also one of the most emotive and politically charged topics in this book. Therefore, make it easy for your assumptions to be varied, so that sensitivity analysis can be done. Make the source and logic for all assumptions clear. Do your best to build your analysis on robust data-quality foundations and if you need to make top-down estimates, get your key stakeholders to be part of that estimating process. It is a journey and requires as much judgement as number crunching to get to the best possible answers. I say best possible, because there can be no definitive right answer. It is about getting the right balance.

By the time you have finished your rightsizing, you will be done with your design work. Now the real work starts because you have to execute that design into reality. Going back to the introduction in Chapter 3.1, there is no point just having designs on paper. Using the architectural metaphor, the drawings only have value if you turn them into buildings that people can live and work in. In other words, you have to make the design real. That is the subject of Part Four of this book.

Remember this

1 Ensure you define and get sign-off for the methods you are going to use to rightsize.

2 Don't use poor magic numbers to deterministically produce the answer. An example is assuming the span of control should be eight.

3 Activity analysis is powerful, will support writing robust business cases and ensures everyone focuses on the right thing.

4 In situations where you have large numbers of variable roles, use driver analysis to estimate the numbers.

5 Sophisticated modelling methods like Monte Carlo simulation have their place in highly complex settings, but in those settings the other three methods should still be applied as a way of triangulating your answers.

Notes

1 Simon, B (1998) Max Ringelmann (1861–1931) et la recherche en machinisme agricole, in *Cahiers d'Histoire et de Philosophie des Sciences, No. 46: Histoire de la méchanique appliquée. Enseignement, recherche et pratiques mécaniciennes en France après 1880*, Fontanon, C (ed), pp 47–55, ENS Editions, Paris

2 *Harvard Business Review* (2012) How many direct reports?, April [accessed online 12 January 2015] https://hbr.org/2012/04/how-many-direct-reports/ar/1

PART FOUR
Making it Real

Introduction

Theories are always very thin and insubstantial;
experience only is tangible. HOSEA BALLOU

What is Making it Real?

Good strategy is strategy that is executed.[1] Up to now, we have been in the world of theory and design, of concepts and how things should work in a stylized and abstract way. If we stop now, I fear there is a large chance that you would be worse off. You would have thrown great concepts around, created a huge amount of work and built large expectations. This book is intended to help you achieve and sustain your competitive edge through effective, data-driven organizational design. It isn't the design, however, that will ensure you get the edge; it is the execution of the design. You know you need to eat fewer calories than you burn to lose weight, but will you actually do it? An architect can draw hundreds of pictures, floor plans and electrical schemas, but if nothing is built, then so what? The only value of a theory is if it works in practice. It is easy to live in the world of theory, plans or designs. It is safe. Changes, scenarios and tweaks can be made without an impact. But, once a design or plan has been decided upon, then what? How do you ensure success? How do you sustain it? How do you mitigate the downside risks?

The first thing is to realize that no matter how good the design is, no matter how much you have thought about it, you will have missed many elements and that the design won't be 100 per cent right. It is going to need to change and you need to be comfortable with that notion. The second thing to realize is that we don't live in a bubble and circumstances will change, so you need to be alert and adaptable. The third thing is: this is a learning process. Every day we learn more. We refine and with luck improve. Lastly, no matter how hard you think it is going to be, it will be harder. But I believe one of the strengths of many of the people who do great things is a kind of forecast optimism bias. They believe they can do more, faster, better than you could realistically expect. And then once they push forward, with more than normal resilience, somehow they achieve it.

Making it Real isn't just about running through all steps in an implementation process. It is about winning the hearts and minds of everyone involved so that they are willing to make it a success. Figure 4.1.1 highlights the importance of moving the perception of change from being uncertain, full of fear and lacking intrinsic motivation for the workforce to one where everyone is full of growing optimism, a clear understanding of what will change and why, together with the highest possible levels of motivation of where you want to move them from and to. The last point is probably the most important. As Daniel Pink wrote in his book *Drive*, there are three things that make a role in the knowledge economy truly engaging: purpose, autonomy and mastery.[2] The micro design creates the structure that ensures that each of these three conditions of achieving highly motivated employees is possible:

- Purpose is provided by the vision and strategy, as outlined in Chapter 2.2, but also in ensuring each employee has meaningful personal objectives, as discussed in Chapter 3.3.

- Autonomy means defining the accountabilities and decisions to strike the right balance between top-down control and the autonomy that so many people desperately seek. Chapter 3.4 discussed how to define the accountabilities using the RAS framework described in Chapter 1.3.

- Mastery is best achieved when employees are working within the flow channel as described in Chapter 3.6. It is not only developing competencies to the highest possible levels and being great at what you do, it is also being sufficiently challenged in the process.

In other words, if you have done the macro and micro designs well, you are positioning yourself perfectly to create an organization of highly motivated and engaged people.

But even with all the strengths and possible upsides, the most important question to tackle is whether you are brave enough and committed enough to go for it. Be under no illusions as to how tough it is likely to be. Structure the work into bite-size chunks so that it doesn't overwhelm you. Learn how to be both brave and realistic. Improve the odds of success and make the process of doing so rewarding. In order to become fit, to become a top

FIGURE 4.1.1   Position the change from uncertainty, fear and unengaged people to optimism, transparency and high levels of motivation

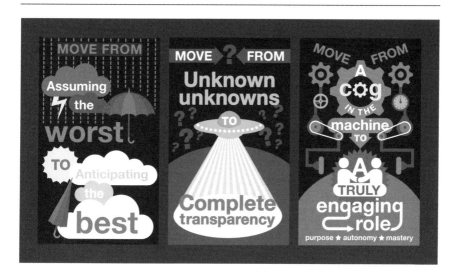

athlete, you have to find a way to enjoy training. Similarly, to get the competitive edge, you have to find a way to enjoy the journey and build in institutional resilience.

Realize the design is only a sketch

Economics is a dismal science. As people often say, put six economists in a room, ask for their opinion, and you will have seven or more opinions. It is not dismal because 'economists' are unintelligent or lazy. It is because the subject is just so hard. Unfortunately, it can't all be captured in mathematical equations, but still we try. We try because we need to improve our understanding and the only way to achieve that understanding is by simplification. On the first day of my economics education we were taught a model of perfect competition where no businesses are large enough to have market power; where there are infinite numbers of buyers and sellers; with no entry or exit barriers; all products are the same; everyone has perfect information and everyone is rational. This model allows would-be economists to learn how firms would maximize their profit and how prices would be set. The model is useful not because it is so accurate – the number of markets that operate 'perfectly' is clearly limited – but because it provides a base against which adding in more complexity can be tested. It enables us to ask: What if there were only one company or piece of imperfect information or product differentiation? With the relaxing of each assumption comes a host of new insights into how the world works. Only once something is understandable, in simple form, can more complexity – more truth – be added.

What is interesting, in the social sciences at least, is that our understanding of this world changes it. For example, option pricing theory has led to more sophisticated instruments, which change how capital is allocated and returns for investors are maximized. In many respects, organization design in large organizations is not too dissimilar. It is an intellectual model of something too complex for us to fully understand. Our model has to be simple enough for one to understand. It is a model of reality, not reality itself. But like option pricing, the model will affect reality. By defining who is responsible for what and how many of a given role are required, it will change how people behave, what they do and how successful the organization will be in achieving its goals. However, it isn't reality. Employees won't and shouldn't just do what is written down in their job spec. The activities described in the activity analysis do not reflect all the activities that happen or should happen. It is a guide. Reality is what all those people actually do on a minute-by-minute basis. It is how decisions are really made during unstructured conversations in corridors, by coffee machines, at the bar or just popping into an office, as well as in those structured meetings.

We try to make our designs more complex, in order to deal with the greater complexity. Multiple reporting lines and complex matrixes are examples of this. But we can't make our design too complex to understand. We shouldn't even try to define everything. The idea is to define enough so that everyone is clear as to what they need to do. Where does their role start and stop relative to others? What should success look and feel like?

Structure and logic for Part Four

The metaphor that is used to structure this section is that of a Formula 1 race team. There are three phases in a race. First, there is the *pre-race* preparation and planning. Second, there is the *in-race* delivery and reacting to events on the ground. Third is the *post-race* tracking of the results, root-cause analysis of what went well and what could be improved, together with celebrating the achievements. The pre-race preparation includes detailing how it will all work with a range of decisions that need to be made. It is where you have the luxury of time to think it all through and aim to maximize your chances of success. It should include practising and 'what ifs'. It is thinking through how it will really work in practice; understanding the impact from all the key angles; planning for empathetic communication. There are two chapters dedicated to this pre-race phase: Chapters 4.3 and 4.4.

Chapter 4.3, HOWWIP or How will it work in practice, deals with 'visioning' the new work, and understanding the issues that will be thrown up, knowing how they will be resolved and understanding the interfaces between various positions and functions. A range of practical team exercises is provided to enable the key players to fully test how the new organization will work and how they will work together.

Chapter 4.4 covers implementation. It starts with how to do the range of impact assessment analyses required. From this understanding is derived the selection process for determining who is to get what job and why. Within this are a number of legal and consultation considerations. We are talking about human impacts and aiming to drive a new organization forward. Good communication is crucial but all too often left as an afterthought. At the end of Chapter 4.4 you will have learnt how to fully transition the entire organization from the as-is to the to-be world, and you will know how to generate a clear audit trail for every judgement and decision made.

Military strategists say that a plan lasts until first contact with the enemy. As soon as the plan starts to be executed, you are in the race. Unforeseen events start to impact and, therefore, change it. Unfortunately, you can't think of everything during the pre-race phase. It is about having the right feedback loops to know when something has changed; to know what to do to stay in the race; to be better at reacting to things than your competitors and take advantage of any changes; to be sufficiently nimble. The micro design phase is an explicit world of two points in time, the as-is and to-be states. This doesn't reflect how things will really be. Time is continuous and ever changing. Therefore, in order to make the design real, you need to have the analytical tools to manage that ongoing evolution. You need to be able to track how you are doing versus the initial set of plans (which become your targets). But as things change, your targets will change too. These become your forecasts.

Chapter 4.5 is about how to plan the supply and demand of your workforce over time, and how to track actuals against these targets and forecasts. To me, workforce planning is just an extension of the micro design and inextricably linked to it. Unfortunately, there is confusion as to what it really is and what the differences are between strategic, operational and tactical workforce planning. This chapter details the definitions of each together with how to do both the strategic and the operational planning. Because we are dealing with people and talent over time, Chapter 4.6 highlights how to do data-driven succession planning. It describes how to ensure you have the right talent in the right roles so that you can manage the evolution of your workforce over time.

This is a book about getting and sustaining the competitive edge. I didn't want it to stop with planning and managing the transition. An organization is only successful if the strategy is being met and the goals are being achieved. To do this, an organization has to get things done. There is a wealth of good practice and I describe how to take advantage of that practice within this broader context in Chapter 4.7. The post-race phase is the reflective phase and is covered in the Chapter 4.8. It deals with how you did. Did you meet the goals and how do you ensure you continue to do so? If you didn't or are not meeting the goals then what was the root cause? However, what is the point of just getting all this work done? We need more than that. What better way to finish than with celebrating and then giving a chance for the organization to rest, recoup and prepare for the next stage in its journey? It isn't all about work. We are human. Our bodies and minds need downtime. Time to rejuvenate. If all has gone well, if we meet or exceed our goals, then celebrate. At the end of the day, when top sports teams win trophies, they sing, spray champagne and party. Why shouldn't we?

Keeping that end in mind and before we get into all this planning, delivery and reviewing, it is worthwhile to take a step back and think through how many things can and will go wrong. Too many implementations go wrong for predictable reasons. Chapter 1.2 mostly focused on the macro and micro challenges. It was too early to focus on all the traps resulting from implementation and making the design real. But it is now time and, therefore, Chapter 4.2 highlights all the common traps with a focus on how to mitigate three specific ones.

Notes

1 Thought to have first been said by Peter Drucker, the founder of modern management.

2 Pink, D H (2011) *Drive: The surprising truth about what motivates us*, Canongate Books Ltd, Edinburgh

Common traps

Man is the only kind of varmint that sets his own trap, baits it, then steps in it. JOHN STEINBECK

Introduction

When it comes to a redesign or transformation there is so much that can go wrong. In some respects it would be a surprise if any implementation was ever 100 per cent successful and was implemented as anticipated. There are traps everywhere and a lot of the Making it Real section deals with how to avoid them. But to avoid them you need to recognize and understand them. In this chapter I begin by outlining some of the signs that indicate when things may not be going to plan. I then highlight some of the common traps you are likely to come across and explore three in detail: not allocating enough resource; too many initiatives; and forgetting the basics. This is the shortest chapter in the book because much of the detail is covered within other chapters. However, I didn't feel I could write a book on design without going into the traps in a little detail. Also, much of dealing with these traps is mindset. If you can begin to predict what's coming and recognize when things are going wrong, then the probability of the success of your design will increase.

Knowing when and what things are going wrong

To ensure an organization design remains on track the first thing is to recognize when things are going wrong. So what are the common signs that something is going wrong during the implementation of a new organization design? This list is not intended to be exhaustive. Common examples include:

- a feeling you are just shifting boxes around org charts rather than implementing real, visible change on the ground;
- challenges from people that jobs are being allocated based on personal connections rather than competencies;

- lots of one-to-one side meetings to share concerns and find out what's really going on;

- meeting mania where people are constantly in meetings with an excessive number of participants;

- initiative fatigue with a feeling of achieving little while being too busy to change that fact;

- absenteeism and attrition increase with key talent leaving for competitors;

- having a lack of clear priorities as to what needs to be done and why it is needed;

- discussions and debates are becoming personal and are damaging relationships.

These are signs that the implementation of the design is being ineffective. So what are the possible root cause factors that drive this? There are countless examples, so I have included a sample, as shown in Figure 4.2.1. The common traps are organized into six broad themes.

There are a lot of things that can go wrong and this list isn't even exhaustive. That is why Making it Real is such a crucial section. It is the make or break time. You have to draw attention to these traps before and during the implementation of the design. To understand the traps specific to your design, before you implement do a post-mortem analysis. Gather your implementation team into a room and imagine you have just finished the design. Then, working backwards through the timeline, ask everyone to say 'what went wrong' and 'what the impact was'. This acts as a great way to uncover possible traps before you start and to document risks and priorities for the implementation. A lot of the chapters throughout this book are designed to deal with many of the specific traps in the areas they cover. However, I want to expand on three generic traps, which I believe can often be the main cause for a design derailing. The three traps I have chosen to address here are:

1 not allocating enough resource;

2 too many initiatives;

3 forgetting the basics.

Not allocating enough resource

Months and months can be spent on doing the macro and micro design, and they often overrun. However, implementation milestones are still expected

FIGURE 4.2.1   List of example traps

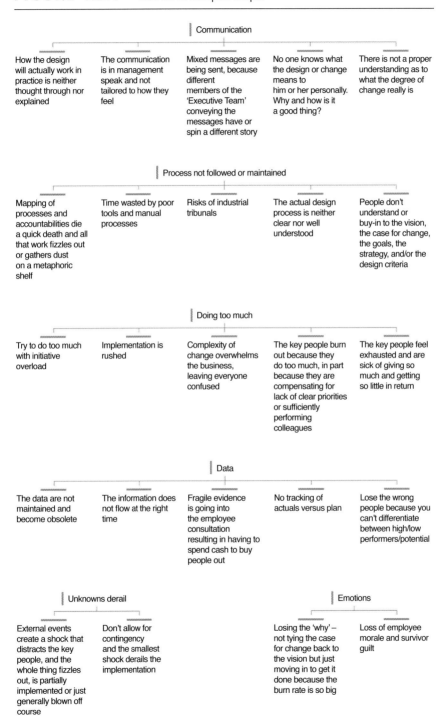

Communication

| How the design will actually work in practice is neither thought through nor explained | The communication is in management speak and not tailored to how they feel | Mixed messages are being sent, because different members of the 'Executive Team' conveying the messages have or spin a different story | No one knows what the design or change means to him or her personally. Why and how is it a good thing? | There is not a proper understanding as to what the degree of change really is |

Process not followed or maintained

| Mapping of processes and accountabilities die a quick death and all that work fizzles out or gathers dust on a metaphoric shelf | Time wasted by poor tools and manual processes | Risks of industrial tribunals | The actual design process is neither clear nor well understood | People don't understand or buy-in to the vision, the case for change, the goals, the strategy, and/or the design criteria |

Doing too much

| Try to do too much with initiative overload | Implementation is rushed | Complexity of change overwhelms the business, leaving everyone confused | The key people burn out because they do too much, in part because they are compensating for lack of clear priorities or sufficiently performing colleagues | The key people feel exhausted and are sick of giving so much and getting so little in return |

Data

| The data are not maintained and become obsolete | The information does not flow at the right time | Fragile evidence is going into the employee consultation resulting in having to spend cash to buy people out | No tracking of actuals versus plan | Lose the wrong people because you can't differentiate between high/low performers/potential |

Unknowns derail

| External events create a shock that distracts the key people, and the whole thing fizzles out, is partially implemented or just generally blown off course | Don't allow for contingency and the smallest shock derails the implementation |

Emotions

| Losing the 'why' – not tying the case for change back to the vision but just moving in to get it done because the burn rate is so big | Loss of employee morale and survivor guilt |

to adhere to original timescales. Because management is involved closely with macro and micro design, and these stages are theoretical, the impact of the delays are not as keenly felt as those working on making the design real. Having put the macro and micro design in place alongside an implementation plan, it is often assumed by management that the design will 'just happen'. All too often senior managers stay clear of the detailed nature of implementation, leaving it to junior resources. The result is that the execution is not managed or tracked properly.

To get an implementation right takes considerable effort. If anything, executive sponsorship needs to be more committed and public than in the macro and micro design. The risk with the macro and micro design is going into too much detail. The risk within Making it Real is not going into enough detail. Making it Real is all about a conscientious, thorough and dogmatic eye for detail and approach to delivery. You will need resilience and you will need to stick at it (something I come back to in the conclusion). There are no hard-and-fast rules here in terms of the numbers of resources needed or the time required (for more on project management read Chapter 3.5). However, before you go into your implementation make sure you have:

- a detailed plan with appropriate staffing;
- significant contingency times in place as not everything will go to plan;
- an appropriate budget – *you can't afford not to.*

Too many initiatives

In January and February 2011 I had the privilege of interviewing a series of senior executives from the world of private equity. They were a mix of members of value enhancement teams, chief experience officers (CXOs) and investment committee decision makers. The focus of the interviews was to acquire an understanding of 'how private equity firms can best ensure they enhance the value of their investments'. One of the questions I asked each interviewee was: 'Why do things fail?' Remarkably, every single person gave the exact same answer:

'Things failed in the past because an organization was trying to do too much.'

They all agreed that too many high-level initiatives and too much change leads to inevitable failure. When I asked what the ideal number of initiatives was for a business at any one time, the highest number given was six. My main takeaway from this was that it is all about choosing your priorities when implementing your design. Go back to your macro design. What are you trying to achieve and what is your case for change? Based on these, pick the most important initiatives to implement first. Be wise in that choice. Don't pick too many and ensure you see them through. And when you think they are done, you are probably only halfway there. To make something real, to make it truly sustainable, takes years of effort. It takes a dogged and relentless commitment to a limited set of initiatives. Less is more. When it comes to implementing your organization design it is all about getting things done (a subject I return to in Chapter 4.7).

Forgetting the basics

When you look across disciplines such as sport, those who are at the top of their game emphasize the same point: they train and train until they can execute their basic skills to perfection without a moment's hesitation. However, when it comes to business, we struggle with the basics. We struggle to communicate effectively, sort our management information, be clear about who is doing what by when, plan and know the plan seamlessly, and fundamentally, be clear about why we are doing what we are aiming to do in the first place.

Getting the basics right means knowing what is core to your organization and ensuring you are world-class at achieving that core. This approach is central to both good strategy and the execution of that strategy. Go back to micro design and define the core goals, objectives, processes and competencies. It might sound simple, but the process of defining which of the elements within the micro design is core will make your design team think and debate more than almost anything else. Try to keep it focused and principled. Once you are clear as to what is truly core, ensure you achieve those objectives, run those processes seamlessly and grow those competencies.

In terms of the organizational design basics, this is a long book with lots of details. But if I was going to prioritize three elements from each section required for the implementation of the design they would be:

Macro:

- A clear vision, strategy, case for change and design criteria.
- A clear target operating model that ties the structural design to the value chain through a high-level accountability matrix (RAS).
- A clear and compelling business case.

Micro:

- A solid understanding of the as-is and to-be organizations, in terms of headcount and cost by role, including the detailing of reporting lines.
- A clear definition of the work required using the Level 1 process map and what each role is responsible for.
- A robust logic for determining the numbers of FTEs required in the to-be model as detailed in Chapter 3.7.

Final thoughts

Murphy's Law is an old adage that states 'anything that can go wrong, will go wrong'. I think this is a very apt phrase when making a design real. No matter how well you plan or how great your design process is, in implementing change and striving to achieve your organization's vision and goals, many things can and will go wrong. There can be an exodus of talent, lawsuits for discrimination and unfair dismissal, paralysis, companywide confusion and a breakdown of trust, to name but a few of the many consequences. These and other issues are caused by a range of bad management practices and most are avoidable. To some extent, you can even plan for the unforeseeable by committing enough of the right resource and allowing enough time.

I think everything I've said in this chapter and everything that I'm going to say in the Making it Real section is just business basics. I hope the remainder of this book will give you a roadmap for effective execution. It isn't just about planning or implementation. It is about achieving the desired results without falling into a range of predictable traps. If I've done my job right, there is no reason to be fooled by these traps because, I hope, enough of them are now clear so that you have sufficient reserves to deal with those that are not clear.

Remember this

1 Watch out for and recognize signs that indicate the design isn't being implemented according to plan.

2 Make sure you think through the possible traps before doing your implementation.

3 Ensure you allocate enough time and resource to the implementation.

4 Have a limited number of priority initiatives at one time so that the implementation doesn't get overloaded and stall.

5 If you have done a good job on the macro and micro design simply focus on getting the basics right for the implementation and the rest will follow.

HOWWIP

> *In theory, there is no difference between theory and practice. But in practice, there is.* ANON

Introduction

I love acronyms because they communicate whole ideas and methods in one short, memorable word. One of my favourites is HOWWIP, which is short for *How will it work in practice?* This acronym came up when doing a particularly complex and detailed project with a colleague and it has stuck with me ever since. The reason why I like it so much is it is a very quick and easy reminder to think through how something will work in reality. Much of this book so far has been focused on theoretical design. This chapter is about making sure the theoretical is really possible, and how to make it work in practice, and I mean *really* work. Does everybody know what he or she is doing from day one of the implementation through to two months down the line?

In reality, the HOWWIP question is one which will have been naturally popping up throughout the design process. Think back to the dreamer, realist and critic in Chapter 2.3. Throughout the steps in the macro and micro phases, the issue of whether something is practical or not will have already been addressed. The reason for spelling it out at this point is to ensure the detail has been thought through. It acts as a natural check on the implementation to head off issues before they arise, and to uncover the answers to the questions that haven't been asked yet.

A large part of Making it Real is getting people's heads around what the design really means to them personally, how they will be affected and how they expect it to work. In this sense, this chapter links very closely with Chapter 4.7 on organizational getting things done. After all, if people don't know what they should be doing, how are they going to get it done? Furthermore, it is the process 'exceptions' that can drive the majority of the work. By bringing the design to life, focus on how the new design will deal with things like:

- What to do when actual performance is adrift from budget?
- When there is an 'event' like a safety incident or an embarrassing PR incident, what happens?

- What happens if the two approvers for a given decision can't agree?
- How does the implementation team hand over to the ongoing service team?

Part of this process is about the interface design; how items of work will be handed from one person to another. Another part is bringing tangible clarity to what can seem like a pretty theoretical design. To see a decision matrix with a set of acronyms such as RAS (responsible, approve, support) is one thing; to understand what 'approve' or 'support' really means in the context of that decision is another. For example, 'approve' the recruiting plan might have the Finance Director, HRD and Business Director with A's for approve. The key is to think through the practicalities of delivering those processes. It anticipates issues and deals with them. The approval process could be that a hire form is filled in by the second Tuesday of every month and signed off in a committee meeting of approvers, or that all roles must be in the budget that is signed off annually, with a separate exception process that requires the CEO to approve. Beyond this, what information needs to be produced by whom? Does HR need to come with job specs and the expected hiring costs? For certain roles, does the requester need to produce a business plan? If yes, what needs to be on that plan?

HOWWIP is both a natural ongoing process through the design and implementation as well as a practical framework for structuring a set of workshops or exercises. In this chapter I will work through three exercises that I have found useful in testing the feasibility of a design implementation. These are simply tools to help you think through exceptions and issues; to discover the sorts of things that will trip the design up so you can prepare effectively for the change to come.

HOWWIP outcomes

Before jumping into the exercises it is worth demonstrating how they fit into the bigger picture, and how they can be documented in a useful manner as part of the overall project. The point of the exercises is to clarify answers to the question 'How will that work?' These answers are worth recording if they are going to be of ongoing use, as people won't remember later on, and the same questions often pop up from numerous sources. Another point is that sometimes a question cannot be answered immediately. By noting it down it gives you the time to think it over before fleshing out the detail, without it being lost and forgotten. I am not suggesting you need to note down everything, and quite often it simply requires adding to existing documentation, but depending on the level of work, independent documentation can be invaluable. There are three documents you can produce:

1 **HOWWIP log.** The HOWWIP log is almost like an FAQ list combined with a car park list. As you are detailing the processes in your workshops, questions and concerns will be raised that you won't have time to deal with immediately. So you 'park' them. Those parked questions get written into a log. So that you can structure it, link the questions to the Level 2 value chain and main activity it relates to. It is helpful to provide a priority rating so that you can manage the order in which questions need to be dealt with, together with an audit trail of when the question was raised, by whom and what the status of the question is. As you answer the questions, document the outcome. Figure 4.3.1 shows a simple example log investigating the efficiency of a sales process for a delivery and support team.

Process descriptors: For those processes which are relatively simple, all you need is a quick one- or two-line descriptor on the steps of a Level 1 value chain process map. The descriptor should give a little more detail so that it is obvious what is meant by each step. If a question was raised in the HOWWIP log, it is also good to include the answer within this descriptor. For example, the process could be 'Annual budget' and the descriptor 'How the annual budget is generated, reviewed, approved and managed in-year'.

FIGURE 4.3.1   HOWWIP issues log example

Item	Nearest Current Activity	Level 2 Activity	Question	Priority	Raised	Closed	Who	Status	Outcome	Comment
					Dates					
1	Solution Design	Proposal	How to flag...	M	Tuesday, 03/03/2015		Rupert/ Peter	Open		Affects sales...
2	New Client Sale	Proposal	Why is it that...	H	Thursday, 02/04/2015	Thursday, 09/04/2015	Rupert	Closed	A level 2 activity...	n/a
3	Issue Management	Issue Triage	Why does Support...	H	Thursday, 02/04/2015		Michael	Open		For example...
4	Customer Care	Monitor Customer Satisfaction	Customers who...	L	Thursday, 02/04/2015		Michael	Open		The worry is that...
5	Solution Design	Data Integration	All too often...	H	Tuesday, 07/04/2015		Ben	Open		A bad data...

2 **Detailed process**. There are going to be instances where the detail is just too complex; where there are loops, branching of activities and systems required to support the process. Where there is clear use for a subset of detailed workflows and the number of positions involved is three or more, then detail the Level 2 process swim-lane map described in Chapter 3.4. In Chapter 3.4 I mentioned how most design only needs to be based on Level 0 and 1 maps. To recap, Level 0 is a summary value chain map used in designing the target operating model while Level 1 is the processes depicted as value chain steps in a hierarchy, with activities, decisions and outcomes listed below each process or subprocess.

Level 2 is a swim lane with owners and icons representing various actions such as: decision; activity; subprocess; and outputs. Figure 4.3.2 shows an example of how a support desk might deal with client issues.

Each row, or what looks like a swim lane, is a function or position. There are a clear start and end, so a sense of timing can be shown and the number of handoffs (interfaces) counted. A 'swim-lane Level 2 process map' details how a process should work. My experience is that these have their time and place, but should be started with caution. They can be confusing, they are

FIGURE 4.3.2   Level 2 process map example

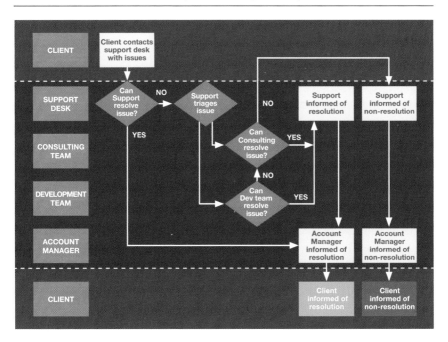

idealistic, they can be hard to follow and they take lots of time to generate. So don't try to define everything as a Level 2 process map. Just do it where: there are lots of handoffs; when a fairly strict process should be followed; where there are loops and complexities. Count the number of handoffs and ask whether that is going to be workable. The number of times that I have seen 15+ handoffs within a single process is pretty remarkable. I've seen processes take three months to execute when it should have been possible to do them in a week.

For example, a few years ago I worked with a pharmaceutical client on its promotional meeting process. The number of meetings reduced by over 50 per cent due to the client's need to meet increasing compliance requirements. The sales and marketing teams had to fill in complex requests, get financial and compliance approvals together, and complete a range of questionnaires. It took months to get decisions through and everyone spent time waiting for everyone else. So we mapped the as-is Level 2 process and saw that there were 16 handoffs. We quantified the times taken and where the bottlenecks were. Once this was done it was pretty straightforward to reengineer the process and identify a simple workflow system that automatically tracked various SLAs to ensure the to-be process would work. Within months, the number of promotional meetings returned to the desired levels.

Exercises

These exercises are simply tools to solicit where the issues will be and get to the point of answering them. A great deal of the purpose in these is simply to encourage people to talk about and to visualize what is ahead of them. I have three simple examples:

Exercise 1 – Talk through the process with cards

Top sportspeople spend a lot of time visualizing each element and scenario. They think through how it will work and feel. This exercise aims to replicate that in a group setting. Take one subprocess that involves interaction at many points within the business – for example, recruitment, L&D or appraisals. For each step, print out the cards described in Chapter 3.4. Lay the cards out in order on the table.

- Define where the process starts and finishes.
- Identify the points where there are handoffs.

- Define in the Inputs; Activities; Outputs at each stage plus any decisions.
- Test that the process will work and that it is clear:
  - List a set of questions concerning how the process will work.
  - Have a group stand up in a small circle with each person in the circle 'acting' one (or more if there are more roles than people in the circle, but always being clear what role each person is 'playing' at any time) of the roles. Start with the first step and then pass a 'who's got the monkey'[1] juggling ball to the person who acts next. The monkey is a metaphor for who is responsible at that point in time.
  - At each step, say: what it is you need; what you will do; and what the outcome will be. By walking the process, each person talks through what they do and how they will do it.
- Write up any orphans (activities or decisions that don't have an owner), gaps, issues and questions on the HOWWIP log.
- Review after the completion of an area to understand the amount of workload that was missing from the original description.

Exercise 2 – Interface ball game

Building on exercise 1, a good game to play is the 'interface ball game'. The main issue this game addresses is sorting how the interfaces between people will work; to understand who does what, and how information and work are transferred between people. The way the game works follows the process described below:

1 A process is chosen. For example, the client issue resolution process illustrated in Figure 4.3.2.

2 Those involved in the process stand up (or someone acts as if they are one of the participants in the process).

3 The facilitator gives a context to a selected situation and then asks practical questions; for example, 'What happens when the client contacts us with an issue?'

4 The person responsible for the first action raises his or her hand and catches a ball thrown by the facilitator (in this instance the Support Manager). The person with the ball then talks through with the group:
  - What they need: 'Detailed description of the issue from the client.'
  - What they do: 'Understand and document the issue for internal purposes.'

    – The outcomes they have generated: 'Resolve the issue within the support team or triage the issue to the consulting or development team.'

5 The person who then needs to pick up the next action raises his or her hand and receives the ball from the first person. They repeat the three points (Need; Do; Outcome).

6 This continues until the process is completed.

For the game to work, it needs to have enough pace; those with the ball need to be succinct and to the point. Short punchy sentences and humility are at a premium. If people are unclear, have a brief discussion and try to resolve the issue. If it is too difficult to resolve, then capture it as an issue for the HOWWIP log and move on. This requires excellent facilitation and documentation skills. Ideally, these are two different people. One capturing the details of what people say; what they need; how it works; concerns and issues. The other, the facilitator, needs to keep the game going and needs to keep it playful. Equally important is picking good processes to talk through. Start with the blatantly obvious and incredibly easy ones. Get everyone familiar and comfortable with how to play and then add complexity.

Exercise 3 – The round robin interface conversations

Another good exercise is to get a group of people together who will be working cross functionally and where there are lots of connection points. The way the game works is everyone has a conversation with everyone else and a facilitator documents the conversations. Each 'date' follows a pattern of both parties writing down:

- What they need from the other person/position (each person is representing a position, but it is ideal for the person who will occupy that position to be preparing and participating in the date).

- Things they are unsure about. For instance, who will be doing something or when something will be done.

The first person then states what he or she needs and the second person seeks clarification or raises an issue if he or she believes that something shouldn't or can't be provided. This is then repeated the other way around. Finally, there is a discussion about the lists of items both parties are unsure about with a goal of resolving as many issues in the list as possible. The key to making this work is good time management and like so many things in life, good preparation. Try to keep each date to 15–30 minutes. Bear in mind that if there are eight positions, then everyone will have seven conversations. So with seven 30-minute conversations, scene setting and coffee breaks, that is a good half-day session. But if done well, 56 detailed interface conversations have taken place in a focused and controlled way. This is far better than everyone scrabbling around independently trying to work it out. (For an example of how to organize this type of session, see the Appendix.)

Below is an example of the type of conversation you are trying to facilitate. This is between a Project Manager (PM) who delivers a client solution and the Support Manager (SM) who will look after the client from that delivery point to discuss the handover and possible ongoing issues:

SM: Prior to the end of a project, I need to know the scope and issues with the client. What did we deliver? What is different? Who are the key stakeholders?

PM: OK – I will provide a detailed list answering each of these questions. In addition, I'll talk you through the key concerns and issues. I will ensure you know who the key users and super users are.

SM: My fear is the support test will become a training desk if we are not careful. So if there are continued user issues down to poor understanding on items that should be covered by the training, would you mind calling the client to verify the issues and test what a solution might be?

PM: That is a great point and valid concern. I will ensure only those who have attended super-user training will be able to call the support desk. Equally, I will test their understanding and will follow up one week after the training to ensure they are comfortable.

These conversations are important because they get right into the detail. Commitments are being made to each other, which can be captured in the process charts as 'Outcomes', Level 2 process maps, if needed, or the Give and Get matrix.

Exercise 4 – Give and Get matrix

Building on Exercise 3 is the Give and Get matrix that summarizes what each position will give to a list of other functions and, therefore, in turn, what it will get in return. Another way to think of this is as an enabler and

FIGURE 4.3.3 Example Give and Get matrix

Get \ Give	ACCOUNT MANAGER	PROJECT MANAGER	SUPPORT TEAM
ACCOUNT MANAGER		→ Project update → Budget update → Overview of proposed solution	→ Product usage report → Customer satisfaction reports → Escalation of issues
PROJECT MANAGER	→ Client deliverables → High-level design → Budget and commercials		→ Product usage report → Client issue report
SUPPORT TEAM	→ Proposal → Commercials	→ Detailed solution design and implementation documentation → Deliverables update	

dependency matrix. What will each position enable another position to do? What does each position depend on from each other one? The way it works best is to create a large matrix on a wall and for those in each position to list what they will give and get. For example, Figure 4.3.3 illustrates a Give and Get matrix for the different people involved in a sales process.

An example of the effectiveness of this technique occurred on a supply chain transformation project in East Africa. My client was growing rapidly and needed to overhaul the processes, physical network and flows, inventory and organization. To transform, we defined 13 projects. Each project had a business case in terms of CapEx and operational investment, benefits, cash flow, payback, Net Present Value (NPV) and Return on Investment (ROI). My concern was that the client would salami-slice the highest ROI projects and those that didn't require much investment. There was a risk that some of the key enabler projects that didn't provide a strong return on their own would be pushed into the long grass, and that the client wouldn't see the strategy as an integrated strategy. But how could we communicate that to the board? What we did was to create the dependency matrix and then we used that matrix to quantify the set of relationships as shown in Figure 4.3.4.

FIGURE 4.3.4 Dependency matrix scatter plot

Impact vs Dependence by Label sized by Investment

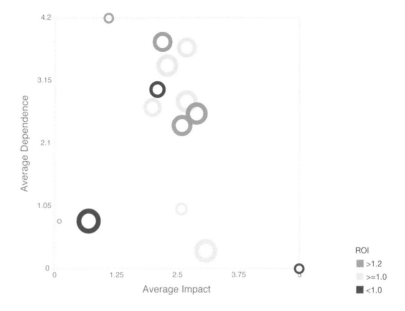

There was only one project that was a true island. It didn't enable any other projects and only relied on one. The island projects are shown in the left-hand corner. There were a couple that were only enablers (bottom right-hand corner) and one that relied on 12 of the 13 others (top-left corner). However, eight of them were a combination of relying on and enabling four to seven of the other projects. Those are the clustered projects in the centre of the scatter plot. The size of the circle reflects the level of investment required while the colour is the ROI, from negative (red) to below the hurdle rate (amber) to above the hurdle rate (green).

Final thoughts

HOWWIP is about how it will work, pure and simple. During the design process, it can all get a little too theoretical. There are hundreds of really simple questions that need answering. Not all those questions can be answered during the design phase, but the HOWWIP aims to address the nitty-gritty of how things will really work.

Embrace the HOWWIP. Embrace making things real and thinking through how stuff will really work. In my experience, it is only at the HOWWIP stage that you know whether the design will really work. It is the place where you will get the 'Oh no!' and 'We really need to work that one out' moments as well as the 'Ah-ha' ones and 'Yes, I can finally see how this is actually going to work.' It is where it all starts to become real.

> ### Remember this
>
> 1 When thinking through the implementation, document the questions and issues that arise so you can flag them and, where possible, address them.
>
> 2 Use process cards to help you work through and summarize processes and handovers.
>
> 3 Facilitate conversations between people at the interface of handovers by using games such as the interface ball game or structured round robin workshops.
>
> 4 Map out the handovers so you can see when and where dependencies interact and ensure they will support each other.
>
> 5 Keep asking *How will it work in practice* throughout every stage of the design.

Note

1 See https://hbr.org/1999/11/management-time-whos-got-the-monkey/ar/1

Implementation

A good idea is about ten per cent implementation and hard work, and luck is 90 per cent. GUY KAWASAKI

Introduction

Once you have done all your detailed design and developed a strong perspective about how it will work, it is time to implement it. This is both a change process and a mechanical one governed by law. It requires you to take everyone with you and for you to follow the right steps at the right time. As soon as employees hear there is change, they will immediately start internalizing a range of questions: What do you really mean by change? How will it affect me? Is my job on the line? Should I get my CV out there? What do I tell my family and friends? It is emotional and the first instinct that most people have is to think about all the downsides. Even those employees who are not directly impacted will still be affected by how those who *are* impacted are treated and the fairness of the process.

What you will notice is that a great deal of the work required in making the change happen actually starts at the early macro and micro stages – this is where all that work comes into its own. One of the big risks is that you see the macro, micro and Making it Real phases as fully sequential. Although one follows another for the most part, this is not strictly the case. For example, the communication and consultation phases need to start way before you get to the implementation. They start right from the beginning, and in reality never stop.

This chapter outlines several important areas of consideration when doing your implementation. I begin by going through how to quantify what will actually change through an impact assessment. I then explore how to develop your communication strategy in a way that is not only thorough, but also truly empathetic so you bring people along the journey with you. The last section focuses on managing the transition and ensuring you run a legal and fair consultation process at group and individual levels. The implementation is where you need to bring all the work and documentation you have done together. There is a lot to think about, process and manage. The place to start is by getting your head around exactly what is going to change from every angle.

Impact assessment

In order to measure the impact on people you have to understand how each person will be affected. In order to aggregate the effect of the change, you need to create a series of common change categories that answer specific questions. The change categories summarize the ways in which people will be affected. Is there risk of redundancy or just a change in desk location? Have elements of the role changed or new accountabilities been added? Example impacts include a change in the reporting lines, responsibilities or content of the role; grade (job level) and reward; salaries; physical location; whom someone will work with.

The starting point with knowing what will change goes back to building the baseline and understanding the as-is from Chapter 3.2. If that data is wrong, then you just compound the risk, manual effort and cost of the implementation. This is a moment you have to have the facts. If you are unclear or inconsistent then those employees you want to keep may leave, and the implementation will become that much harder.

Understanding impact

The goal here is to quantify how every person in the organization is impacted. The aim, therefore, is to flag for every employee what the impact is. You start by listing each possible impact area. For example, if there is a change in reporting line, are they at risk? If there is no change, it is also useful to flag that there is no impact. Figure 4.4.1 shows an example for all the employees reporting to a given manager, in this case Johnny Gomez. The first row shows that Scott Knowles is at risk while Bailey Johnson has a significant change in his responsibilities and a change in his reporting line.

FIGURE 4.4.1   Manager's team impact table

Full Name	Role	As-Is Manager Name	FTE Impact	Role Change	Relocation	Reduction in Pay
○ Scott Knowles	Recruitment Specialist	Johnny Gomez	-1			
○ Mohammed Sanderson	HR Manager	Johnny Gomez	0	✓		
○ Harvey Morris	Assistant Recuitment Specialist	Johnny Gomez	0			✓
○ Donna Lawrence	Assistant Recuitment Specialist	Johnny Gomez	0			✓
○ Bailey Johnson	Learning & Development Specialist	Johnny Gomez	0	✓	✓	
○ Bryan Korn	Assistant Recuitment Specialist	Johnny Gomez	0			
○ Mia Tomlinson	Compensation Administrator	Johnny Gomez	-1			
○ Riley Norton	Assistant HR Manager - South	Johnny Gomez	0			

Once you have this individual analysis, it should be easy to aggregate the information. I suggest you do this at the planning group level (a planning group is a cluster of similar roles rolled up. For more on planning groups see Chapter 4.5.). Slice and dice the data. Test it and ensure all bases are covered. The types of question that commonly need answering include calculating:

1 Headcount and Full-Time Equivalent (FTE) changes.

2 What is the change in total employee cost? The total cost typically includes elements like base pay, pension, healthcare, car allowance and tax. It can include allocations for direct attributable costs such as IT, property (their desk) and telecommunications.

3 The cost of redundancy. This is often driven by tenure, salary and grade.

4 Average depth and spans of control.

5 Relocation costs.

For each measure that you are aggregating, it helps to slice the data by each of the key dimensions, for example by function, grade, location, tenure, gender, age.

This is why having an accurate as-is is so crucial. Because it is about people, you have to do everything to avoid making a mistake while recognizing that mistakes will probably be made. Getting something wrong means sending a strong signal that you just don't care about your people. On top of that, it will possibly open you up to greater risk of an employment tribunal, decrease your credibility as a management team and raise questions that if you are wrong about something so fundamental what else might be wrong?

A good example of how this could affect the impact assessment is not putting everyone in the same role at risk. If the number of full-time employees (FTEs) required for a given position is reduced, then all those in that role are at risk. A common issue is the lack of consistency of job titles. For example, one organization I worked with had 75,000 employees with over 14,000 job titles and yet thousands were doing the same role. It is remarkable how many different titles you can give to 'Personal Assistant' or 'PA' or 'Exec Assistant' or 'Secretary'. This type of ratio of job titles versus employees is common across organizations. I commonly see a ratio of employees to job titles as low as 2:1. In other words, for roughly every two employees there is a separate job title. Make sure you have been clear in your baseline and maintained strict rules to make your life easier now and decrease the risk of making a mistake.

Quantifying impact for roles

One of the hardest elements to understand is whether the role of a person has changed. A change means a substantive difference in accountabilities. For instance, you could define substantive as being a greater than 25 per cent impact (measured by time) on the time required to do the work (the activities). If it is less than 25 per cent, then it isn't significant. Technically, the trick to doing this is mapping employees into both as-is and to-be role and process trees. By doing an Individual Activity Assessment (IAA), you know what each employee currently does. A similar IAA is used to define the to-be accountabilities (see Chapter 3.4 for more information on how to do this). So, as long as the data structure of the IAA and to-be processes are the same, you will know if their responsibilities have changed and in what proportion. Practically, you should triage the areas addressed. Take out those unaffected and those completely changed (for example, outsourced *en bloc*, or eliminated due to technology). There will typically be only a few areas where the impact of the change is complex.

Figure 4.4.2 gives an example analysis to quantify the change of activities in each function for the to-be design. In this case there are four categories for which no change is needed (green), where productivity improvement is required (yellow), where activities need outsourcing (amber) or need to be stopped (red). For example, the Commercial function has 46 distinct activities, 17 of which won't change for the new design, 15 where more productivity is needed, 10 that will be outsourced and four that will be stopped altogether.

FIGURE 4.4.2   Processes impacted

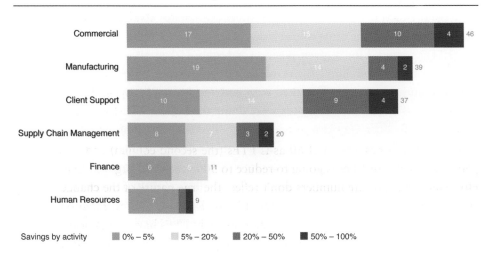

FIGURE 4.4.3   Aggregated people impact by location for an example value stream (Commercial)

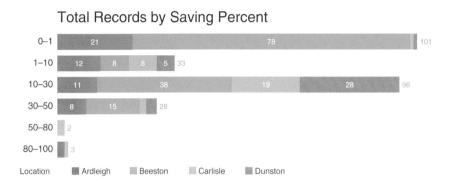

Total Records by Saving Percent

Location		
■ Ardleigh	■ Beeston	▨ Carlisle	■ Dunston

Assuming the IAA is done, you can quickly see the number of employees impacted by these changes. Looking now from the people perspective, Figure 4.4.3 shows that within the Commercial function, 101 people have no impact while 33 have less than 10 per cent change to their role. The colour highlights the numbers within the Commercial function as they are broken down by their specific locations (for example, regions). We can see that 78 in the blue location are not impacted, while 15 are impacted 30–50 per cent of their time. In other words, 15 people who work in the blue location and within the Commercial function are going to have their work reduced by 30–50 per cent. Assuming the average is 40 per cent, this represents a total of six FTEs who are at risk within their current positions.

The point then is getting down to the individual level. Who are those with a greater than 30 per cent impact and where are they based? Figure 4.4.4 gives an example of just that. Each person is coloured by planning group.

Quantifying impact across dimensions

As noted above, there are several ways in which each employee can be impacted. Figure 4.4.5 shows by site how these can be aggregated. Having defined at the individual level the impact flags, you can now aggregate the change.

This example has a total of 60 as-is FTEs (the second column) and it is planned that this number is going to reduce to 50 in the to-be organization. However, the aggregate numbers don't reflect the true nature of the change as there are a total 20 FTEs at risk and 10 new FTEs (new roles) required resulting in a net 10 FTE change. In addition, eight FTEs have a significant change in their work, of which four currently work in Foxfields. In this

FIGURE 4.4.4   People impact listed by location and planning group

Location

	Ardleigh (10)	Beeston (15)	Carlisle (5)	Dunston (3)
Saving Percent 30–50 (8)	○ Thomas Lee ○ Omar Webb ○ Gracie Doyle ○ Eloise Jenkins ○ Steven Bias ○ Rick Jones ○ Harry Manning ○ Luca Carroll	○ Frances Bush ○ Bryan Korn ○ Bill Ha ○ Libby Lucas ○ Donna Lawrence ○ Sebastian Coates ○ Mohammed Sanderson ○ Mia Tomlinson ○ Jessica Talbot ○ Riley Norton ○ Elise Morris ○ Charlie Mellor ○ Gracie Oliver ○ Harvey Morris ○ Bailey Johnson	○ Tegan Murray ○ Thomas Richard	○ Tyler Swift ○ Amelia Yates ○ Andrew Williams
	8	15	2	3
50–80 (2)			○ Logan Price ○ Sienna Miah	
			2	
100–80 (3)	○ Spencer Sinclair ○ Joseph McCool		○ Lora Williams	
	2		1	

Category   ■ Account Manager   ■ Line worker type A   ■ Line worker type B   ■ Line worker type C   Supply Chain Manager   ■ Warehouse Worker

FIGURE 4.4.5   Aggregate impact numbers by impact type by site

Site	As-Is	To-Be	Roles Changes Change	Exit	Relocation Change	From	To	Reporting Change	Reduction in Pay
Ardleigh	4	3	−1	1	0	1	1	2	2
Beeston	2	0	−2	0	0	2	0	1	1
Carlisle	10	17	7	0	1	3	10	9	7
Dunston	3	0	−3	0	0	3	0	3	2
EastLancs	16	13	−3	6	3	1	2	4	0
Foxfields	25	17	−8	13	4	3	6	8	3
Total	60	50	−10	20	8	13	19	27	15

example, there is also a large relative degree of roles moving location with three roles leaving Foxfields and six new ones arriving. In total there are significant levels of reporting line changes with 27 people changing their manager. Now that you know exactly who is impacted in what way, how are you going to communicate the change?

Communication

I will be the first to admit that I have messed up at this stage on many occasions. I have thought it all through only to miss fundamental points. I have tried lots of different approaches in different circumstances and what seemed good in theory was, in reality, disappointing and even the cause of significant issues. The worst situation in which I was personally involved was the first time I ran a redundancy programme. My company's growth had stalled after 24 months of spectacular expansion due to a particularly bad sales quarter. We had to make cuts. Not drastic cuts, just corrective cuts. After management discussions and negotiations we established where we needed to get our cost base down, what roles needed to be reduced, our selection criteria and finally the names. The key communication messages were then agreed:

- We needed to make reductions because sales were insufficient and to ensure we returned to profit.

- We needed to give reassurance that the business was still strong: we had a great reputation; loyal clients; a committed team; a strong balance sheet; and the backing of investors.

My plan was:

- Tell everyone at once on a Tuesday afternoon at 3.00 pm.

- The managers to follow up with their teams and conduct one-to-ones with people who were worried.

What went wrong and what did I learn?

The main issue was my speech. It was not so much what I said, but how I said it. I rehearsed the whole thing and wrote down exactly what I was going to say. During the rehearsals, I was coached by a couple of members of my senior team. But when I spoke the words I wasn't myself. I didn't talk to the team and instead I gave this prepared speech. I wasn't authentic. I didn't look everyone in the eyes and spell out from the heart why and how we were going to get out of the situation we found ourselves in. I spoke the words but didn't build empathy, resulting in a lack of trust and creation of unnecessary distance. I spoke from the head, not the heart. I also didn't drive the message home. I didn't follow up with smaller groups and I didn't repeat the key points. My team had follow-up meetings, but it wasn't enough. Everyone radiated fear and frustration. It is easy to communicate when times are good. When times are tough, it is easy to fall into silence. My final takeaway from this experience is that after the process I didn't sufficiently talk through what we did wrong or what we would do to avoid being in this situation again. What did I learn? What was to be the plan moving forward? How were we going to regroup? Having gone through complex and straining processes you need time to reflect and learn. This is something I come back to in Chapter 4.8.

Communication is clearly a huge topic: one far too large for a single subchapter in a book. Hundreds if not thousands of books must have been written on communication. What I am going to do is talk through my top tips and perspectives that are relevant for organization design.

Build real empathy

Of the tips, this first one is by far the most important and most certainly the hardest. As Stephen Covey says in his book *The 7 Habits of Highly Effective People*, one of the habits is to 'seek first to understand, then be understood'.[1] You need to aim to feel what it is like from your employees' perspective, not yours. A useful framework for this is the WIFM and WAMI analysis. (WIFM: 'What's in it for me?' WAMI is 'What is against my interest?'

Asking these questions across the board helps to articulate how your audience will feel and probably react. The WAMI is actually easier to investigate because most of the time people look at the downsides and the negatives. If you know what people are interested in and expecting before you start the communication process then it's much easier to frame and articulate the messages in the right way.

Acknowledge and plan for the communication challenge from the start

Accept that communication starts from the first moment a project gets discussed. As soon as a decision is made to do something, and that is mentioned from one person to another, communication has started. From the first second of your design process, start by thinking and planning through who is told what, and when. Don't forget that we humans are experts at reading body language and picking up on a vibe that something is up. Assume that once more than a handful of people know, something will get out. So, as much as you try to lead and influence the process, recognize that it is not one you can possibly fully control.

If there are going to be redundancies, then think through the consultation process. The mechanics of this is discussed in more detail in 'Transition management and consultation' below. But don't wait until the end to signal that this is a possibility if you need to take unions and/or your works council with you, and make the consultation process real. Start early, even if off the record you have the trust of your union/works council colleagues. The key is to build trust. Trust is hard earned and easy to lose. This is a tightrope you are going to need to walk. Remember that case for change in Part Two. You must consider how you leverage and build on it together with how you link the design to the design criteria that follow from that.

The design process is a communication process

By its very nature, you will need to engage with people who are going to be affected by the design. The more professional, open (in terms of being open to the ideas of those involved in the process) and logical/fact driven the process is, the better. Be serious and take care to reach the right answers for the right reasons. The number of times decisions are made on a whim or political horse-trading between power brokers is hard to believe and this must be avoided. If the design criteria say 'what' is most important, deciding 'who' is to be involved is a way of you saying who *you* think is important. Choose wisely.

Make it as fact- and reason-based as possible

People want to know the reason why and don't want to be treated like children. It is easy to dumb things down too much. If those affected can understand why, then they will be far better equipped to deal with it. I have had to let quite a few people go over the years for various reasons, be it redundancy or performance reasons. When the reasons behind the decision were clearly explained, the person was far more likely to deal with the news effectively. In order to make sure that your messages are as reason-based as possible, you need to consider:

- What are the design criteria and how did they translate into the design?
- What is the business case? How does it enable the strategy of the business?
- If employees are going to be put at risk, what are the objective selection criteria? What are you doing to provide other opportunities or support?

The worst thing is a lingering death. So when you make the final decisions, make them clearly and move quickly. Be generous in the pay-out and support. If you are quick and fair, the speed will pay for your generosity. If the process is fact-based, you will also do a much better job of retaining the good people who are often let go during a redundancy process. Why are they let go? It is often simply too complicated to assemble all the information and make fact-based decisions across thousands of people. As a result, many companies have been through the experience of wholesale redundancy packages followed by hiring back experienced people as contractors or consultants because they had specific knowledge that was needed. A data-driven approach, particularly when it comes to historical performance and competency data, will give you the best chance of reducing or eliminating these issues, resulting in a better outcome in quality of people retained, and a lower cost of subsequent rehires.

Communication map and tracker

A communication map lists who is being communicated to, how and when. As always, I propose that you make it visual and review it from various perspectives. The mechanism is for every employee whom you want to communicate to, to know what the change is going to be from all angles. Use your Impact Assessment to segment the workforce by the nature of their impact. For each impact, think through what the communication approach, messages and support need to be. By detailing how each employee is impacted, you can tailor your communication to him or her. For example:

- Those who have a change in reporting lines will need to know who their new manager is.

- Those with changes in accountabilities may be losing elements of their work that they love. They will need to understand why and how this will help their career development.

- Those at risk of redundancy will have thousands of thoughts rushing through minds: 'How am I going to find another job?' 'What kind of package am I likely to get?' 'How am I going to pay my rent or mortgage?' 'What are my family and friends going to say?' They are going to need lots of support through the process.

- Some may just be confused, even though the change doesn't affect them directly. Explain the business case and what it will mean for them.

It is good to know who has been communicated to and if there were any escalated issues resulting from the process. Implement a tracker so you can monitor the execution of your communication plan. For example, for each segment or group of employees, define the type of communication method, type of message, timing and responsibility for delivery. As the plan is delivered, each person responsible can then update his or her progress together with any issues requiring escalation. The key is to define what are the messages, who gives them, when and how. For each segment, think through what mix of communication channels will best be used. Example channels include town hall presentations; team meetings; one-to-one meetings; breakfast or lunch Q&A meetings; video; short e-mails that emphasize key points; posters; intranet. For in-person communication, it is useful to create speaking briefs of the key points.

Listen

Remember that good communication is two-way. You have two ears and one mouth for a reason (as many of our grandparents will have taught us). But organization-wide listening isn't easy. It requires the creation of listening tools such as fast-feedback surveys (for example, five simple questions that take two minutes to complete where the analysis is automatically generated so that action can be immediate). It requires giving the person receiving the message time to receive, reflect, understand it and then respond with questions, comments, ideas or simply a burst of emotion. If you provide a feedback loop and don't act on it, you are going to make the situation worse. Like all these obvious points, it is about having the discipline to actually follow through with the action. Simply said, and hard to do well.

Transition management and consultation

Transition management is the process of determining which employees get what role in the new organization and the physical process of making that happen. It often involves running a consultation process. At the end of the process, the to-be organization needs to be populated. Some employees will be automatically transferred as their roles are not at risk, there is no change, and their roles won't be open for others to apply for them. This is called opt-in. An example of this is likely to be the CEO. For the remaining roles, it is common practice that employees will have to apply for the roles they desire. In order to manage this, a workflow process is needed. The consequences will be populating the to-be organization and the management of those who need to be made redundant (Figure 4.4.6).

Assessment and selection process

The assessment and selection process determines who is going to get what position. The first step is defining the inputs to the process: the assessment mechanism; the HR consultation policies; processes; and precedents. Then

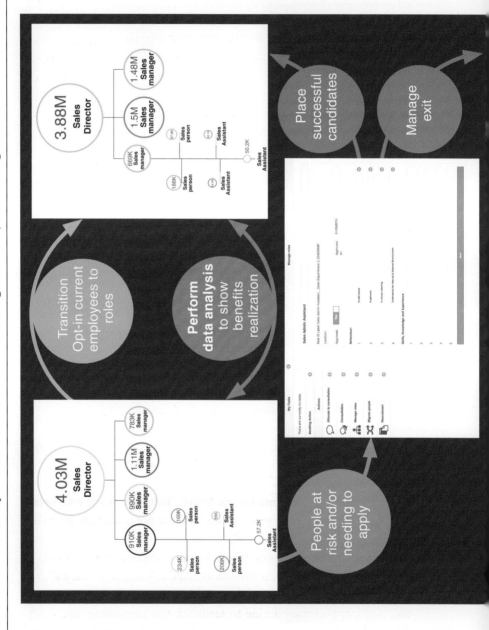

you need to think about how the general and individual consultation processes work (I go into this more detail later in the chapter) and what your selection rules will be. For example, which people can be 'automatically matched' versus going through either a select-in or select-out process? With a select-in there are typically large numbers of people competing for the positions. For instance, you may have 60 people vying for 30 positions. A select-out is simpler with only a small number at risk, for example 22 people vying for 20 positions. In the select-out, you transfer all and determine which 'two of the two' should be removed.

The biggest issue to overcome is what the assessment mechanism is going to be. There is a range of mechanisms for you to select from:

- Historical data such as performance scores. If you have competency and objective management in place as described in Chapters 3.3 and 3.6, then perfect. Unfortunately, the majority of organizations have poor historical data. If there has been a merger, then this may be irrelevant in any event.

- Generated data aims to collect the sorts of data specified in Chapter 3.6 so that a judgement can be made about who is best capable to do each role. These typically break down into a set of technical role-specific competencies and general behaviours. Mechanisms for collecting this data can include:
  - employees' self-assessments;
  - interviews;
  - manager assessment and surveys of each of their team;
  - committee reviews;
  - third-party standardized tests;
  - assessment centre testing.

These mechanisms are not mutually exclusive. You may want employees to do a self-assessment so that you can see where there is alignment or risk of a large variation in perception. Whatever the method of collecting the assessment data, I think it is crucial to run a well-structured calibration process by a committee of well-informed managers. The role of the calibration process is to verify that each of the judgements is robust and consistent. Once this is done, you may decide to feedback the assessment and verify that each employee agrees or at least has a chance to challenge it. An exception process can be run to deal with the most contentious issues. Lastly, a decision has to be made.

Define assessment and the implementation process

What is the implementation process going to be? In what sequence will the planning groups, geographies and functions be rolled out? What are the timetable and programme roadmap? What is the consultation and appeals process? The key thing is to define the process and get legal advice. Figure 4.4.7 provides an example I received from the law firm Kemp Little.

General consultation

In works council or union environments, formal consultation is required. This normally causes extreme levels of anguish. It is often seen as doing battle with the devil or a reason for people not to do many of the things deemed crucial by management. From the other perspective, those sitting on the works council or union side, it is all too often seen as paying lip service. They see a disingenuous management team that is not acting in their employees' best interests. I've seen how general consultations can spiral into acrimonious strikes.

I am not an industrial relations expert but have spoken with many who are, and on both sides of the fence. What is interesting is their views are exactly the same and pretty simple. Again, it is all about trust. From the union's perspective that means the consultation is genuine. That, in turn, means that the decisions are not yet taken and they have a genuine chance at influencing the outcome, which means involving them early enough in the process. From the management's perspective, it means they can share thoughts and options without being held to ransom. They can have a personal relationship and rapport between the two parties, which can pay large dividends. There is an element of negotiation and an element of give and take without either side fully devolving everything they hear. To gain trust you need to have an open mind, but equally not be easily intimidated. You must see arguments from both sides and represent various perspectives without blatantly pushing your own agenda. Once a relationship is broken, it is almost impossible to fix and once a negative spiral is started, it is hard to stop.

Legal consultation

Getting your head around the legal requirements of redundancy can be a challenge. It is an area of great risk for organizations. So it is worth getting right. When putting together your consultation process I suggest you write

FIGURE 4.4.7 Example individual redundancy consultation process from Kemp Little

Individual redundancy consultation

Town Hall Meeting

- Arrange town meeting
- Present current situation
- Present what you are doing about it
- Explain the implications, eg:
- Select redundencies
- Sorts of numbers impacted
- Explain the process
- What the steps are?
- How long it will take?
- What everyone should do?
- The support you will provide

First consultation meeting

- Discuss with employees
- Nature of the proposal
- Business reasons behind the proposal
- Impact on the employee's role
- Consultation process to be followed, including proposed selection procedure and criteria (if relevant)
- Whether there are any ways of avoiding or mitigating the impact
- Suitable alternative vacancies
- Redundancy package
- Allow the employee an opportunity to comment
- Respond to comments raised or agree on points to be taken away for consideration

Second consultation meeting

- Run through the matters discussed in the first meeting
- Provide feedback on points raising in the first meeting (if any)
- Take further feedback (if any)
- Encourage the employee to apply for any suitable alternative vacancies
- Allow the employee an opportunity to comment
- Respond to comments raised or agree on points to be taken away for consideration

Apply the selection criteria (if applicable)

- Objective criteria
- More than one person scoring
- Moderated scores
- Consider whether it is necessary to make reasonable adjustments for disabilities or to avoid other discrimination

Final consultation meeting

- Decide if there is another role
- Decide whether to proceed
- Decide final terms

Gate to proceed

- If applicable: Communicate the employee's score
- Reconsider suitable alternative vacancies. If none:
- If applicable: Allow them an opportunity to comment on the scoring
- If applicable: Respond to comments raised or agree on points to be taken away for consideration (if any)
- Confirm the outcome
- Provide support through the termination process

it up and get legal input to make sure you are doing it properly for your jurisdiction. Figure 4.4.7, provided by Kathryn Dooks, Employment Partner at the City of London law firm Kemp Little, demonstrates what this could look like. Depending on whether you have redundancies across more than one jurisdiction can add significant complexity to the legal landscape you have to navigate. So in this section I highlight two important considerations if this is the case, and then investigate three common traps to avoid in the redundancy process.

Considering variation in redundancy processes across jurisdictions

When dealing with redundancy across jurisdictions, careful planning of the consultation in each jurisdiction is essential. Alison Dixon, a senior employment lawyer in the International HR Services team at the City firm Bird & Bird, says that although the law that requires employers to consult collectively in the case of mass redundancies is likely to be similar across EU jurisdictions (as it derives from European Directives), the way in which the law has been implemented in each country varies quite significantly. For example, the threshold number of proposed redundancies that will trigger the obligation to consult on a collective basis differs from country to country. In Germany, the applicable threshold depends on the number of employees at the relevant establishment, while in France it is 10 or more redundancies within a 30-day period; in the UK the trigger is 20 or more over a 90-day period. There may also be additional obligations to consult with a European Works Council. The legal consequences of failure to comply with local duties to inform and consult range from financial penalties payable to the affected employees (UK) through to injunctions preventing the redundancies from being implemented (Germany) and criminal penalties (Belgium and France).

There are also strict requirements about when the duty to consult arises, which vary across Europe, meaning that in some countries the duty will be triggered at an earlier stage in the process than in others. Management and HR need to be educated about these requirements at a very early stage in the planning process, in order to avoid inadvertently triggering a duty to commence consultations in any particular country before the business is ready to do so, or even undermining the validity of the consultations altogether. Communications with staff or their representative bodies need to be carefully coordinated across the affected jurisdictions to avoid this type of problem. A staff communication (or even an e-mail between members of senior management) that is perfectly innocuous in one jurisdiction (such as the UK, which is one of the more permissive jurisdictions) may be a complete no-no in another (such as France, where the legal regime tends to be much more protective of employees). A famous example of a business getting it completely wrong is that of Marks & Spencer's exit from Europe in 2001. They announced their closure plans to staff before consulting with the appropriate staff representatives. This resulted in the French courts ordering them to suspend the redundancy process in a blaze of terrible publicity, which included the French Prime Minister commenting that M&S should be punished and protests on the streets of Paris.

Clearly, central management and HR need to fully understand the legal landscape in each country where redundancies are proposed, and both the legal and practical risks associated with non-compliance, in order to come up with the most effective plan. For businesses unaccustomed to the regimes in mainland Europe, it can come as a shock to learn that non-compliance with consultation requirements can result not only in financial penalties but also lengthy and costly delays to the process. It is much better for that realization to come during the planning stage than when those plans are being executed.

Three common legal traps to avoid

The process is one thing. But what are some of the traps to be avoided? With this in mind, I asked Kathryn Dooks to add some more experiences and reflections.

Coordinate your consultation process across the organization

A common error in a restructuring context is to make a decision to close down one function of the business and to refocus the business by growing a different function. Employers often recruit for the growing function before starting to consult on the redundancies in the function that is being closed down, leading to accusations that the consultation process is a sham and that the restructuring is a done deal. This frequently arises from an (sometimes erroneous) assumption that the redundant employee does not have the skills and experience to undertake the duties of the expanding function. Employers should discuss the employee's transferrable skills and experience as part of the consultation process; they will not be aware of all of their employees' skills and reasonable retraining should be offered. Give each employee a chance to express interest in all open roles, not just those in his or her area.

For example, one of Kathryn's clients in the media sector was scaling down its administrative function while at the same time growing its marketing function. The client recruited for the marketing roles before putting the administration roles at risk of redundancy, and the administration staff who were at risk of redundancy claimed that they had the skills to carry out the marketing roles (or could have done with reasonable retraining) and that the redundancy consultation process was therefore unfair. This resulted in a litigation process that awarded significant costs. Given that only a small handful of people were involved, the client could easily have postponed the recruitment in the marketing function and started the redundancy consultation process earlier, enabling management to discuss the vacancies with the administration employees to determine whether they had appropriate skills and experience for the roles.

Avoid grounds for constructive unfair dismissal claims

Employers often hire a new member of staff to slot into the structure over the head of an existing employee without consulting the existing employee (particularly in a rapidly growing business). This can result in a change of reporting line, team size, perceived status or responsibility for the existing employee, which may lead the existing employee to resign and claim constructive unfair dismissal. However, if the employer had taken the time to consult with the existing employee about its plans and the reasons behind them prior to recruitment of the new employee, there would have been greater chance of persuading the employee of the merit of the proposal and less chance of a successful constructive unfair dismissal claim.

Ensure selection processes are fair

When reducing the size of a function rather than eliminating it altogether, ensure you avoid discrimination issues arising from the selection process and criteria being applied. This most commonly arises where an employee is disabled or has been on a period of maternity leave during the period being assessed for the selection process. When the employers score the employee as part of the selection process, they often fail to take account of the disadvantage to the employee arising from the disability or maternity leave and don't make adjustments accordingly. Apparent maternity discrimination (or other types) can arise inadvertently where, for example, it just happens that a large proportion of those selected for redundancy are on maternity leave. Pull your numbers together by each group, consider the risk and consider how a situation would look in front of a tribunal judge. Employers also need to take care not to go too far the other way and to overcompensate for the impact of one group leading to allegations from the other. It is always best to seek advice on the criteria used and any adjustments proposed in this context.

From a process perspective, it is common for employers to think that HR managers should handle the process on their own. This can lead employees to think that management is shirking responsibility for its decisions and avoiding difficult conversations. It always best if the message is being delivered by the individual's line manager or a senior member of management with an HR manager supporting and being present in the room. Last impressions matter and how you treat those leaving the organization will have a significant bearing on how your organization will be viewed by the outside world and by those who remain. It is a process that needs to be run both efficiently and with empathy. Above all, ensure that all decision-making is carefully documented, can be justified on objective grounds and is fair, and that the process is well managed.

Collateral

Before you start the implementation process, you need to ensure the design and all the logic for the decisions you are making are effectively documented. The reality, however, is that the documentation process never stops because the detailed design never stops. The consultation process will throw up legitimate issues that will result in subtle changes. Equally, as days turn to weeks and months, events will force change too. You will need to react to that change and many of the detailed designs will evolve. The process of documenting the design is, therefore, an ongoing rather than one-off activity. I believe the discipline required to do the micro design should become a core ongoing competence, only more so, as Chapters 4.5 and 4.6 demonstrate.

One of the greatest clichés about management consultants is that they write huge PowerPoint reports which end up collecting dust on a shelf somewhere. How the vision of all that labour eroding in value over time used to depress me! When you do this work, you put in a great deal of effort. If the collateral from the detailed micro design is not maintained then, eventually, it will erode and die. And so will the benefits. The design cannot be a static solution documented for all time in hundreds of PowerPoint slides and Excel files. An organization is constantly evolving and, therefore, the information about the organization needs to be updated in electronic form, too. The information needs to be easy to share and drill into detail. It needs to support all the remaining elements of executing the design on an ongoing basis.

Final thoughts

The essence of this chapter is pretty simple. Know what is going to change and make that change happen in a structured and fair way. Knowing what is going to change needs to happen at the individual level first and then be aggregated up. This is the impact assessment. Inversely, the communication and consultation processes need to start at the aggregate level and then be implemented at the individual employee level.

But the art of this isn't so much the how but the when. The when for a great number of the elements is right from the start of the macro design process. That is when the communication starts. However, there is a catch-22. If you start too early with general consultation and don't have enough answers to specific questions you might send unfounded fear through the ranks. But if you wait until everything is worked out, you will at best break trust and at worst have missed an angle of thought that could have led to a far better outcome or you will need to do lots of re-working. It is a bit of a tightrope walk. No matter what, if you break trust it is hard to get it back. So be thoughtful both in your timing and in developing strong relation-ships with those with whom you need to consult at the general level. For the individual consultation process, be fair and clear. Have a well-structured process that protects you both legally and minimizes risks, but is also effi-cient so that you can move forward into getting the value from the to-be design.

Implementation requires both the soft and hard sides of management. The ability to be empathetic and to communicate accordingly versus the hard-nosed process management of those at risk through the application and redundancy processes within the law. There is a lot of information that needs to be managed. You need to have your systems and processes in place. Each person will want to know what the design looks like, what his or her role will be and how he or she fits into the bigger picture. To support that, you will need to move beyond the traditional PowerPoint and Excel documentation. Equally, you will need to be able to track progress on a daily basis as there are lots of moving parts and a complex set of anxious stakeholders. Once done, it will be time to move to managing the ongoing to-be or new 'business as usual' world. That to-be world won't be static. It needs ongoing management if you are going to achieve the goals you set yourself.

1 Build a comprehensive and detailed impact assessment at the aggregate and individual levels of the organization.

2 When communicating change, be as true to yourself as possible. If you don't, people won't believe in you or follow you on the journey.

3 Use all the hard work building your baseline to understand why things are changing and support your communication with the facts.

4 Be clear and fair about your assessment and selection criteria and consultation processes. Where necessary, bring in professional support to avoid legal traps.

5 Document the process and keep the design collateral up to date so you have an audit trail and can keep tracking progress.

Note

1 Covey, S R (1990) *The 7 Habits of Highly Effective People: Powerful Lessons in Personal Change*, Simon & Schuster, New York

Workforce planning

> *A goal without a plan is just a wish.*
>
> **ANTOINE DE SAINT-EXUPÉRY**

Introduction

How do you know that you are getting the right people, doing the right things, at the right time, in the right numbers and with the required skills? How do you manage this over time? What is your governance process for dealing with changes and how do you keep a grip on basics like budget versus actuals? How is your forecast of headcount or salary cost changing?

These are all pretty fundamental questions and beyond the reach of most people to answer. If there is one area of poor organizational performance across all industries, it has to be workforce planning (WFP). At one conference I attended in the summer of 2014, the final keynote speaker asked 100+ senior HR practitioners, 'Has anyone here even come close to getting workforce planning to work?' She said that if any of them had, she would bite off their hands and pay whatever figure came into their heads for the answer. No one put up a hand.

Workforce planning is a really tough problem. For any significant business, the numbers of employees involved and the change and complexity mean it can't really be done using manual tools like Excel. However, according to the Aberdeen Group in their May 2014 research paper, over 50 per cent of organizations still have manual or spreadsheet-based workforce planning processes.[1]

In this chapter, I look to illuminate how to move forward in the workforce planning journey. I explore what workforce planning is, breaking it down into three types: strategic, operational and tactical (often referred to as scheduling). I then explore how workforce planning is related and connected to the organizational design and, in turn, how good design supports good workforce planning. In the final section I explain how to build a plan at the strategic and operational levels and maintain that plan in order to deal with changes over time, governance and making decisions such as approval to hire.

What we really mean by workforce planning

I have found that everyone has a slightly different understanding as to what workforce planning means. When I hear people talk about workforce planning I often hear questions like:

- How many people do we have for a given age?
- What is the gender or diversity split?
- What is the split of permanent versus contract labour by factory?
- How many open posts are there?

This is not workforce planning; it is HR analytics as described in Chapter 3.2. Workforce planning is about the demand and supply of 'workers' (be they permanent or temporary; full time or part time) required for each time period (by year, month, week). Workforce planning has two components: supply and demand. It is about knowing the gap between actuals (the supply) and plan (the demand). It is about knowing why there is a gap. What is the root cause? Is it because you didn't recruit the number specified in the plan? Is the churn rate higher than was assumed? Has the plan has changed? Only when you know why you are off plan in any given area are you in a position to actually do something about it. I will return to this later in the chapter in 'Workforce planning in practice'. However, for now I want to define three types of workforce planning.

Breaking down the term 'workforce planning' helps to identify the different values you get from the activities associated with it. Each type of workforce planning requires a different approach, set of skills and is often done by different teams. What differentiates the different types is their time horizons and the level of granularity they are done at:

- **Strategic workforce planning**: looking forward 18 months to multiple years into the future. Done at the workforce planning group level.

- **Operational workforce planning**: looking forward monthly to 12–18 months into the future. Done at position level.

- **Tactical workforce management** (sometimes referred to as scheduling): looking forward within the day to the coming weeks or a maximum of one quarter into the future. Done at employee daily schedule level.

Strategic workforce planning

Strategic workforce planning looks forward multiple years. The drivers behind the need to do strategic workforce planning include external factors and business and operating model changes. For example, external factors could include wide-ranging social changes. A classic example is that of the medical profession in Western industrialized countries in the 1960s. A combination of increasing wealth and technological advances in medicine (along with other factors such as state-funded procedures in Commonwealth countries) led to a greater demand for medical treatment and personnel. The surge of demand was beyond the service that the numbers of doctors could provide, a problem characterized by the press as national doctor shortages. Spotting that there was a gap in the domestic supply of medical personnel, many countries created new medical schools to increase the intake of students and the 'talent' to meet public demand.[2] Other examples of these acute long-term shortages in talent include the number of nuclear scientists within the nuclear power industry or experienced mine engineers in remote regions of Australia. They are the sorts of trends that are hard to spot with an in-year or even in-decade perspective. The consequence of missing them can be fatal.

Another driver for strategic workforce planning is a change in operating model. For example, in the early 2000s I worked with a public sector client attempting a digital transformation in order to achieve a new range of goals and targets based on a radical shift in policy. The change was so big that all front-line staff needed weeks of training, on both the new major IT system being put in place and the new processes. We had to take into account a number of factors in the transformation:

- What was the training and learning curve going to be?
- What might be the productivity levels per agent (the number of cases they could deal with) or what might be the likely range?
- The estimate of data migration and the speed at which clients (certain members of the public) could be transitioned from old to new.
- How many agents for how long would need to work on the old system, and how fast would the ramp-up to the new system be?
- Lastly, there was a whole range of exceptions resulting in more work. These exceptions were workarounds because the standard system couldn't deal with certain elements of complexity that the new legislation and government policy drove.

The risks were high. One workaround alone, because of a complex piece of legislation, resulted in 360,000 work days of extra effort. Over a five-year period, this amounted to an additional 340 staff alone. The demand for the workforce grew from 12,000 people to well over 16,000 within one year. However, according to the business case this would need to be reduced to 8,700 post-implementation. Given this was a government agency, redundancy packages were not an option and attrition was low. The gap between the target and actual demand was too big, highlighting that either many of the policies or the business case and targets needed to change. The strategy of the entire agency rested on getting right many of the fundamentals highlighted above. And, in this instance, I wonder how funding for such a large programme could ever have been made without understanding this type of workforce impact.

In all instances of strategic workforce planning, because it is done so far into the future it doesn't need to be done at a detailed position level. It is useful to chunk the level of analysis up a level to workforce planning groups. A planning group is a group of workers who are broadly fungible. They have similar competencies and can do each other's work. Not all planning groups are created equal. Some take a long time to replace with limited labour markets and/or a lengthy learning curve to master the skills required to do the job. The above-mentioned nuclear physicist and drillers in the mining industry are two good examples. Furthermore, the impact that each planning group has can vary significantly too. Certain planning groups are core to the competitive position of the organization and it is, therefore, critical that they are directly employed, while others are hard to find and train. In many cases roles may be better 'bought in' from external sources, such as professional service firms or agencies, to meet this demand. The planning groups can, therefore, be segmented into four categories as shown in Figure 4.5.1.

The profile of the various WFP segments can be plotted into a matrix, as illustrated in Figure 4.5.1. When demand forecasting you can leverage many of the methods as described in Chapter 3.7. These segments can inform the complexity and level of effort you place into planning. The lower-priority segments (closer to the left-hand corner of Figure 4.5.1) are more easily rectified on an operational basis so strategic planning errors are less critical.

Operational planning

Operational workforce planning encompasses a medium-term view; for example, ensuring you have the required workforce to meet annual objectives

FIGURE 4.5.1   Workforce planning groups

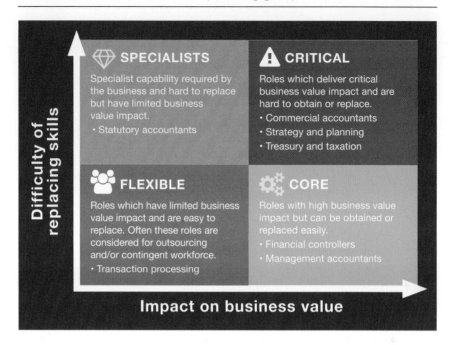

of operational business plans. It is done from a position perspective, the level that you recruit at. For example, what is the change in the recruitment list? What does the pipeline look like for the next 12 months? This element of workforce planning is, therefore, an input into the resourcing/recruitment function. I regard a budget as an operational plan and the process of the annual budget cycle falls within this scope.

Tactical workforce management or scheduling

This is the day-to-day view. It is reacting to unforeseen changes. A key member of staff leaves. Attrition suddenly jumps and you need to get a contractor in. Someone is sick for two weeks; how do you cover that? Who needs to work which shift? How to manage the nursing roster? How to do this falls outside the scope of this book; the activity is more transactional while this book is strategic and operational. However, if you would like to know more about this transactional activity, I suggest looking at how software packages like Quintiq, Primavera, Kronos or SAP do it.

How micro design helps to drive workforce planning

Having clarified the different types of workforce planning, it is worth outlining how workforce planning fits into the work already done in the micro design. There is a large synergy between the two given they are both focused on numbers of people, which roles, competencies required and when they will be needed. Micro design needs to be regarded as an input into workforce planning. It is more strategic in nature in terms of defining where you need to get to. Workforce planning and management are about how you get there. You could use the analogy of micro design being like a balance sheet at a fixed point in time, while workforce planning represents the cash flow, with volumes that constantly change and are tracked over time as the business changes. They are symbiotic. Workforce planning without a clear micro design is like driving somewhere without a map.

With micro design the questions are: What is the as-is situation and the to-be design? How and where do they differ? What are the improvements? How big is the change? What is the impact going to be? They are about two points in time and a variance between those two points. With micro design I am interested in the differences between these two points. With workforce planning, it is the number of FTEs over time. Each month is likely to have a subtly different view. Demands are shifted out or urgently pulled forward. It is tied up in budgeting and forecasting; for example you want to slice the required number of FTEs by role and then by geography for each month (or quarter).

Once the to-be numbers are signed off, it is the role of the workforce planner to get the organization from the as-is to the to-be state. It is about the transition of those states. Again, in all probability the exact envisaged to-be numbers will never be reached because too much will change as time evolves. During the micro design you just can't envisage every angle, nuance or eventuality. The whole concept of steady state is, therefore, a bit of a misnomer.

The micro design is the platform from which you plan your workforce plan. It should define your workforce planning groups, roles and positions. It defines what each role means by defining each role's objectives, accountabilities and competencies, together with where each set of roles sits organizationally and, therefore, defining the positions. As a reminder, a position is a role that reports to the same person in the same geography. The job description is done at the role level. Planning is done at the position level.

Once you have the demand, WFP is then about the 'how' of filling the positions, or in other words ensuring supply of labour. In doing this you can take a simple headcount perspective, or, as much WFP literature advocates, you can look at competencies too. While I agree that taking a competency-based approach is more valuable, I accept that it's already extremely hard to do workforce planning well at the 'headcount' tracking level. Trying to predict the quantity of competencies required and available over time in practice may be too much. It is definitely much easier to see it as a journey and at least begin at the headcount level.

Good micro design should make the implementation of workforce planning and management workable. This is essential when it comes to implementing your design. Having said this, in all likelihood those doing the micro design may not be doing the workforce planning and certainly won't be doing the workforce management as often they come from different parts of the business. Therefore, make sure those doing the design understand their impact on the implementation and those executing the workforce plan understand the design.

Workforce planning in practice

A useful way to approach workforce planning, regardless of the type of planning, is to think in terms of supply and demand. Workforce planning is governed by these two forces. The first aspect of workforce planning is the demand for resources. The demand is done at the position level. Each position has a title, set of reporting lines, desired start and end dates (exception: permanent positions will not have end dates) and approval status. The demand is, in effect, the workforce plan. It is what is required by the business unit, function, location and job families. In practice, this will look different depending on the type of workforce planning you are doing.

Strategic workforce planning is conducted by scenario modelling the future needs of the business. Business managers need the ability to think through what type and number of resources they need by answering a series of questions; for example:

- What does a given scenario look like?
- How big would the change be?
- How does it compare with a different scenario or the current headcount?

In contrast, operational workforce planning can be thought of in terms of how you manage that budget. Plans are drawn up by business managers in accordance with the strategic plans and the more immediate demands of the business. Once they have the most appropriate plan they will seek sign-off through the appropriate governance mechanisms. The operational plan will continually change, from small alterations in start dates to changes in business requirements and hiring freezes. The only thing you can know for certain is that the actuals will invariably vary from the plan.

Knowing your resource supply versus demand

The second aspect of workforce planning is the supply of resources. This is the current headcount and known changes to the headcount:

- Who are the known leavers?
- When do contracts for temporary labour end?
- When are the new starters scheduled to join?
- How long does it take to hire each role?
- Is it better to recruit internally or externally?

Once resource demand and supply are known, the business needs to understand gaps.

Doing strategic workforce planning

From a strategic workforce planning perspective the key is making it comprehensible and avoiding too much detail. As highlighted earlier in the chapter, you plan based on your planning group whether at a subfunction or geographical level. Think through potential reasons for change, both external and internal and how they might affect the workforce. For example:

- How many people do you need in sales by country each year in order to meet the growth aspirations of the business?
- With the new FSA regulations, how big should the compliance function become?
- Given the age profile of each oncologist in London, how many people will need to be trained and qualified to meet the exodus in 10 years' time?
- Given the number of new mines that are opening up in South America, how many project managers and rock engineers are needed?

If you want to be more precise in your plans you can also start to do driver-based planning in a similar way to driver-based rightsizing as outlined in

Chapter 3.7. This is where you use drivers to help you estimate the number of FTEs required. For example, if the number of quality engineers is a function of the number of developers, then if the number of developers doubles the number of quality engineers probably also needs to double. Just like the rightsizing debate, the level of sophistication you should go to depends on materiality and complexity and whether a more precise answer is likely to be significantly different from a less sophisticated one.

An example of strategic workforce planning done well was a project undertaken by a large retail bank. The bank was facing substantial pressure on revenue and margins, driven by a change in customer behaviour linked to the economic climate and the uptake of digital and substantially increased competitive pressure. The bank recognized that it needed to change the way it did business and focused on several substantial changes to its business model:

- changes to the way it segmented customers and how these different customer segments would use the bank away from branches to ATMs, contact centres, internet and mobile;

- changes in product mix that customers would buy;

- changes in productivity driven by Lean Six Sigma improvements.

The implications of these business changes was that to deliver the business plan, the workforce needed to change in:

- the numbers of workforce required in each category (for example, fewer branch staff, more private bankers, more digital staff);

- the skills required of the existing and future workforce within each category.

A strategic workforce plan was produced that converted the required business results into workforce requirements (demand) and compared that with a projection of the workforce available (supply) for each workforce category. This was based on a number of different scenarios around the pace and extent of business change.

The plan identified gaps in some critical areas of workforce (for example, private bankers) and some surpluses in other areas (for example, bank branch staff). A series of workforce interventions was identified to help better match the workforce to the new business model. For example, the bank had scaled back its graduate intake programme as a cost reduction measure. The strategic workforce plan showed that it would be cheaper and more effective to reinvest in that programme than to try to address some of the workforce gaps from the open market. It was estimated that the value of these interventions was worth tens of millions of pounds in cost avoidance and margin enhancement.

Doing operational workforce planning

A good way to think about operational workforce planning supply and demand is people and position planning. People and position planning cuts through to the core of what most people call workforce planning. It is more than planning, though: it is the execution of the plan. It goes into the month-to-month management of an ever-shifting workforce. For instance, where is there a need for a position that is not currently filled? Where is there risk of redundancy? Where has resource been requested but not fulfilled?

To conduct workforce planning you need to link resource supply (current headcount in each position) with resource demand (demand for each position). You can then model and plan resource demand, assess whether demand can be met with current resource supply (headcount), or alternatively plan additional resource. Every current resource will have a known position. The workforce plan will show the business need for each position. A summary of this methodology is illustrated in Figure 4.5.2.

FIGURE 4.5.2 People supply and position demand in operational workforce planning

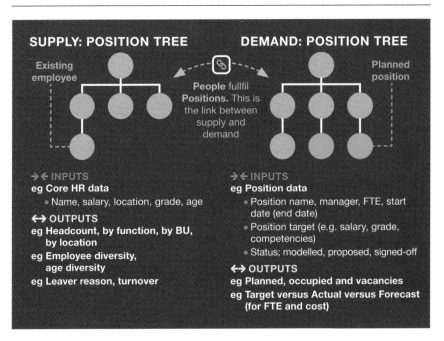

On a practical note, if you haven't done the micro phase already and are jumping straight into WPF, then one of the problems you may face is a proliferation of job titles. When starting off with any given client, it is extremely common to see one job title for every two employees. The highest ratio I have seen is only 1:7. So the first step is to clean this. One way to deal with this issue is to try to simplify the data by bringing it up a level; for example, bringing job titles up to job family level and working from there.

In terms of a methodology this is all well and good, but the key is to be able to workforce plan and analyse your workforce on an ongoing basis, to see where the gaps are early in the process and identify where you can fill them from. A good source of inspiration in doing this well can be taken from sales and operational planning (S&OP). Good supply chain teams have a pretty robust calendar routine. Multiple functions are pooled together at fixed points during the year, month or week. Forecasts are frozen x days out. The decisions that need to be made are clear, as is the information to make those decisions. It is about being efficient with everyone's time and that means pre-work, clear agendas and expected outcomes. To get this kind of ongoing holistic approach:

1 Use your baseline data to gain an understanding for the organizational as-is; for example, actual headcount.

2 Integrate your various organizational functions, aligning and synchronizing them to create a people forecast.

3 Plan accordingly within a specified time frame based on organizational demand to create a budget.

If you do this rigidly you can start to get a view similar to Figure 4.5.3 and begin to understand whether your actuals, budget and forecasts are synchronized and on track. Remember that the customers for workforce management are inside the business, not outside. They are related to and driven by the business strategy, while the demand comes specifically from requests to hire or plans to hire over a period of time. The demand plans need to be compared with the supply. You should ideally factor in time to retire analysis; the impact of attrition, or even the attrition levels by area and planning groups.

The maths is simple. What is difficult is getting the right metadata tags, understanding how to deal with temporal data and knowing the basics; for example: What is the attrition by role, area, group, grade, tenure or high performers? Which roles are hardest to recruit for and how long do they take to fill? What are the internal supply options for each role versus recruiting

FIGURE 4.5.3   Tracking of the workforce supply and demand over time

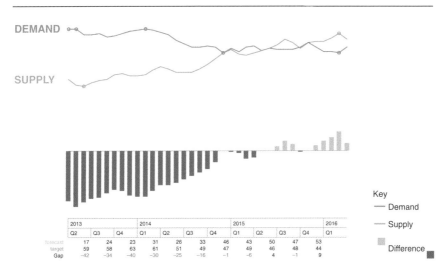

	2013			2014				2015				2016
	Q2	Q3	Q4	Q1	Q2	Q3	Q4	Q1	Q2	Q3	Q4	Q1
forecast	17	24	23	31	26	33	46	43	50	47	53	
target	59	58	63	61	51	49	47	49	46	48	44	
Gap	−42	−34	−40	−30	−25	−16	−1	−6	4	−1	9	

Key
— Demand
— Supply
■ Difference

outside? In this context, thinking about succession planning becomes a subset of workforce planning. Succession planning can be thought of as cultivating the long-term supply of core and strategic workforce planning segments. Chapter 4.6 goes into more detail about this. The result of all this is a picture of demand and supply over time, as shown in Figure 4.5.3. This graph also shows the gaps and the detailed numbers.

With this sort of analysis you can really start to understand the drivers of change and how they impact your organization. It can reduce the debates about whether plans should be altered and why decisions were taken in the past, because people can see how the organization has fluctuated and is fluctuating over time. It puts you in the best position possible to make quick, agile decisions to ensure you get the most value from your existing and future workforce based on business opportunities and risks.

Final thoughts

Workforce planning is one of those areas where the theory is easy but the execution is fraught. To execute requires strong metadata control of elements like roles and grade definitions. It then requires implementing a process and system so that the theory can be operationalized. In this book, I don't delve into systems implementations; it is about concepts and practices. However, I hope this chapter gives you, at the most basic level, what workforce planning actually means, and an insight into what is required to get a plan in place. From here, the challenge is creating a plan specific to your organization and design, and implementing it.

A lot of thinking in this chapter has been inspired by best practice in the supply chain function. Companies put huge amounts of investment into their supply chain capabilities. They know that it is about a combination of people, process and systems so they invest in all three areas. They know it can be a great source of sustainable competitive advantage and they know there is no quick fix. It takes years to build a truly world-class supply chain capability and it may require targeted outside help. It certainly requires continued senior leadership support, budget and a focused team. Mostly, however, it requires a long-term commitment to excellence. To do workforce planning well you can learn from all these things. It requires perseverance, resilience, dedication and investment. It isn't a quick-win space. But then again, things of real value rarely are.

Remember this

1 Ensure clarity regarding the differences between types of strategic and operational workforce planning and tactical workforce management, and if you can, make time for the strategic and operational – they're worth it!

2 Make sure you have a good understanding of both the demand and supply of your workforce over time.

3 Keep things simple, and at the strategic level use workforce planning groups and segment these so that you spend your effort on the most critical areas.

4 Think of operational planning as people and position planning to help match your supply and demand.

5 Ensure you have a clear process for tracking, approving, managing and then linking into the resourcing/recruitment functions.

Notes

1 Aberdeen Group (2014) Workforce Planning: Mapping the Road to Success, Research report 5 May 2014, [Online] http://www.aberdeen.com/research/9265/RR-workforce-planning-success.aspx/content.aspx

2 Wright, D, Flis, N and Gupta, M (2008) The 'Brain Drain' of physicians: historical antecedents to an ethical debate, c. 1960–79, *Philosophy, Ethics and Humanities in Medicine*, 3 (24), pp 1–8

Talent management, succession development and succession planning

> *Change the name of the process from succession planning to succession development.* MARSHALL GOLDSMITH

Introduction

Succession planning is a hot topic and is high up the agenda for many senior HR leaders. This is no surprise given that attracting the right talent is crucial to your organization's success. However, despite all the discussions about talent management and succession planning I believe there are three major issues with the way most organizations approach succession planning:

1 There is not enough of a long-term focus.

2 There is too much attention given to only top levels of the organization.

3 The focus is on *planning* rather than *development*.[1]

I believe people are overly obsessed with the top organizational tiers of management or Top 150 in large multinationals. In a survey conducted by Ernst & Young in 2007 on the greying US workforce, 41 per cent of employers reported that their middle management ranks would be hit the hardest by mass retirements, yet 75 per cent of the same companies reported having succession planning that focused on senior positions only.[2] I believe there needs to be a systematic process of improvement that goes much deeper than just the top level. Too often, succession planning is regarded as a one-off activity. However, as Marshall Goldsmith argues, the focus should be on development rather than planning. You should focus on improving existing talent to minimize the impact when key people leave. Alongside this, I believe a far longer view should be taken of the flow of talent over time to give you time to develop that talent and help individuals fulfil their potential.

This chapter is linked closely with the ideas of competency management and workforce planning. If competencies define the talent you currently need and have, then talent management is about managing and nurturing that talent for your future workforce. In this chapter I begin by highlighting the importance of succession planning. I then outline two approaches to succession planning: the first based on defining priority and risk to focus plans; and the second a focus on individual talent-driven succession planning. I end on how to implement succession planning in practice, bringing together the work done on competencies (Chapter 3.6) and workforce planning (Chapter 4.5). Throughout this chapter remember that talent does not mean one type of talent, or a misguided focus on leadership, but a full range of focused skills and behaviours across the organization based on a particular role. The question is: Given your set of roles today and your roles in the future, how do you spot talent suitable for those future roles throughout the organization?

Why all the hype?

Why the obsession with succession? If someone leaves, why not just recruit from the outside? Does it really have a material impact on an organization's performance? Can it really be a source of competitive edge? My view is, it can and that the hype about this crucial topic is justified. In 2011 New Zealand won the Rugby World Cup for the first time since 1987. It had a highly capped and ageing team, and with the World Cup being its seemingly singular focus there was a big question about whether it could sustain its success. Since then, it has sustained a win rate of over 80 per cent and at the time of writing has a 100 per cent winning streak. The secret? Talent management.

New Zealand faces an uphill struggle when it comes to achieving and sustaining success. It is a country with a population of only four million so talent is at a premium in comparison with other top rugby nations, such as England and France. So New Zealand has had to put a real focus on attracting and developing talent. Its approach demonstrates three areas where organizations could significantly improve their talent management processes:

1   **Have a long-term perspective.** New Zealand invested heavily in all stages of talent development, introducing special non-contact forms of the game so that talent can be nurtured from as early as the age of three.

2   **Ensure structured development.** The talent system is not simply a plan but a structured system focused on developing talent. Each age group is introduced to different forms of the game with a focus on particular skills and aspects of the game to stretch them. There are apprenticeship programmes for the national team in order to ease talent in gradually, planning and managing succession.

3   **A focus beyond top talent.** Just as organizations shouldn't focus on the top level of management, New Zealand has built a system which goes beyond simply picking out the stars, by building talent which supports the whole team and the landscape of New Zealand rugby as a whole.

What New Zealand has done so well is executed a succession plan. The country's ability to foster and grow talent is not simply paying lip service but has become part of the culture through rigorous thinking and disciplined development. Organizations should take all these lessons on board if they are going to make a difference. As Jim Collins argues in his book *Good to Great*,[3] a good way of thinking about it is to get the right people on the bus, sitting in the right seats. Thinking about organization strategically means defining the 'seats' in the right numbers at the right level, and ensuring a flow of talent in the future capable of filling those seats. Succession development, like so many things in business, is often talked about but not implemented. In addition, the focus will be only on the top team. Who are the successors to the main board members and senior executives? In my view, this is all too little, too late. It needs to be much deeper and far-reaching down through the organization if there is any chance of developing talent in the long term.

Succession planning represents an area for significant performance improvement in organizations. According to the Corporate Research Forum (CRF), 'Planning for Succession in Changing Times' report, 'only 56% of those surveyed said they are satisfied with their organization's ability to fill senior positions, and 42% are actively dissatisfied with it'.[4] According to the recent KPMG report 'Rethinking Human Resources in a Changing World': 'Executives see succession planning rising up the HR function's to-do list over the next three years (20% compared with 18% for the past three years), but only 22% of executives think their HR department "excels" in succession planning.'[5]

The rest of this chapter sets out an approach to address the challenges organizations currently face in this area. I start by returning to the platform you have been given to succession plan effectively given the competency management done in Chapter 3.6. I then explore two different methods for succession planning: first, a priority- and risk-driven approach; and second, a way to do that alongside talent-driven planning. I finish by looking at how to implement talent and succession planning in practice.

Approaches to succession planning

The starting point for succession planning means understanding the attributes required for each role and the attributes that each employee holds. In this respect, succession planning is closely linked with the fundamentals of competency management (Chapter 3.6). In Chapter 3.6 I highlighted the analytical limitations of the box grid. So, are there other analytical frameworks that can really make this process more fact-driven and robust with any hope of being better than manager gut feeling?

A good place to start is with competency management. Start by systematically understanding the required competencies for each role and assessing the level of competence that each person has. In a similar way to creating the summary process cards in Chapter 3.3, every individual could have his or her summary competencies against a role's competencies in one 'competency passport'. With this, you could focus on gaps and desired areas of improvement. However, this only gives the context of an employee's current role. By extending the thought process to other roles, you should be able to see the gap in competencies versus all roles. This could apply beyond competencies. For example, you could incorporate 'skills and experience' rather than the 'attributes, aptitude and behaviours' which are behind competencies. I am wary of placing too much emphasis on skills or experience as people will rise only to the level of their incompetence. It may solve today's problem but it will not solve tomorrow's. I believe that the attributes and behaviours wrapped up in competencies are more innate and harder to develop than skills and experience, which only require time to develop. Through your succession planning process you want to be able to determine who, according to your measures, is the closest fit and, therefore, the best candidate for succession. For those who are potential successors, what are the things that they most need to work on? How are they progressing? Which skills are in the shortest supply? In this section I demonstrate two approaches to help answer these questions. The first takes a short-term priority- and risk-driven perspective, while the second focuses on a longer-term talent-based approach.

Priority- and risk-driven planning

Succession planning is not a simple case of competency mapping. In the more immediate term, succession planning should also take a priority- and risk-based approach. You need to know where focus is required, which roles will be hardest to replace owing to key technical skill or leadership, and whether any of those roles are at high risk of departure. This is not just about senior leaders, as often key roles can be at a low level. So you need to investigate flight risks across all the key roles regardless of the level at which they sit. Then you need to know which roles already have a large set of potential successors in place.

One way of thinking through flight risk is demonstrated in the fishbone diagram in Figure 4.6.1. The fishbone diagram is a causal diagram created by Kaoru Ishikawa in 1968 that shows the causes of a specific event.[6] In it, we are asking, what factors act as a good prediction of flight risk? For example, if the tenure in a role is high and the attrition of the team that role is in is high, then all things remaining equal, they are more likely to leave. It is common for companies to rely solely on the perspective of the manager. My perspective is that the view of the manager is only one data source. The manager's perception can be skewed by personal relationships, a lack of information or having the wrong motives. For example, one inter-national software firm I worked with initially used to place sales talent within a nine-box grid approach, based on manager reports. When it combined sales and finance data with manager placements it found that manager perceptions of top performers were not in line with their perfor-mance numbers. The lesson is to incorporate managerial feedback with data from across the organization, such as performance scores, sales records, 360 feedback, and so on, to build a comprehensive understanding.

Using the risk mapping process highlighted in Figure 4.6.1, you can utilize a wide range of data to investigate which employees are in what risk and impact categories. In other words, you can narrow down the focus of discussion and action by plotting your employees into high, medium or low 'flight impact' versus 'risk' categories. In this case, it would be a 33 pivot graph, but in reality it doesn't matter how you cut the data. The flight impact score for the organization, if employees leave, is a combination of 'business

FIGURE 4.6.1 Illustrative flight risk fishbone root causes

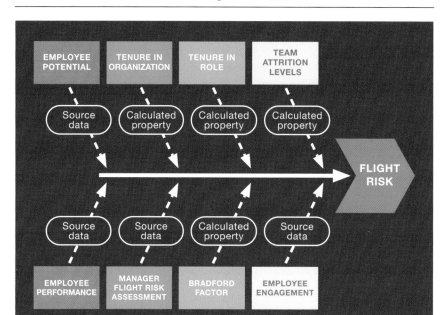

impact' and 'time to productivity' measures, as outlined in Chapter 4.5 for workforce planning groups. Having completed this analysis, the key employees to focus on first are the high-high employees. These are those mostly likely to leave, resulting in the worst impact. While initially this approach has a naturally short-term view, when it is combined with a talent-based approach you can begin to think long term about where future employees could sit in the organization and where the development priorities need to be.

Talent-driven planning

Life isn't static, and you need to try to plan a long way into the future. What if you could predict which groups of employees are most likely to be able to step up into the senior roles? What if there was a body of research with practical uses that could help plan five, 10 or even 20 years into the future? Well, I believe there is. One way to think about the long term is to make predictions on where people could end up. The best predictor of the future is the past. So by looking at the speed of progress and development of your talent pool, you can start to think through five to 20 years hence.

A useful approach is to make your predictions based on 'stratified systems theory'. The idea, put simply, is that every employee is at a given 'stratum'. Elliott Jaques, a Canadian organizational psychologist, defined these levels as corresponding to naturally occurring levels of cognitive capability or complexity of information processing that are a part of human nature.[7] As Ken Shepard, the President at Global Organization Design Society, explained it to me, you can judge what 'stratum' people are in by their mental models and how they frame things. This can be shown by how they answer questions such as 'What is your view on the legalization of drugs?' together with the time horizon in which they look forward (is their horizon tomorrow, next month, next year or what is going to happen in 10–20 years?), and the type of mental models they hold (simplistic to complex to a 'meta model' of the world). Training and experience are required to identify where people sit and are not in the scope of this book. But simply, a Stratum I person would say to the drugs question, 'It is bad,' whereas those higher up have ever increasing levels of articulation and even meta models for answering the same questions.

It is typical practice to relate the stratum to the level someone is in. Is the person a front-line employee doing manual work or the CEO of a major corporation? A short explanation of each stratum from Elliott Jaques is:

- **Stratum I**: These jobs might include shopfloor operator, sales clerk, or general police officer; most work is routine, and supervision is commonplace for new tasks. Such jobs are good fits for Level 1 people, who think forward with a time horizon of one day to three months.

- **Stratum II**: First-line managers, shopfloor supervisors, middle managers, proprietors of some small businesses and police inspectors have a felt-fair pay level of one-and-one-half times what a Stratum I employee might get. This job fits people with a three-month to one-year time horizon and who can handle assignments that take that long a time to fulfil.

- **Stratum III**: Department heads, workshop managers, owners of multistore franchises and police chief inspectors would make felt-fair pay that was three times that of a Stratum I employee. Stratum III managers typically know personally all the people below them in a hierarchy. Many professionals with high technical skill levels operate at this level, managing just a few people. People with a time horizon of one to two years can handle this.

FIGURE 4.6.2   Illustrative stratum model predictions

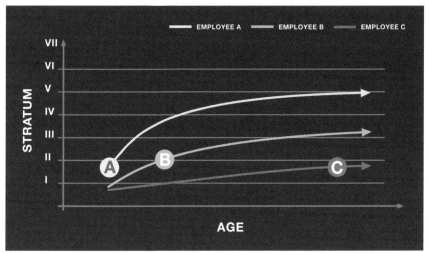

- **Stratum IV**: A plant manager, editor of a large media operation, lab manager, or any line leader with responsibility for diverse constituencies would earn felt-fair pay six times that of Stratum I. Appropriate time horizon: two to five years.

- **Stratum V**: Positions at this level include divisional executives of large companies, business-unit heads (at the vice presidential level), production directors and CEOs of 5,000-employee organizations. Most 'zealot' jobs are probably Stratum V positions. Felt-fair pay: 12 times Stratum I. Time horizon: five to 20 years.

As Donald V Fowke wrote in *Thinking About Organization Strategically*: 'High potential employees are those who will be capable of general management, or equivalent Stratum IV functional roles, before they are 43 years old. This means they will need to make the turn from front-line manager to manager of managers by 27 years of age.'[8] Around 40 per cent of all employees/ people in society will only ever be Stratum I, with another 40 per cent only reaching Stratum II. Almost no one, ever, makes it to Stratum VIII. Those individuals include Steve Jobs (CEO of Apple, 1997–2011) and Jack Welch (chairman and CEO of General Electric, 1981–2001).

What I like about this model is how practical it can be. Based on where someone is and his or her age, the future trajectory can be mapped along an arc. Mapping where employees sit and their age gives you a good place to start long-term workforce and succession planning. Think through attrition and the population sizes and form a view as to how much talent could make the cut in five, 10 or 20 years' time. Imagine three people: Person A, Person B and Person C as shown in Figure 4.6.2. Person B has a slightly higher score than Person A, but is expected to max out at Stratum IV (which is still very senior), while person A is destined to be capable of becoming a Group VP and possibly even a CEO, even though Person B has roughly the same score as Person C. Another interesting point highlighted to me about this model is the insight that you should never have anyone manage someone else in the same stratum or more than one level away. For example, if the manager is at Stratum III, he or she should only manage those who are in Stratum II. In addition, each role demands a given level of person to fulfil it. But that doesn't necessarily mean the person in that role actually hits that level. He or she could be a Stratum II or IV. Therefore, that person won't perform well enough OR will be frightfully bored. Based on the research of 59,000 manager – direct reporting line relationships in 76 organizations by Ronald G Capelle from Capelle Associates, 36 per cent of managers are in a compression relationship.[9] What that means is that 36 per cent of everyone's manager is at the same stratum as those they are managing, resulting in over micro-management and doing too much of their teams' jobs because they are not fully capable of doing their own job.

A Level 1 salesperson is transactional: 'You give me the cash and I give you the product.' The transaction time is extremely short. The Level 2 salesperson is a relationship manager: someone looking after a range of accounts with a one to 12 month time horizon. The Level 3 salesperson, therefore, is the territory manager. However, too often the territory manager is actually spending large amounts of time babysitting the relationship managers and doing too much of the actual work. This issue of Level 3 managers spending too much time doing Level 2 work is pervasive. According to Capelle, about 50 per cent of the time spent by professionals is doing lower-level work, with a conservative cost estimate of $10,000 per position.

Although to follow anything dogmatically is dangerous, I believe stratified systems theory is a useful framework. You must remember, however, that it isn't the final answer. It is about mapping out employees' potential in terms of where they are likely to be at a given point in time, not necessarily what *will* happen. If only social science could give us anything that deterministic. There are risks in doing this work. Does the process open you up to employment tribunals and does it become a demotivator? One of my previous clients in a highly regulated, government and unionized environment said she wouldn't touch it with a barge pole. Her perspective was that it runs the risk of putting employees in different 'potential' buckets. By saying someone is a successor doesn't mean he or she would get the job, but some may not see it that way. It isn't recruitment but it could be viewed as a de facto decision; it is driven by favouritism and doesn't follow the proper recruitment selection processes. Marshall Goldsmith in his '4 Tips for Efficient Succession Planning' HBR Blog Network said it nicely:

> While development plans and succession charts aren't promises, they are often communicated as such and can lead to frustration if they aren't realistic. Bottom line, don't jerk around high-performing leaders with unrealistic development expectations. Only give the promise of succession if there is a realistic chance of its happening! [that is, it's about having the real conversations].
>
> *Harvard Business Review* 2009[10]

Like all pieces of analysis, more complexity and refinement can be added. You also need to think about what the business needs in terms of talent as the business model and operating model evolve and, therefore, what the required attributes are of the future workforce, and whether you should develop your existing talent or seek new talent. Everything is possible, but not everything is desirable. Each piece of additional accuracy in the model means collecting more data, involving more discussions, effort and time. There always has to be compromise between accuracy and practicality.

Implementing talent and succession planning

I have developed several principles and frameworks that impact on talent and succession management from some of the previous chapters. They include:

- Competency (Chapter 3.6):
  - The need to define a competency hierarchy and then set target competencies for each position.
  - Run a process that assesses each employee against those target competencies.
  - Understand the gaps from the employee level up to the overall organizational level, sliced by a range of dimensions; for example, function, grade, location and even recruitment channel, manager, time in grade.
- Workforce planning (Chapter 4.5):
  - Define workforce planning (WFP) groups based on broadly fungible positions.

- Map these WFP groups by two dimensions. The 'time to productivity' and the 'strategic impact'. Where are the biggest issues?
- So far in this chapter:
  - Determine the flight risk of each employee and the impact of him or her leaving (combining the two dimensions from the WFP segments above).
  - Map each position to the Jaques system theory strata (levels).
  - Assess each person's level (this should, therefore, be part of the competency mapping process, and form 'just' another view of competency levels).
  - Determine whether there are misalignments. For instance, the manager and team are either at the same level (they are compressed) or too far apart (there is a gap).

Assuming that you have all this information, what can and should you do with it?

Identify risks and opportunities

For each workforce planning group, and especially the strategic ones, which groups have the greatest risk? Which have the greatest number of high potentials coming through and where do you need to recruit from the outside?

Develop and improve

The first step is development, led by the managers and other leaders within the organization. Are the managers aware of the gaps in their teams? Are the managers adequately trained in how to mentor and coach their teams? Where managers don't have the skill or time to mentor their teams, do you have alternative mentors or coaches? Do you have a culture of providing constant feedback? I believe it is only possible to master skills with constant focus and support, purposeful repetition and an environment that tolerates mistakes. This fits within the conditions of flow as explained in Chapter 3.6. It is fundamentally a core role of management to ensure managers constantly improve their teams. This process needs to be supported by HR, but it isn't HR who is responsible.

The next step is more formal, centrally led, training and development. From a competency perspective, those competencies with the greatest gaps should feed into the training needs assessment. Group the poorly performing and most critical competency gaps into bundles of what can effectively become training courses. Which courses have added the greatest impact? If you know when the various employees have attended their training courses, can you find evidence that they are more likely to attain their objectives? Can you find a positive correlation between gained competencies and hitting desired KPIs? Another method to test the value of training is through follow-up surveys sent several months after the training with specific business outcome questions.

Beyond this, the range of options to address improving your talent and mitigating the risks is endless and falls into what can commonly be regarded as good business practice. Some other common activities include improving recruitment practices through more tailored skills and behaviour assessments; understanding which recruitment channels and types of candidates deliver the best results; ensuring there is an open learning culture... The list is endless and begins to fall outside the scope of this book. Like many good practices, they are often easier said than done. Chapter 4.7 provides a range of tools to help you pull your thoughts together, create a plan and then use a range of tools to ensure those plans are executed.

Final thoughts

Once you get your competitive edge, can you keep it? Any review of the fall of the mightiest firms over the past 100+ years clearly shows most can't. In order to sustain it, you are going to need to sustain employing great people. That means creating a culture of building a talent pipeline and ensuring succession planning becomes a core management process. It is going to need to become part of your culture. Talent is a big topic in HR circles. I don't think anyone doubts its importance and the idea that there is a war for talent is no longer new. But the common practice I see is to focus too narrowly and in too much of a subjective way. It should start by knowing what type of talent you need. That is defined by the list of competencies (skills, experience and behaviours) required for each role (the demand). From there, it is about looking forward and working out the development needs of those people deemed to be critical successes. The importance of each role in terms of succession planning relates to the risk of those in that role leaving (the flight risk) and the impact that will have. The impact doesn't just relate to how close the role is to the CEO. Some roles may be senior but easy to replace while others are far more junior but almost impossible to replace and take years to develop.

> ### Remember this
>
> 1 Ensure you have effectively mapped employee and role attributes to compare and see the gaps.
>
> 2 Prioritize and focus effort by assessing where high-impact staff are at high risk through analysing a range of data.
>
> 3 Create a long-term view by predicting individual success and facilitating development to fulfil potential where possible.
>
> 4 Invest in and take practical steps to ensure structured development.
>
> 5 Connect inputs in talent development such as training and recruitment with outputs such as performance and career progression to understand effective methods.

Notes

1 Goldsmith, M [accessed 17 February 2015] 4 Tips for Efficient Succession Planning, *Harvard Business Review* [Online] http://blogs.hbr.org/2009/05/change-succession-planning-to/

2 Ernst & Young LLP [accessed 17 February 2015] 2007 Aging US Workforce Survey: Challenges and Responses – An Ongoing Review [Online] http://www.plansponsor.com/uploadfiles/ErnstandYoung.pdf

3 Collins, J (2001) *Good to Great*, Random House

4 Hirsh, W (2012) Planning for succession in changing times, Report, Corporate Research Forum

5 Rethinking human resources in a changing world by KPMG (2012) Global study commissioned by KPMG and conducted by the Economics Intelligence Unit of 418 executive.

6 Ishikawa, K (1976) *Guide to Quality Control*, Asian Productivity Organization, Tokyo

7 Jaques, E (1971) Time-span handbook: The use of time-span of discretion to measure the level of work in employment roles and to arrange an equitable payment structure, Heinemann, London

8 Fowke, D V (nd) *Thinking About Organization Strategically: A Systems Approach to Strategy, Structure and Staffing*, New Management Network, Ontario [Online] http://www.new-management-network.com/publications/Thinking%20About%20Organization%20Strategically.pdf

9 Capelle, G (2014) *Optimizing Organization Design*, Jossey-Bass, San Francisco

10 Goldsmith, M [accessed 21 February 2015] Harvard Business School blog [Online] https://hbr.org/2009/05/change-succession-planning-to/

Organizational getting things done

Plans are only good intentions unless they immediately degenerate into hard work. **PETER DRUCKER**

Introduction

A lot of this book has been focused on planning and implementing your organization design over time. No matter how good your design or plans look on paper, at the end of the day, achieving your strategy through successful design comes down to getting things done on the ground. Too often, great ideas and well-intentioned initiatives go from *sizzle* to *fizzle*. They start off with drive and enthusiasm and over time become lost in the general black hole of stuff that needs to be done day to day. The same blockers to making design plans a reality rear their heads again and again. For instance:

- People don't know what they and others are responsible for or what deadlines they are working to. One part of a project gets finished but fails to be passed on to the next person, so the project slips between the gaps.

- Leaders flit from one priority to another giving impetus to one initiative without any consistency, resulting in activities being dropped for no reason but a whim.

- The wrong activities in an organization are perceived to be a sign of being busy. For example, people's days are full of overly long, unnecessary meetings.

- People politics means the conversations that need to happen are avoided and sidelined for the comfort of tomorrow, which never comes.

- People can't get access to the right information when they need it, resulting in a stream of e-mails back and forth as people search for that key document.

Getting and sustaining the organizational edge mean addressing these issues, not just to implement plans, but also to create a culture of continuous improvement. This requires leveraging your organizational structure to ensure responsibilities and decision-making processes are clear, while putting ways of working and resources in place to maximize organizational networks and information flows for individuals and teams.

The micro design you have done sets the context for this, but it isn't sufficient on its own. In Chapter 3.5 I listed the three levels of project planning and management. That chapter detailed how to create a summary map and integrated plan when project planning. In this chapter I want to address how on a day-to-day basis you can manage and get the hundreds if not thousands of tasks done. I start by highlighting the power of the list as a way of bringing discipline to individual and team ways of working. I apply the idea of using the dynamic lists when implementing a complex set of activities and plans across individuals and teams, through the example of an agile software approach to development. I then explore how you can use the processes and outputs from a data-driven approach to help remove traditional barriers to getting things done using the examples of meetings, office politics and resources. Throughout the chapter, while the techniques I am discussing are applied in the context of implementing an organization design, I hope they also give inspiration and ways of working more broadly across the organization, and on an ongoing basis.

The power of the list

The focus of this book is the organization as a whole, as a functioning system. However, an organization only gets as much done as its people get done – both as individuals and as teams. In building a framework for organizational 'getting things done' I have taken my main inspiration from the power of the list. The idea of creating lists is by no means revolutionary, but it is undoubtedly extremely effective. In this section I will explore how lists can help ways of working on both an individual and a team level, before applying these techniques to the complex ways of working in an organization. Creating lists is extremely effective. Benefits include:

- **Reduced stress.** Brings a feeling of control by having all activities and tasks in one place. There is less worry that you will forget something or waste time doing the wrong things.

- **Increased focus**. Gives you the opportunity to make better choices about where to focus your attention and time, taking into account your context.

- **Improved delivery**. Helps you keep commitments as you will be able to remember them, and prioritize so that you can stick to them.

As Atul Gawande says in *The Checklist Manifesto*, checklists help navigate the complexities of the world around us.[1] He illustrates the power of the checklist from the medical profession to skyscraper construction. He highlights the power of the list as a reminder and a resource of empowerment for workers. For example, he explores how a simple five-point checklist, including simple activities such as 'washing hands with soap', when implemented at the intensive care unit at Johns Hopkins Hospital in Baltimore prevented an estimated 43 infections and eight deaths over 27 months. And when it was later implemented at another ICU in Michigan infections decreased by 66 per cent within three months.

On an individual level, one of the best methods for effectiveness is David Allen's *Getting Things Done: The art of stress-free productivity*.[2] It may be over 10 years old but it sets out a fantastic method for structuring everything you need to get done. In the context of this book I have set the four broad steps to this approach as part of a weekly review, but if you want to learn more I would recommend it as an excellent read.

1 Set out all your objectives, responsibilities, projects/initiatives. Build them in a hierarchical list.

2 Organize the list into a set of context-specific buckets. For example:
   - how urgent;
   - how time consuming;
   - whether it requires input or work from another person.

3 Process the inputs and review options for next actions.

4 Do actions and maintain steps 1–3.

These steps help map out the week(s) ahead and give priority to the things that need to be done. If a new urgent task hits the list, then you have the means rapidly to know what is going to be impacted. These two examples are, on the one hand, extremely useful to help follow static rigorous procedures and, on the other, help to organize yourself on a personal level. However, in the context of the day-to-day life within an organization, you need a way of combining the flexible and evolving nature of David Allen's approach with the thoroughness and simplicity of Atul Gawande's checklist. You need a way of managing the detailed daily workflows and handovers, and a process to monitor progress on a continuous basis.

Getting things done in a team

As I argued in Chapter 2.3, employees are connected day to day through organizational networks. It is these networks that facilitate getting things done. The organizational hierarchy isn't there to manage the detailed daily workflows. For many roles, the manager cannot manage all the elements of work. Teams need to self-manage and get things done. This does not mean simply creating lists in Excel, which get left to gather dust, but creating a resource that is intuitive and dynamic for both individuals and teams. In the context of any project, you need a way of itemizing all the things that need to get done, updating them and passing them between people, as well as a process to monitor the progress on a continuous basis. One way of achieving this is to use an agile approach to working.

The interactive backlog

An example of an agile approach is in software development. The idea is to maximize team resources, while maintaining a fluid list of actions and priorities to cope with the, sometimes unpredictable, nature of software development. Teams start with a backlog, a list of all the functionality that needs to be built. Each item is given a score as to how much effort it will take (called complexity points). Each element of the backlog is given a property. Prioritizing is easily done by physically ranking each element in the list from most important at the top to least popular at the bottom. The next step is to create a generic process flow. For example: prioritize, design, build, test, release. All the items sit within a backlog until a decision is made to prioritize them onto someone's specific list of actions. Once each person has finished, that person will transfer it to the next person's in-tray. For example, the designer finishes the design and hands it off to the developer. If the design isn't clear enough, they will have a conversation and perhaps even hand back the specific piece of work in question. This process of handing the work between everyone's lists continues until the person responsible for releasing it does just that. In agile development, at any time a new item can be added to the list and the prioritization of that list can be changed. The only time the backlog can't be changed is during a 'sprint'. A sprint is a fixed

FIGURE 4.7.1   Example Kanban

Status

Not Started (18)		On Hold (4)	For Approval (4)	Booked / Ordered (14)		In Progress (5)	Complete (4)
Letterhead Creative	Events stand design Creative	Branded mugs Directors	Water bottles Directors	Business cards Creative	DJ HR	Video Creative	Branded bottle openers Creative
Business cards Creative		Employee Surprise HR	Drinks Directors	Bags Creative	kayak HR	Group Train tickets HR	Lensbury Creative
Case Studies Creative		Office chairs HR	Canapes Directors	Meeting room signs Creative	Reception upgrade HR	Transport HR	Table sweets HR
Flyers/One pagers Creative		Kitchen upgrade HR	Posters Directors	Logo above sofa Creative	Metal Pillars HR	Paint HR	Coffee table book HR
Brochures Creative				Wall sign in hallway Creative	Office Clean - Sunday HR	New lights for darkside HR	
White papers Creative				Vinyl installation Creative			
Pop up banners Creative				Brand A5 document Directors			
Compliment slips & Envelopes Creative				Dance off (Bounce) HR			
Website Creative				Catering HR			

Owner   ■ Creative   ▨ Directors   ▨ HR

period of time in which to complete detailed design, development, testing and releasing of the software code. The goal at the end of each sprint is to have functional, fully useable software.

Figure 4.7.1 shows an example of a backlog from a member of my team. For simplicity's sake (the technical software backlog is too complex for a book like this), the example here is a backlog for a list of activities related to launching a new brand. Each column is a stage in the process with the colour depicting who owns it. Once a task is done it gets passed across. The list can be changed dynamically and viewed by all. If the list is too large and things aren't moving through, then everyone in the team can see there is a problem. In many ways, the backlog is exactly the same as a Kanban system for scheduling work. 'Kanban' means signboard or billboard in Japanese, and was a method developed by Tajichi Ohno to improve efficiency across the production process. The system ensures that production is demand-led, with Kanbans alerting suppliers to produce and deliver a particular material based on consumption. What is great about this process is that it is easy for everyone to see everything at any point in time: the list of things everyone is working on, how long they have had it, the history of that work item and where it will go next. It is extremely intuitive and brings together individual and team ways of working so they can see what they have achieved and what still needs to be done.

The waterfall method

Another approach is the waterfall method. This is very different from the agile approach described above. It is used when the final requirement of what needs to be 'built' is fully understood and doesn't change. In software development, for example, it has the same summary steps: design; build; test and fix; release. However, unlike the agile method these steps are all done in sequence. You design the entire solution first, then the development team builds the whole thing, then it is all tested, and so on. The waterfall method should only be used when there is complete clarity in what you are trying to achieve or build. It gives you less agility but a greater sense of control. You know exactly what you are getting before you start 'digging' the foundations. However, if there are aspects subject to change, or you are learning as you go, the traditional waterfall will not give you the flexibility you need.

Tracking and management

One of the greatest benefits of using this type of agile approach across organizational work is that it provides a huge amount of information, allowing you to hone and improve your ways of working. For example, each day the amount of work completed is known as each person either completes what he or she has done or gives a percentage complete at the specific action (backlog) level. This then makes it easier to know how much time and effort specific pieces of work will take in the future. It also means that when you meet as a team, you can easily and quickly review what has been achieved, areas for concern, and what needs to get done next and with what priority. For example, Figure 4.2.7 shows a burndown chart highlighting how much work has been done versus the plan. After each sprint, the number of complexity points delivered (the output) can be compared with the plan and historical actuals. The team can then do a sprint review as to why it might have missed a certain goal, what the learning is and how to improve for the next sprint. Because the length of a sprint is relatively short (typically two weeks, but can be as long as four weeks and as short as one), the feedback loops mean that what has been learnt can be rapidly applied.

Applying an agile approach

In terms of bringing this type of approach from software development across other organizational ways of working, I do not believe in being too prescriptive. Each team will have its own ways of working and its own networks.

FIGURE 4.7.2   Example burndown chart

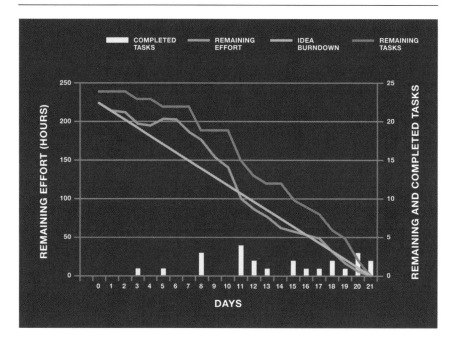

What I want to pull out is that the agile approach is a great way of making sure everyone knows what they should be doing, how they could be doing it, and of tracking progress. It helps facilitate networks of people working with each other across functions, projects and other boundaries. For example, let's return to Chapter 4.6. Part of the challenge for many individuals and organizations is the sheer amount of stuff that is on at one time and 'needs' to get done. By having a dynamic list assigned to people it will highlight conflicts and where there are bottlenecks or simply just too much to do.

Although this is applicable for every level of the organization it does undoubtedly start at the top. If you are the leader, you set the tone and standards. People will model their behaviour on their seniors, set the examples and tone. Once it gets out of hand, like so many things that are cultural, it is hard to pull it back. For example, use your visual implementation plan/checklist to focus your own activities and instructions. When reading Bob Woodward's book, *State of Denial*, I was struck by his story on the number of instructions Donald Rumsfeld would write and send. Called 'snowflakes', they would be written on white paper and seemingly come from the heavens! We have all been guilty of sending out requests or instructions either to get something off our plate or in the heat of the moment. However, rather than getting things done, because these instructions come from on high, all other priorities are temporarily parked. The result? Nothing ever gets finished, or certainly not as efficiently as it could have been. The direction and motivation from leaders need to be prioritized and managed based on an awareness of what is going on the organization, who has time currently and what activities would suit them. Your implementation plan/checklist gives you a good opportunity to check whether your instructions are an urgent priority or can wait to be discussed and added to the list of things to do longer term.

Using a data-driven approach to get things done

In many ways, getting things done happens by building a particular organizational culture. Culture, although linked to organization design, is an entire subject in its own right. However, I do want to demonstrate how using the processes and outputs from a data-driven approach, both from the above section and explored in the earlier chapters of the book, can be applied in practice to get things done in the day to day.

Meetings

Meetings are one of my bugbears. The phrase 'I'm back-to-back all day' is extremely common in large organizations. All too often meetings don't have a clear purpose, agenda, outcomes or mechanisms for following up on actions or recording decisions made. We have all been that person sitting there wondering quite why we are there, and thinking through all the more useful things we could be doing. Part of this comes back to roles being unclear. If it is unclear who makes the decisions or who is responsible for doing the job at hand, then it is no surprise that a large group of people is involved. Here are three ways to use the materials and approaches outlined in this book to get more from your meetings:

1 Get the right people in the room: A lot of this book has focused on bringing clarity to decision-making. Techniques like the implementation/ project plan detailed earlier in this chapter are an excellent way of ensuring people know whom they need to turn to if they want answers, and who the people responsible and involved in the process are.

2 Ensure the right information is in place for decisions to be made: A big issue for a lot of meetings is preparation. If the meeting is to make a decision, then what information is required should be clearly understood prior to the meeting and prepared. If the meeting is a routine one, like a weekly sales or finance review, then the information and agenda should be standardized. For example, create a dashboard, which covers all the 'business as usual' questions.

3 Use live data and analysis: By bringing high-level visualizations, as well as the ability to drill into the data behind them, into the meeting, you can answer questions as they are raised rather than being a subject for another day. It allows decision makers to concentrate on the same information and engage with it. Meetings become more efficient and focused, with better decisions being made from the information available.

Politics

As I highlighted right at the start of this book in Chapter 1.2, politics are probably the biggest barrier to getting things done. Shared ambition to achieve the same results means information gets shared easily and freely with decisions motivated by getting the best solution. In contrast, a lack of trust will result in your organization struggling and losing its edge. When people play politics, then what could be decided in minutes can take months, years or simply never be resolved. An organization becomes paralysed. This is one of the biggest cancers within any organization. Typically, it isn't anyone's fault. If a group of individuals don't like each other, trust each other and/or want the same thing, then that organization will fail. To a certain extent, politics are not something you can necessarily control. It comes down to personalities and egos. However, you can set up ways to put yourself in a position to help avoid the problem or at least expose it:

- Clear goals and objectives: Having a shared ambition is something which often grows with teams rather than being immediately internalized. However, you have to set yourself up for success by effectively communicating both the high-level organizational goals and individual objectives (Chapters 2.2 and 3.2). If employees know in which direction they are pulling it gives them a much better chance of being inspired and pulling together.

- Being clear on responsibilities: By ensuring you have clear responsibilities for both processes and day-to-day project management, it is more difficult for things to slip through the gaps. Transparency over who is doing what will uncover quickly where projects stall and make it difficult for people to excuse continually blocking things.

- Tracking progress: Half the battle is simply knowing when something is going wrong. Having a data-driven approach means you can track how things are progressing against plans, whether objectives, plans or projects. Transparency over where things are going wrong facilitates feedback loops for both employees and managers to have a conversation about where there may be problems, and uncover political issues early on.

There are many tell-tale signs of office politics. For example, look out for lengthy papers or e-mails to justify decisions, or outside mediators being used to drive consensus, or the amount of time spent talking about people rather than on the task at hand. Sometimes a point of no return gets passed. No amount of process design, team building events, objective setting, or off-sites will be able to redress the situation. Once relationships are beyond repair, the only way to sort the situation out is for a person or group to leave either that team or the organization. It is easy to see why so many mergers struggle. Cultures can be very different and difficult to bridge. There is no doubt that office politics is a tough problem to solve: it is emotional and can be very difficult to resolve without conflict. In this regard, there is no immediate solution, except to be strict and bold in cutting it out at the first sign. It is worth it – trust is very hard to rebuild.

Resources

The final area I want to explore is that of resources. Initiatives are often slowed down, or stalled by the inability to get access to the right information when needed. This wastes people's time and pulls them off their focused activities. There are many content management systems out there, but it doesn't matter how good a system is, it is only as good as the processes behind using it. Therefore, think through which resources are needed by whom and when:

- Make the most of your Kanbans/backlog: These give a great overview of all the work that is going to be done both over the long term of a project and the immediate future. Have an initial and then weekly review where you reaffirm priorities: who deals with them and what they are going to need to get them done. That means all the resources can be put in place from the start, or at least before they hinder someone from achieving something.

- Don't forget your data collection methods: Sometimes you simply need to extract information from across the organization. So don't forget the methods discussed in the data goldmine (Chapter 3.1). Using pulse surveys and webforms are a great way of getting information from a wide range of sources quickly.

- Ensure plans are documented and in a shared location: Many of the materials employees will need, when it comes specifically to the implementation of the design, are the documents you created at the beginning whether they are the design criteria, process maps or objectives hierarchies. This is where all that hard work pays off. If all of these are well documented and advertised in a shared location it will make it much easier for people to implement the design along the lines it was intended.

Final thoughts:
Use the right management tools

We are what we do every day. From an organizational context, we are not only what we do as individuals, but also how we work with those around us. Part Three of this book, 'Micro design', is all about defining who does what and the numbers of people required to do it. Part Four, Making it Real, is about actually doing it. Not all activities need to be managed this way. If the role is transactional (for example, first line phone support) then you will have other metrics to understand the effectiveness of the work (for example response times, customer satisfaction, time to resolve, resolutions percentages). Like many of the tools and methods discussed in this book, it is about using the right tool in the appropriate context. I find many of the concepts explained in this chapter particularly useful for work that doesn't fit within strict everyday processes. It is not a surprise that the amount of literature and people talking about self-organizing teams is on the increase. It is because the level of detail required to manage all the work is too great. In the future, teams will be given a set of tools to manage the work and provide the appropriate levels of transparency as to their progress.

As I have highlighted throughout the book, and the focus of the next and final chapter, measuring and tracking are fundamentally important to getting things done and understanding progress and effectiveness in real terms.

How many of the 'event' objectives have been done on time as described in Chapter 3.3? How many critical actions, for example those to mitigate a significant risk as explained in Chapter 3.5, haven't progressed since the last review? How many items does each person have on his or her plate within the next review period? In a team context, tracking the work and making this process transparent means people can see where the blockages are, who is responsible for what and, if it's with them, when they need to get things done by. If a set of priority actions has been stuck with someone for months but non-priority actions are done or you don't know what that person has done, then he or she either has too much work, doesn't agree with the priorities, or doesn't have the skills or resources to do the work. Either way, you can do something about it, and make sure things get done!

Remember this

1 Get the most from your organizational hierarchy and networks by ensuring responsibilities are clear and transparent.

2 Use interactive lists to help teams and individuals allocate work between each other.

3 Track progress to see where blockages are and which areas need focus or support.

4 Make the most of the data-driven processes and outputs you have been applying throughout the book to drive effective ways of working.

5 As a leader, set the example and tone. Be brave, and when office politics arise, tackle the situation as early as possible.

Notes

1 Gawande, A (2009) *The Checklist Manifesto*, Profile Books

2 Allen, D (2001) *Good to Great*, Piatkus Books

Sustaining the edge

I've missed more than 9,000 shots in my career. I've lost almost 300 games. 26 times, I've been trusted to take the game-winning shot and missed. I've failed over and over and over again in my life. And that is why I succeed.

MICHAEL JORDAN

Introduction

This is the last chapter of a big journey. In this book I have mapped out a path to enable organizations to achieve the competitive edge through organizational data and analytics. However, one of the greatest challenges still to come is sustaining that edge over the course of time. In reality, organization design is not and should not be thought of as a one-off. You will always need to improve ways of working, review and adjust plans and meet new targets if you are going to stay ahead of the competition and continue to fulfil your organizational potential. It is hard work. It requires constant discipline. It is a test of endurance.

In this final chapter I want to explore how you can sustain performance by continuously tracking your organization and performance against plans. While implementing each of the steps within Part Two (Macro design), Part Three (Micro design) and Part Four (Making it Real), you need to ask yourself: How well did we do? What are the areas that didn't meet our expectations and why? What can we learn from those experiences? and How do we know we have actually learnt the right lessons? Equally, you need to know when and where you have succeeded so you can celebrate, reflect on your achievements and take a well-earned rest. Throughout this final chapter I revisit the key themes in the book, and finish with a note on what the future may hold and how you can prepare to make the most of it.

Tracking the system

In Chapter 4.7 I talked about getting things done. But how do you know when you have actually achieved something? How do you know if you won or lost? How do you know when all the small day-to-day things you do add up to something bigger, something worth talking about and something worth celebrating? Your vision should be inspirational, it should get you out of bed every day and motivate your work. However, if you never feel like you are getting closer to your vision, it can be demoralizing and can start to lose its value. Unfortunately, organizational success isn't always simple to define. Unlike in sport there is no single score, no level playing field, and no referee to call time. It is up to you to know when you have scored a goal, or won an important battle.

So, have you got any closer to your vision? Have you achieved the goals and high-level objectives you set yourself? If you are off track, by how much and where? I find it remarkable how much effort goes into developing detailed business plans. Having heated arguments as to what should or shouldn't be done. Or making commitments, in many cases to investors, and then just leaving the outcome to the team without much, if any, control as to whether those plans have been achieved or not. The reason for this can be a simple case of getting bogged down in the detail and the day-to-day issues. But you have to take a step back and track against high-level targets, otherwise there's just no point in them. This is why the combination of high-level ambition and detailed plans is so important. The business plan in Part Two is connected to the detailed plans in Part Three, which are then fulfilled in Part Four, Making it Real. You need to bring everything back to the macro level so you can see your overall direction of travel.

Target versus actuals versus forecast

The world is constantly moving. No matter how thorough the budgeting process, assumptions made will turn out to be wrong. There will be changes to the organization. These changes need to be controlled and understood. But as priorities and facts move so do the numbers and sometimes structures. Sales in one area may lead to a bigger team or a new technology may change a set of processes. No matter what the reason, it has to be possible for the team to tweak the to-be design, for that to go through an approval process and then be accepted by the powers that be. What happens over time is typically an increasing divergence between the target and forecast. Questions will always be raised as to 'why' and 'where'. Why are they different, what has changed and how? Where are they different? Is it a particular function or location? To know the answers you have to track the system.

Tracking the organizational system and connecting it to your high-level objectives and plans mean understanding your organizational inputs in the context of business outputs. For example, tracking headcount reveals an input to the system, while organizational objectives are a specific output against which to measure the inputs. It is these outputs that, when rolled up, will help you identify how close you are to fulfilling your high-level objectives and goals as a business. As discussed in detail throughout the book, this means collecting the data, visualizing that data, understanding what is happening and where to facilitate a conversation. Figure 4.8.1 is an example of tracking the actual headcount versus both the target and forecast numbers. The target is the original target laid out in the final business case. The board members will have these numbers firmly in their minds. The forecast is the view of what the headcount will be, given everything that is known at the time of producing the report. Knowing how, where and why the forecast deviates from the target is crucial to keeping everyone informed as to how the organization is evolving. Answering the question of where the change is requires the ability to slice the data by geography, function, job levels and workforce planning groups. Knowing where will then help to answer the 'why' question.

Beyond headcount tracking

Tracking should be deeper than just monitoring headcount or cost. Those are just inputs, not outcomes. You could track your headcount and cost targets perfectly, but dramatically miss all the key outcomes like profit, revenue growth, customer satisfaction, or employee retention. Using the methods explored in Chapter 3.2 I showed how you can visualize the goal and objectives hierarchy using the BRAG colouring scheme. However, that just shows a static view. Figure 4.8.2 shows the tracking of the BRAG status over time with the percentage in each BRAG category. The ability to see performance over time combined with the ability to drill quickly into where you are ahead or behind brings the whole picture to life. These sorts of reports stimulate conversations about how to get even better or how the team can close the gap if there is one.

The limitation of this type of analysis is that it shows the aggregate score. So what does performance look like for each person? Figure 4.8.3 shows four objectives and how they are progressing over time. The first two have consistently been on or over the target in the blue-green zones. However,

FIGURE 4.8.1   Headcount tracking of target versus actual versus forecast

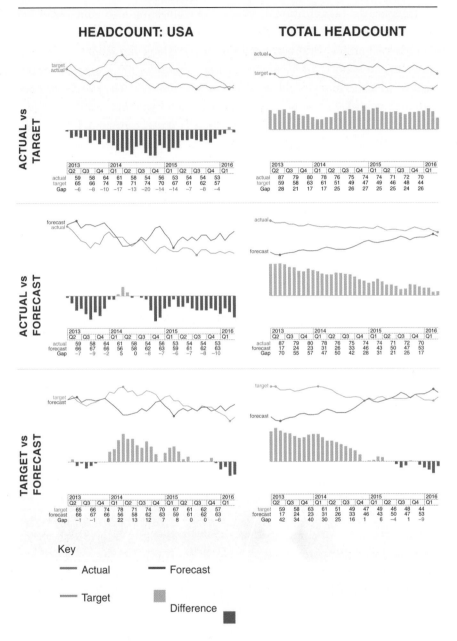

FIGURE 4.8.2   Summary objectives BRAG status

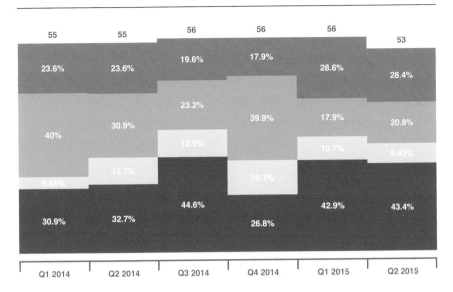

FIGURE 4.8.3   Individual objectives BRAG status

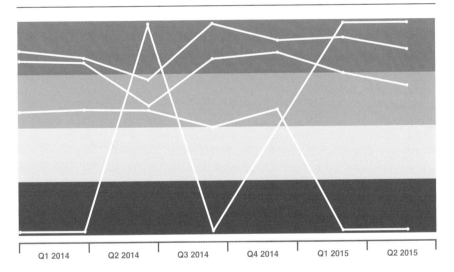

the third objective, having been on target, has suddenly deteriorated and the final objective is completely volatile.

This analysis gives you the basis to start really digging and asking in-depth questions to uncover correlations. Go back to the objectives tree and find the relevant numbers linked to employees. For example, is there a relationship between the tenure of their roles? If you look at your inputs in headcount, where are the high performers coming from? Where do they sit in the organization? Are they reporting to a manager who has others in the team who are behind? Has their absence suddenly increased? Are they overloaded with objectives? All of these questions uncover correlations so that you can find the root causes for high or low performance. By knowing how far off plan you are, who is responsible for what, and by doing root cause analysis as to why, then it should be possible to learn lessons for future planning exercises and to rectify the underlying issues moving forward. This analysis facilitates conversations to find out the reasons for where the problem areas are, and if there are any lessons to take away from those high-performing objectives that can be applied to other areas.

This brings me back to many of the key themes already explored in this book. You need to be sure of your plans and what targets you want to hit. You then need to capture the actuals; make the human process of entering data and the effort to produce analysis as close to effortless as possible to make this happen. The goal is to make sure these routines are as automated as possible. Take away the friction so that the extra effort adds exponential value. This type of capability should be organization wide. Then make the time to sit back and analyse, to have relevant conversations and come out with practical, sensible actions. The act of tracking will lead to business improvements. Instead of the famous saying, 'What gets measured gets done,' I prefer 'What gets tracked gets improved.' The good thing is that the more you improve your data and reporting, the better your understanding of the as-is and the easier it is understand and show where the change is needed.

Celebrating, reflecting and resting

Along the journey, one of the most important things is to take time to celebrate. I love how sportsmen and women celebrate. Sporting celebrations are iconic. The classic dropping to the knees of the Wimbledon champion, the crying gold medallist at the Olympics, the pile-up after a football team has won a penalty shootout. The reaction is instinctive and automatic. So why can it be so rare for the majority of us at work? I believe that if you achieve something remarkable, you should celebrate that fact. If someone else achieves something, celebrate that too. Not all moments are equal. It is those special moments that we remember most. However, it is those little moments where you achieve a small victory that can be the most important. A great organization has to be one that knows how to celebrate. It builds relationships and trust. Celebrating completes the feedback loop, giving deserved recognition to someone for a job well done.

Data and analytics are at the heart of this book. So I couldn't help but advocate a data-driven approach to celebrating! One of the best company away days I ever attended began with communicating the company's year in numbers through a dynamic data visualization. We collected the numbers for the year from across functions, and where appropriate added a percentage change from the number the year before. Everyone could see all the numbers in one place and each function leader stood up in turn to talk through what the numbers meant as the visualization rotated through each number. It was uplifting, transparent and, given we are an analytics company, was a great way of bringing the year's report to life for everyone. Figure 4.8.4 shows the visualization we used.

FIGURE 4.8.4 Organization-wide results by numbers

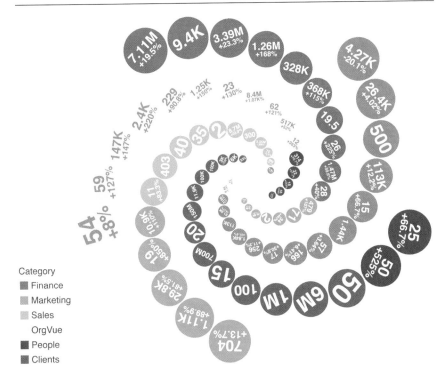

Category
- Finance
- Marketing
- Sales
- OrgVue
- People
- Clients

Alongside celebration, you need a chance to rest and reflect on what you have done and achieved. As Margaret J Wheatley, an author on organizational behaviour, sums up beautifully: 'Without reflection, we go blindly on our way, creating more unintended consequences, and failing to achieve anything useful.'[1] Rest and reflection are integral to keeping the human psychology system working well and I believe the organizational system is no different. The American actress Helen Hayes said, 'If you rest you rust.' With all due respect, I think this is nonsense. I am all for hard work, but without rest you simply burn out. I have seen it happen many times and it is terrible to witness. We are all human. We are all fallible. That means we can't perform at our peak performance indefinitely. You have to take time out, not only to recharge your batteries but also to give you the chance to learn. Mull over what has happened, internalizing it and absorbing the lessons. Without reflection, we just continue as we were, repeating the same old mistakes. As the University of Washington advises in their tips with respect to HR benefits: 'Rest is an important part of a healthy lifestyle for all ages. It rejuvenates your body and mind, regulates your mood, and is linked to learning and memory function. On the other hand, not getting enough rest can negatively affect your mood, immune system, memory, and stress level.'[2] In these 21 chapters, I have extolled the virtues of data, analytics, discipline, hard work and ambition; but only to a point. People are not robots and cannot physically or emotionally keep going indefinitely. You have to find your balance.

Final thoughts

At the beginning of this book I said that I am writing for ambitious people: those who want to do something remarkable and create organizations that do truly remarkable things. To do this requires the mastery of a broad range of skills and knowledge: from analytical systems thinking and modelling to communication and the ability to get things done. It requires thinking on multiple levels: from the vision, linking that right through to each person's role and the competencies required for that role. It requires the right approach: hard work, discipline and the ability to embrace a challenge.

Looking to the future, organizations will continue to become more complex and organizational change will continue to accelerate. Those who do not change their approach to how they design and manage the organization are going to feel the cost. It will become increasingly difficult to know what everyone is doing, who is good at what, how many people you need, and what the impact of your organization design and people is on the business. Organizations have to act to face the challenge of being unable to understand their complexity.

The information is there, and data-driven techniques offer an opportunity to cut through that complexity. Data and analytics are new sources of competitive advantage for any businesses. Mapping, connecting and tracking the organizational system are increasingly going to be the difference between success and failure. Those businesses that can make all the connections across their system, from their vision to the value chain, to ensuring the right people do the right things so that customers can best be served, will come out on top. Those organizations that continue to follow this approach will stay at the top and thoroughly enjoy the experience.

Notes

1 Wheatley, M [accessed 14 March 2015] It's An Interconnected World Shambhala Sun, April 2002 [Online] http://www.margaretwheatley.com/articles/interconnected.html

2 University of Washington [accessed 14 March 2015] The Importance of Rest and Relaxation [Online] https://www.washington.edu/admin/hr/benefits/publications/carelink/tipsheets/rest-relax.pdf

APPENDIX

Data Warehouse

A database specifically designed to support data analysis and reporting (Business Intelligence). A data warehouse typically integrates data from multiple sources and may aggregate historical data to support fast analytical queries.

Transactional Database

A transactional database captures, modifies or deletes data in real time. Typically a business application or website connects directly to a transactional database. Unlike a data warehouse which is structured for reporting purposes, a transactional database is structured to allow for quick modification, addition or deletion of individual data records and to guarantee data integrity. An example of a transactional database is a standard HR payroll system.

Relational Database

A database made up from a series of tables, typically having a formal relationship between each other. An example of a relational database is Microsoft SQL Server.

Relational Database Management system (RDBMS)

Software System to manage databases, allowing users to interact with the system to create, modify, update and administer the database, An example of a RDBMS is Microsoft SQL Server.

Graph Database

A type of NoSQL database (see below) that uses graph structures with nodes, edges and properties to represent and store data. It is particularly useful for associative queries - people who know X also know Y. An example of a graph database is Neo4J.

→ Node: An entity or item such as people, objectives or projects.

→ Property: Information connected to each node. Example properties for a people dataset may include age, role, department and salary.

→ Edge: The connection/relationship between nodes or nodes and properties. Edges are the key to graph databases as they allow you to explore and uncover relationships in the data.

Measure

Data which represent numeric values, which may be used as business metrics and key performance indicators. For instance, number of FTEs, salary, age, etc.

Dimension

Data which categorize data in order to enable users to answer business questions. Dimensions spell out the who, what, where, when, why and how of the situation. They add context and meaning to measures. Commonly used dimensions are customers, products and time periods.

Cube

A cube is a set of organized and summarized data in the form of a multidimensional structure defined by dimensions and measures. It is built on top of a data warehouse and intends to speed up reports by storing precalculated aggregates of data.

Dimensional Modelling

Performed to design and structure the measures and dimensions collected in a data warehouse required to answer business questions. Measures are structured into what are known as Facts and are joined to Dimensions in a so-called Star schema to support easy and rapid reporting. For example, you would look at Headcount (Fact) By Location (Dimension) By Date (Dimension).

Schema

A database schema is a way to logically and formally group database objects such as tables (a collection of data fields of formalized types), views and indexes. One can think of a schema as a rigid container of objects with explicit relationships. Both transactional and warehousing databases use schemas to hold data.

? Query

Queries are the primary mechanism for retrieving information from a database and consist of questions presented to the database in a common, formal language format. Many database management systems use the Structured Query Language (SQL) standard query format.

SQL

SQL Stands for Structured Query Language, used to query and manipulate databases

NoSQL

Stands for Not Only SQL and is used to encompass a wide range of different database technologies that differ from the traditional relational databases that are based upon SQL. Examples of these databases include Graph, Document, Key-Value and Column. Often these types of database have less formal schemas than SQL databases, and thus better support semi-structured rather than highly structured data.

View

A view in database systems is simply the representation of a query (SQL) statement that is stored in memory so that it can easily be re-used. The main benefits of using views are:

→ Improved security: by allowing access to only the information that is relevant.

→ Improved usability: by presenting users and application developers with data in a more easily understood form than in the base tables.

→ Improved consistency: by centralizing the definition of common queries in the database.

ETL

Stands for Extract, Transform and Load. This is the typical process that data go through when being loaded into a data storage system such as a data warehouse. Data are extracted from multiple data sources, transformed into the correct structure, aggregation and calculated values before being loaded into the data warehouse.

INDEX

Page numbers in *italic* indicate figures or tables